I0124699

Macbrair Robert Maxwell

The Africans at home

Being a popular description of Africa and the Africans

Macbrair Robert Maxwell

The Africans at home
Being a popular description of Africa and the Africans

ISBN/EAN: 9783337202606

Printed in Europe, USA, Canada, Australia, Japan

Cover: Foto ©Andreas Hilbeck / pixelio.de

More available books at **www.hansebooks.com**

THE AFRICANS AT HOME

BEING A POPULAR DESCRIPTION OF

AFRICA AND THE AFRICANS

CONDENSED FROM THE ACCOUNTS OF AFRICAN TRAVELLERS FROM THE TIME OF MUNGO PARK TO THE PRESENT DAY

BY

THE REV. R. M. MACBRAIR, M.A.

Author of the Mandingo and Foola Grammars &c.

WITH MAP AND NUMEROUS ILLUSTRATIONS

LONDON

LONGMAN, GREEN, LONGMAN, AND ROBERTS

1861

PREFACE.

THIS book is a pictorial description of Africa. We ask the reader to accompany us through the interior of that continent, whilst we point out to him whatever is peculiar to the different countries and their inhabitants. By thus travelling over several thousands of miles, in the short time required for perusing this volume, he will get a view of various Negroes, Moors, Arabs, and mixed races, in their own places of abode. He will become acquainted with their peculiar customs and manners, the characteristics of each country, and its natural phenomena. We hope that we have omitted nothing of importance which would tend to depict the condition of the " Africans at Home."

These pages contain the condensed information supplied by thirty or forty volumes of travels, some of portentous size. All these narratives contain much that was personal to the heroic men who penetrated into regions before unknown to Europeans.

It is interesting to follow the individuals of this
gallant band, through their laborious researches, their
difficulties and privations, and the dangers or sufferings which they had constantly to endure.   But
many of them perished in their enterprise, and had
not an opportunity of doing justice to their own
journals, or their jottings of what they had seen
and heard.   Some have not had the power of writing
an interesting book.   Others have furnished a good
account of their own wanderings, which were necessarily limited to one part of this vast continent.

The Author does not wish to appear as a traveller,
using the pronoun " I."   His experiences of Africa
are not worthy of being mentioned along with those of
real discoverers.   Yet no one could have written this
book, without having previously visited that country.
Everything in Africa is different from what is seen
in Europe.   The colour of the sky, the air, the land,
the seasons, the rains, the animals (and we speak
feelingly of *insects*), the length of the grass, the
fields, the trees, the colour of the people, their dress
or want of dress, their habitations, food, amusements,
and occupations,—all is strangely diverse from what
Europeans have been accustomed to.   A very sensible man, who had always lived in an inland county
of England until he went to Western Africa, said that
when he landed in that country, he became so
bewildered that he did not recover the proper use
of his senses for a fortnight.

The Author has been in both the east and west sides of Africa; but he, confessedly, did not penetrate far into the interior. Yet he obtained a general idea of its atmospheric phenomena, the character of the people, their simple mode of living, their ignorance and cunning, their rude arts and incipient commerce. He gained a good deal of information from free converse with the natives, who are capital talkers, and some of them, such as pilgrims and traders, considerable peregrinators. With this preparation of mind, he has appropriated to himself the researches of many travellers, and incorporated them with his own previous knowledge. This justifies his using the familiar pronoun "we," in acting as an expositor of Africa to those who will accept his guidance.

In order to save repetition, and to give our readers a connected view of the numerous countries of Africa, we describe them in regular order. Beginning from the west, we take a long journey to the east, through the densest parts of the population; occasionally stopping to notice what is on either hand, to the north and south of our route. Thus, we make excursions to visit the Moors, to brave the perils of the Great and Little Deserts, to see what lies south of the Niger and Lake Chad, to trace this noble river through most of its course, and to view the bloody lands of Dahomey and Ashantee. Arriving in the east, we look at Darfur, Nubia, and Abyssinia; not forgetting to visit the source of the Blue Nile. We manage also to take a peep at Harar and the adjacent country, towards the Red Sea. Imagining ourselves back in Sennaar, we pass to the south in the company of Negro slaves and Arab merchants; and we thus rapidly traverse the burning latitudes of the equator, till we reach the lake regions recently visited by Captains Burton and Speke. A stride westward brings us into the countries lately discovered by the indefatigable and intrepid Livingstone. We get a few jottings from his rich stores of information, all down the middle of the continent, till we pass the deserts inhabited by Bushmen, and reach the out-skirts of Cape Colony; where we take leave of the courteous reader.

We have tried to enliven our style by the inser-tion of authentic anecdotes, and by varying the manner of description. For this purpose, we have sometimes employed the first and second persons plural, "we" and "you," in delineating places and circumstances where neither we nor our readers ever imagined ourselves to be placed: and we have adopted a few short extracts from published volumes, in which the pronoun "I" has been used with good effect. Subjects of natural history peculiar to Africa have been scattered as much as possible through the narrative. Minute details of religious creeds and ceremonies have been avoided; as also of the history, wars, and political changes of different tribes: for these are of little interest to the general reader, and add nothing to his stock of useful information.

Africa is a large place; and no one can be said to understand geography and the different races of men without some knowledge of this immense region. The present volume will give a bird's-eye view of this continent; and from its size and style, may be read with interest, or even as a source of amusement, by those who would shrink from perusing a number of large or erudite works. But in order to become well acquainted with any particular part of Africa, and especially if you have any intention of travelling in that country, you must have recourse to the original authorities.

It is a puzzling matter to know how to write the names of African places, since different travellers spell them in different ways. Mungo Park and the first British adventurers adopted the orthography congenial with an English pronunciation: and the names, as they gave them, were inserted in our maps. But Dr. Barth, Captain Burton, Dr. Livingstone, and others, have followed the continental mode of writing the vowel sounds; and our mappers have inserted the names of newly-discovered places, as they have been thus severally furnished. Hence the orthography of our African maps is a medley of confusion, since some words must be read after the English, some after the Italian manner of pronunciation. In the present volume, we have endeavoured to harmonise these two modes of spelling, so as to make the names easy to an English reader, and enable him to recognise them on any good map, if he will attend to the following simple observations.

We always use *oo* in the *middle* of a name, though some travellers write *ou*, and others *u*: but in deference to the new style we chang the *oo final* into *u*; as in Fooladu, which Park wrote Fooladoo, and others write Fuladu. Word ending in *a* are to be pronounced as if it were *ah*, which is the old method of spelling; thus Park wrote Foolah and Fellattah, which are now spelt without the *h*. Final *ee* and *ie* are the same sound, which Barth expresses by the continental *i*, as Ashantee or Ashanti, Birnie or Birni (we think the first best for an English map). Final *ey, ay, é, e*, are intended for the same sound, and ought probably to have been all written *eh;* but *we* cannot venture upon making so sweeping a change. Our final *i* must be read as *ih* or short *ie*. Therefore, if our readers will pronounce every African name terminating in a single vowel *as if it had an* h *after it*, they will be pretty correct. (Pronounce Foola, Jenne, Kirri, Bornu, as if they were Foolah, Jenneh, Kirrih, Bornuh).

For most of the illustrations which embellish this

volume, we are indebted to those works from which much of the narrative has been gleaned; so that they may be regarded as correct drawings.

We trust that this attempt to give a familiar description of Africa will meet with public approval, and will induce many persons to become acquainted with a most interesting subject, from which they may have been hitherto deterred by want of a condensed and lively account of the "The Africans at Home." We have not enlarged upon the *cotton* question, important as it is at the present epoch; but we have pointed out in the narrative how this plant flourishes in most parts of Central Africa, so that it might be grown there in sufficient quantity to supply the present wants of the world.

CONTENTS.

CHAP. VII.

CHAP. VIII.

CHAP. IX.

CHAP. X.

CHAP. XI.

CHAP. XII.

LIST OF ILLUSTRATIONS.

MAP.

ILLUSTRATIONS (AS SEPARATE PLATES).

ILLUSTRATIONS IN THE TEXT.

Map of
AFRICA
to accompany
"THE AFRICANS AT HOME"

English Miles
100 300   400   600   800

Geographical Miles
100 200   400   600   800

THE AFRICANS AT HOME.

CHAPTER I.

Long before a voyager comes within sight of Western
Africa, he feels the influence of that parched and
sandy region. The genial air of the trade-wind is
exchanged for a hot and oppressive atmosphere. If
the land-breeze happens to blow, it is laden with particles of fine dust which cover the vessel at a great
distance from the coast. The azure sky assumes a
yellowish hue from the reflection of glistening sand :
and the blue waters of the ocean become of a lighter

B

colour. Those huge creatures which swim round
your vessel, as it sluggishly approaches the shore, are
the much dreaded sharks; which have not learned to
distinguish one ship from another, but hope that yours
may be a slaver, from which some dead Negro may
be thrown overboard, to their advantage.

The promontory before us is Cape Verd; and the
rest of the coast lies low. We must take care not to
keep too near to it, lest we should be becalmed in the
bay. Many poor seamen have been thus land-locked,
till they have perished of fever, or their hapless craft
has become a wreck. This accident seldom happens
in sailing to the Gambia, as captains know to keep
away from this inhospitable shore: but it is not an
unusual casualty when leaving the coast. It is a sad,
sad thing, to be thus detained within the purlieus of
destruction, unable to move away, till the fate which
you dread slowly overtakes you. We have heard it
described by two survivors of a gallant crew. Their
vessel lay within sight of shore, as if drawn to it by a
magnet; and the sails hung motionless, or sometimes
faintly flapped as if to mock their hopes. A tropical
sun poured down his flaming heat on their fainting
bodies, which had been exhausted by the African
fever. This disease broke out afresh, and no succour
was at hand. The dispirited crew gave themselves up
to hopelessness, and one after another perished, till
the enervated survivors were obliged to let the vessel drift as she listed, and their lives were saved by
her being wrecked on a reef of sand. The natives
proved more merciful than was anticipated; they

contented themselves with the spoils of the ship, and
saved the two surviving mariners.

The discoloured water tells us that we are entering
the wide mouth of the Gambia. Its stream must be
very sluggish, as the tide rises in it for five hundred
miles. A gentle sea-breeze helps us to creep forward, and enables us to reach St. Mary's before night-
fall, when this wind ceases. We anchor in the channel; for here is no wharf, pier, or other landing
place : and we are conveyed ashore in boats.

The town of Bathurst has some good houses, built
of stone and shell lime. These buildings, being
ranged along the beach, present a pretty appearance,
with their piazzas and whitewashed fronts. Here is
a British colony, the seat of government, and the
emporium of European merchandise for this district of
Africa. But the little island of St. Mary's, on which
it is situated, lies very low, and is swampy during
the rainy season. The last-named evil might probably
be palliated by some good engineering. If the land
were entirely cleared and drained, the inhabitants
would be saved from miasma, and many lives might
be preserved. But the British government has never
seemed to think how many emigrants, governors,
officers, or missionaries perish in that land which has
been designated " the white man's grave." Still it is
possible that, by a different line of policy, Bathurst
might now have been a little African Calcutta, expor-
ting to England large quantities of cotton, coffee, and
indigo, besides other precious commodities.

There are also some native " towns " or villages on

St. Mary's where all kinds of Africans are protected,
and many liberated slaves are settled. Let us enter
one of these little towns; it consists of a few broad
streets, along both sides of which the houses or huts
of the negroes are erected. Each is built in a yard or
garden belonging to its tenant; but all differ in shape,
size, and appearance. Here is a neat one, inhabited
by a Jollof. It is an oblong, divided into two chambers, and whitewashed : it has a hut or two behind it,
which serve for a "cook-house" and store-room. The
sitting-room contains a few articles of European furniture, manufactured in Africa, and two or three
books lie on a shelf, including a Bible, Prayer-book,
and hymn book. These books, or rather the truths
which they teach, have made the dwelling to be
so neat. Many years ago, the lamented Sir Charles
Macarthy was walking with a missionary near some
huts, and pointing to them, he said : " Some of your
people live there ;" the other answered, " How do you
know, Governor? " His reply was, "Because the houses
are whitewashed." It is hard to persuade the Negro
to change his old customs and indolent habits, and
still more difficult to give him a love of cleanliness,
temperance, industry, honesty and domestic order,
until he comes under the power of true religion. All
the native dwellings in this town are not so good as
the one we have seen ; and there are "towns" on the
island little better than those on the continent.

The Jollofs are a fine race of men, and when
christianised, they are brave, faithful, and generous;
good samples of what Africans can become. Some

of the most industrious and skilful mechanics of
Bathurst are of this tribe. Their hands built much

JOLLOF CHIEF.

of this town, including the merchants' houses, the
spacious residence of the governor, and the noble
hospital. Perhaps we shall hereafter meet with them
in a ruder state of life.

Before leaving the island, let us look at these
oyster-trees. What! Do oysters grow on trees, like
apples or pears? Not exactly; yet it is true enough
that they grow on trees; and if you look, you will find
the lower parts of these mangroves covered with shell-
fish. This fact of natural history puzzles a stranger,
till he learns how it comes to pass. The mangrove
grows in brackish water, lining the sides of the river
and creeks as far as salt-water reaches. Then,
as there are oyster-beds in the small creek which
separates one side of the island from the mainland,
the fish adhere to the lower branches of the trees instead of rocks, when the tide is high. At low water
they are exposed to view, and are gathered to be eaten
or to be burnt into lime.

A largish vessel is ready to sail up the river,
freighted with a variety of merchandise. As she
will stop at several native towns on the banks, we
shall take a passage in her; and thus we shall have
opportunities of seeing the Africans in their own
homes. There are small craft built entirely for the
river trade by some of those Jollofs whom we saw,
which can sail up all the way to Fatatenda. But a
ship of 200 or 300 tons burden can manage to reach
Macarthy's island, about 250 miles up the stream.

It is far from unpleasant to perform a river voyage
during the cool season of the year, which lasts for
three or four months. Of course, you live on deck.
An awning affords shelter from the sun by day,
and from the moon and dew by night. For eight
months of the year there is no fear of rain, nor does

a dark cloud blacken the sky. The sea-breeze wafts you up the stream for some days; then you must trust mainly to the tide and boats. When the land-breeze blows, you must cast anchor, and must always stop whilst the tide ebbs. The air is now fresh and cool, till the sun approaches the zenith, when you are glad to be under the shade for a few hours, the temperature being at about 80° Fahrenheit. The nights are very pleasant when you are in mid-stream, away from the torments of mosquitoes, and from too close proximity with the natives. You are then free from all fear of disturbance, and can enjoy the magnificent solitudes of nature, particularly when the moon lights up the landscape, and casts shadows from the vast trees which line the river.

We stop at Jillifree, one of the chief trading places in the kingdom of Barra (though the sovereignty of the bank has been ceded to Great Britain). The town is surrounded with a mud wall, to keep out wild beasts during the night, and to prevent a surprise by some marauding chieftain. The dwellings of the people consist of huts, huddled together in a number of small enclosures or yards, also formed of mud walls. Each head of a family has one of these enclosures, in which huts are erected according to the number of his wives and other wants. The hut consists of a round room, made of mud and thatched with grass. The better kind have a double wall, including between them a narrow circular space, which serves for an outer or sitting apartment. They have no windows,

and only one low door, which admits the light and
lets out the smoke.

In order to visit a native trader, we have to pass
through a number of small winding alleys, between
mud walls, with an occasional door leading into a
yard. A stranger would not easily find his way out
again, for it is a labyrinth. At length the gentleman's door is reached, and we are ushered into a
space containing huts of all sizes, erected without any
regard to order or appearance, like a number of large
bee-hives fallen from the clouds. There is a hut for
the master, a hut for each of the women and her
children, huts for cooking, a hut for horses, a hut for
stores and merchandise — a motley group!

These huts are almost as bare inside as they are
unsightly without. A few domestic utensils, and a
wicker platform for a bedstead, compose the usual
furniture. The Negroes are mere children of nature;
their wants are few and easily supplied. When a
man can purchase three or four wives he becomes a
gentleman; for the ladies and slaves (if he have any)
cultivate his farm and provide for all the wants of the
household. He can hunt, barter, smoke, drink, fight,
and gossip at pleasure.

Our voyage soon becomes monotonous, on account
of those perpetual mangroves, which form an impenetrable forest on either bank for about 150 miles.
This tree, as we have said, grows in the stream, above
low-water mark. It propagates by letting down shoots
from its upper parts, which take root, if they can find
room, and form new stems. As the tops of the roots

are not covered with earth, they have a singular appearance when the tide leaves them, exhibiting a
confused mass of twisted and tortuous fibres, rising

MANGROVE.

into cones, on the tops of which the trunks seem to
be perched. You cannot find mould enough amongst
them to make a grave.

We are glad to reach a break in the mangroves,

caused by a creek, much resembling a canal, the
sides of which are also lined with this interminable
tree.   It is only a few yards wide, and branches meet
over head.   The vessel anchors at the mouth of the
creek, and in the morning we row up in a boat.   It
seems gloomy, for the sun's beams rarely penetrate
the thick foliage with which we are overhung.
There is not a rustle of the leaves or any other
sound to be heard, except the chattering of monkeys
over head, and the more distinct cry of the hawk or
eagle.

AFRICAN EAGLE.

At last, after rowing for a couple
of miles, we land at an open space;
and on climbing up the bank are
presented with a new panorama.
The sun shines brightly on large
fields, studded with occasional
trees. Birds of exquisite plumage,
but wanting song, fly about the
bushes. In the distance is a small
town.   Whilst the supercargo is
trading with the Negroes — rather
a long business — we shall go to
visit this poor settlement.   It is
surrounded with a low stockade, and the huts are of
the meanest kind.

The villagers crowd to see a white man, which is
an uncommon sight in this outlandish place.   They
are mostly clad in a single garment; the men in a
loose shirt or smock, the women in a cloth wrapped
round their waist.   The former have a small cap ;

the latter have their hair bound up in a coloured handkerchief. The children run about in nature's attire. We wished to see the chief; but found that he was asleep on a mat outside his hut. As no one but his wife durst awake him, we sent for this important personage. She was an ugly, haggard creature; and in no way to be distinguished from the other women. They were all in their *dishabille* or ordinary clothes; for in full dress they would have had another cloth thrown over their shoulders and bosom, with necklaces, bracelets, or other ornaments. The men, also, would have worn loose trowsers or drawers.

The chief was awakened, but not to right reason; for he was drunk. He was almost blind, had few teeth, was almost naked, and presented a most unsightly form of humanity. He tried to understand what was said by our interpreter in his own language, but could not. A jester sat by his side and seemed alone to have the privilege of making free with him. These buffoons have certain immunities and privileges during life, but their dead bodies are not interred in the ground, but deposited in the hollow trunk of a monkey-bread tree. They amuse their patron by singing, jesting, making antics, and attempts at music. It is singular that the same custom of having court buffoons should exist in uncivilised Africa, which used to prevail in Germany and other parts of civilised Europe. In this place, we had a very meagre specimen of Negro life at home.

Look at one of those celebrated monkey-bread

trees! It is the Baobab or *Adansonia digitata*,
which though found in Abyssinia and some other
warm regions, seems to flourish most in Western
Africa. Its size is enormous, the trunk sometimes
reaching to thirty feet in diameter. But its height
does not correspond with its thickness, seldom exceeding seventy feet. Its lateral branches shoot out and
droop down, so as to form a beautiful shade of verdure, impenetrable by the sun, extending more than
twenty yards from every side of the trunk. The
roots also are of great length. Unlike most African
trees, the baobab has a soft, light coloured wood,
easily perforated by wild bees, who make it a
favourite place for hiving. Both the leaves and the
juice of the fruit are used by the natives medicinally.
The fruit itself, being acid and agreeable, constitutes
an important article of food and of commerce. The
tree grows very slowly and attains an immense age,
not becoming very large till it has lived a thousand
years.

After being exposed to the heat of mid-day sun in
Africa, you will be glad to find yourself again upon
the water, under the friendly shelter of the mangroves.
Yet these woody creeks have caused the death of
hundreds or thousands of British seamen. Vessels
often go up them during the rainy season, to load
timber, which is cut on the higher lands, and brought
to the banks by natives. After labouring all day in
the heat, and stimulating his exertions with plenty of
rum, the sailor lies down to sleep upon deck. He
could not breathe in the cabin. He inhales noxious

malaria, and is seized with fever. Myriads of mosquitoes destroy his rest, and render the usual medicines abortive. If he cannot be hurried down to St. Mary's hospital, his doom is certain: sometimes he reaches it too late, for nature is exhausted.

The Negro works, but not like an Englishman; he takes it easy, and husbands his strength. He appears indolent, and is often blamed as such: but indolence is a relative term. To labour in tropical Africa as one does in England would be infatuation. The British captain kills his men by making them do the work which black limbs ought to perform. But he has no patience with the "lazy lubberly Niggers," who tell him: "Plenty of time, Massa, to-morrow come after to-day." The captain thinks that the Negro has no just notion of the value of time; and in this he is correct. Yet the Negro also is right in thinking health to be more valuable than time.

At length the mangroves are left behind, and the face of the open country appears from the deck of the vessel. There is not, indeed, much to be seen, except extensive plains and woodlands, with an occasional mud town or village peeping through the trees, yet few and far between. Whilst the vessel is at anchor waiting for the tide, let us take a ramble to a small town at no great distance from the river's bank.

This pure balmy air is delicious. Were it not quite so hot out of the shade, the weather would be altogether desirable. But, in January, we must take this mixture of hot days and cool evenings with thankfulness: for months of scorching heat are fast ap-

proaching.   We soon enter a wood of large trees, not
very close together, and often with a small space
clear of foliage.   The boughs are almost vocal with the
chattering of monkeys, who seem to be talking about
the strangers, and expressing their displeasure at one
intruding into their domains.   The open areas swarm
with paroquets and other birds of richest plumage.
But our attention must not be too much taken up
with what is going on overhead; we must also look
to our feet, and take care not to tread upon a snake.
For this is a land of serpents.   See, there is one
about four feet long, skulking in the lower branches
of the tree which we are approaching!   Our black
lads rush at it with their sticks; and the frightened
creature, taken by storm, is soon disabled and knocked
on the head.   The boys would not be so brave if alone
and unarmed.

It is a small settlement of Mandingoes that we
have reached.   In the structure of its dwellings, it
does not differ much from those which we have
already described.   As strangers, we do not enter it
at once, but sit under the *palaver* tree, till the chief
or somebody else comes to gossip with us, and perhaps invite us in.   There is generally a wide-spreading tree, often the tabba-tree, beside an African
village, under which a platform of cane-work is
erected, called the *bentang*.   This answers the same
purpose as the " gate " or gateway used to do in
eastern towns.   It is a public lounging-place, where
the men gossip, dispute, hear lawsuits, transact public
business, receive strangers, and perform all other

things which require much *palaver* or *talkee*. And Negroes are capital talkers. Here comes the chief and a few others!

MANDINGO.

The Mandingoes are tall, slender, and often handsome. Their hair is woolly and their skin quite dark; but they have not the flat nose and thick lips of the Negro proper. They are nimble, active in war, and enterprising in commerce. Their disposition is naturally gentle and cheerful; so that when they become Mahometans, they do not show that religious rancour and intolerance which the Moors and Felattas exhibit. They are simple in their habits, credulous, and fond of flattery. Mungo Park found fault that they had an insurmountable propensity to steal from him, and to get possession of the few effects which he possessed. He, indeed, made some excuse for them, in the great temptation to which they were exposed when they saw his goods, which, though paltry in an Englishman's eyes, were a fortune in their estimation. We fear that this covetous and thievish propensity is common to human nature; it certainly prevails amongst every nation, tribe, and order of men in Africa. We question, moreover, how long a man would be able to carry a bag of gold or precious things through England, or even through the streets of London, if there were no police to protect him, and no laws to punish any one who might rob him of his treasures.

The Mandingo language is simple, but harmonious, abounding in vowels and liquids, so that it has a smoothness and mellowness of pronunciation like the Italian. But the structure of the language is thoroughly eastern. In some of its grammatical forms it resembles the Hebrew and Syriac; its most peculiar sound is of the Malay family; its manner of interrogation is similar to the Chinese; and in the composition of some verbs it is like the Persian. A few religious terms have been borrowed from the

Arabic, and some articles of foreign manufacture are called after their European names.

The men who have come to the bentang are armed with spears, which they generally carry with them, as the country is in a very unquiet state, and men-stealers prowl about. Being seated under the palaver tree, we talk about the news of the day, the English and the Mandingoes. They parry off any particular questions concerning their own town and its inhabitants, being suspicious of the object of our visit. Instead of inviting us inside the village, they bring us some milk in a calabash, and we give them in return a little tobacco, which they eagerly receive.

All the men wear *greegrees* or amulets : the chief has his breast well-nigh covered with them. The *greegree* is familiar to the sight and to the ear of a sojourner in Africa from the day that he lands in Senegambia. But here is a favourable opportunity for having the matter explained, since a notorious greegree maker lives in this town. Let us, in assumed ignorance, ask the chief what is the use of those leathern things that are suspended round his neck, and fastened like bracelets round his arms? They are generally of a square or oblong shape; but some resemble a horn, others are round, and of other forms. He replies, that they are *greegrees*, and that whilst he wears them, he will be secure from injury. Then why wear so many; would not one be sufficient? "Yes, one potent greegree, like those which I have, will save me from harm. But harm is of different kinds, and so there are different kinds of greegrees to protect from different sorts of evil. This greegree is strong against a fever; this other will keep me from danger on a journey; this other will prevent my being injured by a gun-shot." " Hold there, friend ! Let me try: let me fire this pistol at you, and see if I cannot wound you?" Of course the chief demurs to such a trial of his amulet, lest some accident should happen. Let us, then, propose that he hang the greegree on the bough of a tree, and that we fire at it as at a target; for surely if it can save him from being hurt, it can save itself from being blown to pieces. At this proposal, he looks rather confused; for in reality he only half believes in his amulet. But the marraboo, or priest, comes to his help, and suggests that the greegree which is available against a black man may not protect against the attempts of a white man. This logic is decisive, and so the matter ends.

Rogues always have a back door by which they may escape. So these marraboos take care to have a subterfuge, by which they may be saved from blame through the failure of their pretensions. The potency of a greegree depends upon the wearer's fulfilling some condition which is attached to it by the maker, so that when it fails, it is easy to show, or at least to affirm, that this condition has been broken. Take the following examples.

A poor fellow was going on a journey into an unhealthy part of the country, and being afraid of the prevailing fever, he bought a strong greegree to save him from its power. Nevertheless, he was assailed by this disease, and had a narrow escape with his life. On his recovery and return home, he went with his friends to upbraid the marraboo who had sold the useless charm, and called him a liar and cheat. "I say that my greegree was good," replied the priest. "Then why was I taken with fever and almost killed?" rejoined the injured man. "My greegree was good," retorted the other, "but you must have spoiled it by your folly. What did I tell you to do, or not to do, when I gave it to you?" "You bade me not eat any goat's flesh; and I was very careful not to do so; I have eaten none." The impostor then asked him where he had been, and on receiving an answer, replied: "Oh you fool! don't you know that a man in that town wished to do you harm, and so he mixed the juice of goat's flesh with your kooskoos, and broke the power of my spell!" There was no possibility of answering such a bold assertion as this, by showing that the thing could not have happened, and the complainants went away crest-fallen.

On another occasion, some natives wished to cross the river when the water was very rough by reason of a strong east wind. Being rather afraid, they applied to a greegree maker who lived not far from the stream for an amulet to ensure their safe return. Of course he furnished them with one. But after transacting their business, on recrossing the river, their canoe was upset, and some of the party were drowned. Indignant at having been imposed upon, they went to the marraboo and informed him of the catastrophe. He heard their story with great patience,

and put sundry questions to them about the accident;
meanwhile rummaging his brain for a plausible excuse
for the failure of his greegree. Then, assuming an
air of injured innocence, he exclaimed, " Did you not
see that the man who steered the canoe got
afraid, and put his paddle down to try and touch the
bottom ? That act spoiled my greegree, and the wind
was able to upset the canoe." The rogue had ascertained that the steersman was among the drowned,
and as he knew that a dead man could not answer
for himself, he cunningly laid the blame upon him,
attributing the catastrophe to his unbelief.

Thus the ignorant Africans are deceived and fleeced
by impostors. It is so all over the world, for where
there are simpletons there will also be knaves. Even
the Mahometan Negroes are not free from this superstition, but most of them wear a greegree, containing, as they think, " the name of God " or some words
from the Koran. These amulets, however, are not
limited to such writings, but are made of a great
variety of articles to which fancy has attributed a
kind of sacredness.

The African has a great dread of the unseen world,
which he supposes to be peopled with genii, fairies, or
evil spirits who wish to play tricks upon men. Hence
the greater part of their religion, if such it may be
called, consists in obviating the designs of these imaginary foes. The heathen marraboos encourage their
superstitious fears, and devise antidotes to the pretended mischief. Mahometan marraboos say that
wearing the name of God must do good, and they

prepare written amulets, which are enclosed in the usual leathern purse or pouch.

It is a common idea in Senegambia, that the superiority of white men depends upon their possessing a more sacred greegree than the Negroes can find; and it is currently supposed that this magic charm consists in a knowledge of the name of Moses's mother! European merchants and sailors are often surprised and confounded at being asked "Who was the mother of Moses?" When they reply in truth, that they do not know (the name only occurs once in the Bible), the African believes that they are wilfully concealing it, and becomes more confirmed in his supposition: for why should they hide it, if they had not a reason for so doing?

Can anything be said about the monkeys, which have been described as peopling the trees of African forests, and chattering about the strangers who visit them? There are a great many species of the *Simia* or ape genus, and several are found in the region of Senegambia. The ourang-outang, that caricature of the human figure, does not seem to be met with in the interior; but it still frequents the districts which border on the gulf of Guinea. Ancient mariners were dreadfully afraid of these animals, which attacked them when landing on the coast, throwing nuts, stones, and sticks at them, and screaming in a frightful manner, so that they were thought to be satyrs or sylvan deities. They are still formidable creatures, when a troop of them meet one or two lone Negroes; for they are very strong, so that several men cannot hold one of them. A Negro boy is said to have been carried off by them, and kept in their society for some months. They behaved very kindly to him, especially the females, who furnished him with plenty of nuts and fruits, and defended him from serpents and beasts of prey.

A person living on the Gambia kept several monkeys taken in the neighbourhood when young. They became quite domesticated, and more familiar than was always agreeable. Their name was "mischief." It was impossible to put them anywhere but they would play some mischievous pranks. They took the eggs out of the hens' nests and sucked them, they milked the goats, they rolled bottles of wine and beer along the floor of the piazza for their amusement, they turned sand-glasses several times and then broke them, apparently to see what was in them, they picked mats and mops to pieces, and delighted to play tricks upon other animals. Though forbidden to enter the rooms of the house, — a prohibition which they well understood,—they would sometimes venture a dash at the cupboard where sugar or sweetmeats were kept, running the risk of a thrashing, which they were conscious of deserving. In fine, they were so intolerably mischievous that at length it was found necessary to destroy them.

Some of these monkeys are rough and shaggy creatures, capable of bearing hardships; others are very delicate, and pine and die if exposed to cold or other severities. The different species live separately ; but they are amazingly numerous, not being much exposed to destruction by other brutes. Their principal enemy is the serpent, which follows them through the boughs of the trees, and glides softly upon them when asleep. Leopards and others of of the feline race also manage to catch monkeys. They themselves live principally upon fruits, leaves, insects, and perhaps the eggs of birds. For though the feathered tribe of Africa seem to have an instinct of building their nests in places where monkeys cannot get at them, yet they do not always succeed in eluding their nimble neighbour, who will rob and destroy their nests for mere mischief's sake. They leap from bough to bough, and from tree to tree, with great activity, even when burdened with their young ones clinging to them; so that they literally follow a traveller through the wood, chattering, making grimaces, and sometimes throwing things at him or shaking the boughs over him. Green monkeys abound in some

GREEN MONKEY.

of the woods which border on the Niger, and from their colour it is almost impossible to see the animals which persist in keeping you company over head.

c 4

As the vessel continues to stop, let us try to procure a little game for dinner. If you are a good sportsman your bag will soon be filled with partridges, guinea fowls, or wild pigeons; for these birds are far from being shy, not having learned to fear the gun. A native may have occasionally shot a bird, but probably not in this immediate neighbourhood, and he never fires at one when on the wing. Blackie is a bad marksman, and he does not know what a good gun means. As iron is very precious in his eyes, he thinks that the value of a gun depends much upon its weight. Another sign of its goodness is its flashing well in the pan. So Blackie goes to a merchant's store, where every article imported from Europe is sold, from a bar of iron or a bale of cloth to a needle and thread. He carries with him some gold, ivory, bees wax, ground-nuts, or other African commodity, to exchange for a gun. He knows the value of his own articles, or at least the merchant does not quarrel with him on their account. "Now show me one good gun." The gentleman offers him a nice light fowling-piece, with which he might manage to kill a bird." "How much him be?" "Thirty dollars," says the merchant. "You tink me fool-man, gib tirty dollars for dis gun: him no weigh notting." The merchant shows him another, which he says will perhaps suit him better. It is of Birmingham manufacture, worth nothing; its prime cost being only a few shillings: but it is heavy, and has a good steel and flint. "This is only five dollars." The Negro feels that it has weight of metal, and his eyes brighten with hope. It is new and clean, makes a good click, and sparkles well when the trigger is drawn. So, after a while, he tries it with a charge of powder. Bravo! How it flashes! The bargain is concluded, and five dollars' worth of goods are given for this trumpery article, which no bird need fear at a distance of many yards; and which will soon need to be repaired, if it does not burst; especially as the owner has no mercy on his powder.

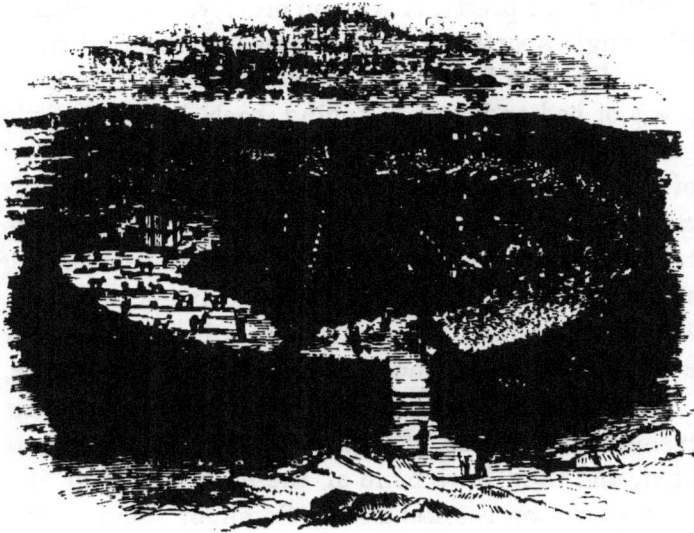

FOOLA VILLAGE.

Perhaps, in this shooting ramble, you may fall in with a village of the pastoral Foolas who abound in this neighbourhood. For there has been no war here for some years; and this timid tribe frequent the most peaceful parts of the country. Let us enter this

village or encampment of theirs and observe it
minutely, for it is different from any town that we
have yet seen.

It is of an oblong shape, fenced with a stockade.
On passing through the gate, you see a long, broad
street before you, with another exit at the farther end.
Cane huts thatched with grass are erected along each
side of the street in a regular manner; in this respect
quite differing from a Mandingo or Jollof town. These
dwellings are pretty, clean, and orderly. They consist
of a single apartment, with a raised platform of cane-
work, like the frame of a couch, to answer the purposes of bed and sofa. Behind each hut is a little
garden, reaching to the barricade of the town. Few
of the men are at home, for they are out herding their
cattle. There is one, however, sitting beside the gate
to keep watch, but employing himself in weaving
strips of cloth in a very primitive manner. Women
are walking about or gossiping, and the children play
with each other, without any impediment of clothing.

The colour of these Foolas is as peculiar as their
customs and modes of living. Their complexion is
light, and they have none of the peculiarities of the
Negro form or countenance. Some of those young
women are fair enough to be Mulattoes or Spaniards,
and are of very handsome shape. You probably never
saw finer specimens of the human frame, except in
statuary. Nor is the work of nature disguised, for the
rotund limbs and graceful figures of these Foolah
girls have no covering. The narrow strip of calico
tied round their loins only prevents their modesty and

yours from being offended, whilst you look at their unartificial gracefulness. But the charms of women in tropical climates fade early, and the demi-nude figure of a matron is far from pleasing.

The pastoral Foolas do not follow agriculture, but only attend to cattle; they are the herdsmen of Western Africa. They have no lands or dwelling-places of their own. They put themselves under the protection of a powerful chieftain, to whom they pay cattle for tribute. When the grass is eaten up in one locality, they emigrate to another; and a removal costs them very little trouble. It is probably on this account that they use cane huts in preference to mud buildings.

The Foolas have a language of their own, though they generally speak Mandingo. It is a very peculiar language, altogether differing in pronunciation and structure from other native dialects. The Mandingo, as we have said, is simple in its grammar, soft and melodious in its sounds. The Jollof is rather guttural, and a little more involved in its syntax. The Foola is altogether complex in its structure, with many intricate changes of number and person, showing that it was once the language of an elegant and probably a learned people. In pronunciation it has a hiatus, like the Kaffir click, which is a strange coincidence. But there are other points of resemblance between the herdsmen of Senegambia and those of South Africa.

Who are these Foolas? How did they come here? They are doubtless the Leucothiopes of Ptolemy and

Pliny, the former placing them near to Foota-Jallon,
the latter to Foota-Foro.   Some think them to be the
remains of the Carthaginians or Phœnicians who
colonised the northern shores of Africa, and were conquered by the Romans and afterwards by the Mahometans.   Many of their words end like Hannibal,
Hasdrubal, Hamilcar, &c.   They are evidently the
relics of a civilised people, and they declare themselves to be descended from *white* men.   Two other
tribes speak the same language with themselves, the
Teucolars and Lowbies, whom we shall meet with
hereafter.

We saw a man weaving at the gate of the Foola
village.   This introduces us to one of the manufactures of Western Africa; and it may be well to describe this art from the beginning.   When the cotton
is gathered from the trees, the women lay a small
quantity of it upon a smooth stone or piece of wood,
and roll out the seeds with an iron spindle.   They
then spin it into thread with the common distaff.   As
may be supposed, the thread is not fine, but it is
strong, and garments made of it are very durable.   It
is woven by men on a narrow loom, so that the lengths
of cloth do not exceed four inches in width.   These
lengths are sown together to make a garment, by
which means it can be made of different colours, by
intermingling strips of blue.

Negroes understand the art of dyeing.   The indigo
plant grows luxuriantly in this country, and blue is
the most common colour used by the people.   The
dye is obtained from the fresh plant, without any pro-

cess of manufacturing it into the indigo of commerce.
The leaves, either fresh or dried in the sun, are put
into a pot, and a very strong ley is poured upon them.
This ley is called by the Mandingoes *sai-gee*, or ash-
water, and it is made by filtering water through
wood ashes (principally of the *Mimosa nitta* and
Mimosa pulverulenta). The leaves remain in the
ley for about four days, during which time it is occasionally stirred; then the pot, which was only half
full, is filled up with the sai-gee, and frequently
stirred during other four days. By this time it has
fermented and thrown up a copper-coloured scum.
It is allowed to rest for another day, and is then fit
for use. The cloth is wetted with cold water, wrung
out, and put into the pot, where it remains for two
hours. Being taken out, it is hung upon a stick,
washed in cold water, beaten with a flat stick, wrung
hard, and again put into the pot. This dipping is
repeated four times a day for four successive days,
when the dyeing is completed, and a very beautiful
colour is obtained. As it requires some little art to
perform this operation successfully, so as to *clear* the
cloth and admit the indigo to all parts of it alike, there
are women who make it their business or profession.
They use no mordant, and yet secure a lasting dye.
When the operation fails, which is seldom the case
in experienced hands, it happens during the ferment-
ing process.

CHAP. II.

Patience in Africa. —Hippopotamus. —Alligators. —Gipsy Foolas. —Macarthy's Island. — A Negro King. — Effects of a Mirror. — Voyage upwards. — A Robin Hood. — His strange Doings, and appalling Greegree. —A British Misadventure. —Visiting the Robber's Den. — African Timber. — White Ants. — Palm Wine. — Fatatenda. — Tedious Trading. — The King of Woolli. — Kooskoos. — Medina. — White Negroes. — Mumbo Jumbo. — Wives.

WE continue our voyage very slowly up the river. The sea-breeze begins to fail us, even by day, so that we cannot proceed whilst the tide ebbs. Whilst it flows, our boats tow us on, and we have the satisfaction of knowing that we do make progress in the right direction. Patience is a very necessary virtue in Africa. You can do nothing in a hurry, except it be to die. All kinds of business and locomotion are performed leisurely. But in sickness you travel at railway speed to reach the last goal. If you would have any enjoyment in Africa, you must get a merry and contented heart, which Solomon says "is a continual feast." Imitate the natives, who make no account of time, and who only try to make themselves comfortable for the present moment. Always remember that "to-morrow comes after to-day."

What is this snorting which we hear in our vicinity, especially in the evening? And that black head which occasionally appears above the water, playing at waterworks like a whale? It is the hippopotamus or river-horse; but the Negroes term it more rightly the river-pig. This is an innocent monster, never injur-

HIPPOPOTAMUS.

ing any one except in revenge. Then its anger is furious. One of them, having been fired at from a boat in the Gambia, rushed forward, and fixing its tusks on either side of the keel crushed the skiff together, as if it had been a nut-shell. Whilst the beast was venting its anger upon the innocent boat,

the guilty men happily escaped by swimming ashore.
We only remember to have seen one herd of these
creatures feeding on the grass, early in the morning;
for they live chiefly in the water, and are very timid
on land.

The ivory of the hippopotamus's tusk is harder
than that of the elephant, and is valued by the
dentist.   The flesh of the young animal is eaten by
natives.   The skin is sometimes made into thongs
and bucklers. A formidable whip for driving donkeys
and camels made from this hide is well known in
Egypt and elsewhere, under the name of *coorbash.*
The animal attains the great size of nearly twelve
feet in length, and is of enormous bulk.   We believe
that it is peculiar to the rivers and lakes of Africa.

Up, up, up the river.   We pass several verdant
isles, the larger inhabited by men, the others by wild
beasts.   We now become very familiar with the sight
of alligators.   They lie in multitudes on the sunny
banks of the stream, and on hearing the least noise
slip into the water.   If you float gently down in
a boat during the heat of the day, you will see them
well ; as you can thus pass by without alarming them,
or disturbing their light slumbers.   At night, they
prowl about, and hesitate not to make a prey of small
animals, and sometimes even of human beings.   But
they will seldom attack a man on shore whilst there
is light.   Ludicrous tales are told by the Negroes of
their dodging the alligator,—which takes much time
in turning its long body,—and even of their catching
it, or getting upon its back. But of course this is mere

talkee. It is commonly said that an alligator cannot bite in the water, when it is not able to rest its tail on the ground. Whether or not this be an apocryphal piece of natural history, we cannot say. We always feared to make the experiment, lest a white body should be more delicate than a black one. For the Negro is bold enough in the water. We have seen lots of children swimming in places abounding with alligators, and sporting themselves there for hours together, like ducklings without fear, and without accident. We had no means of inquiring of Mr· Alligator, if he was frightened at the children's splashing, or if he thought them too nimble for him to catch, or if they were in too deep water for him to rest his tail on the ground. The fact of their being there was patent: and it was as certain, that the same urchins would not have dared to wade in the margin of the river by day, or to have passed near it by night. The eggs of this reptile are often found in the sand: they are large, strong flavoured, and anything but delicate eating.

Landing near a small town, in order to dispose of some cargo, we fell in with some Loubies or Gipsy Foolas. They are a stunted and ill-looking set of people; roving about, making and selling calabashes, canoes, and other pieces of wood-work. Two or three women came and offered to sell some calabashes. These are bowls, made of the rind or shell of the fruit of a large gourd, something like a pumpkin. It is cut into two hemispheres; the inside is taken out; and the thick rind is scraped, polished, and perhaps

carved. Those offered to us for sale were very pretty,
and we wished to buy one or two. But with what
kind of money? The black ladies wished for beads
in exchange. Not being merchants, we did not happen
to have any of these female ornaments on hand. We
had " cut-moneys," that is, quarter pieces of a dollar,
which is current coin with the traders of the Gambia.
But the women said they did not know how to buy
or sell cut-monies. We replied, that money would
purchase food and clothes, but that beads were useless, as they could not be eaten or drunk. They
laughed at this philosophy, and went away with their
calabashes.

Where did these Loubies come from? Nobody
can tell. There are gipsies in all lands, most of them
descended from an Arab stock; the blood of Ishmael
being mixed with that of the people among whom
his children dwell. According to this theory, the
Loubies are descendants of some wandering Arabs,
who sojourned amongst the pastoral Foolas when
they were a powerful nation. This hypothesis may
be as near the truth as any other.

Now we reach Macarthy's island, where we may
take a little rest; as it is a British colony, the out-
post of civilisation and Christianity on the western
part of Senegambia. The island is about six miles in
length, and a mile and a half wide in its broadest part.
It was bought from the King of Catabar by the unfortunate Sir Charles Macarthy; from whom it has
obtained its European name. The natives call it
Jinjinberry. Its soil is in general rich and productive.

Many parts are woody; as only the valuable part of
the timber has been cut down. A considerable portion
of the land is flooded during the rainy season. A little
clearing and good engineering would probably make
it a healthy station, and save many valuable lives. But
this would cost money!

Some thousands of liberated Africans have been
sent to this island and located here, for whose be-
hoof the Wesleyan Missionary Society maintain a
small establishment, chiefly conducted by native
teachers from St. Mary's or Sierra Leone. The settlement has a commandant, and a small military force
of native soldiers; and several merchants of St.
Mary's have stores here, to facilitate their trading with
the interior. The principal town is called Fort St.
George.

On such an island there are no native "lions" to
be seen. Stay! here is one: no less a personage than
his majesty, the king of Catabar, who has come to
visit his English friends. A royal visit! what does
it mean in this outlandish part of the world? Why,
he has come to receive presents, or, in plain language,
to beg. Not that he personally asks for anything,
unless there should be some article to which he takes
a great fancy: but his attendants have no modesty
in soliciting presents for their sovereign and themselves.

It is worth while to see how so great a king as that
of Catabar conducts himself on a visit: so let us step
into a British house which he has entered. He is a
tall fine looking person (twenty years ago), still in

youthful manhood; but his face does not bespeak
much wisdom or talent: and we afterwards hear
that his reputation does not stand very high either
for council or war.   He is well-dressed in African
fashion; but most of his attendants are uncouth
mortals, poorly attired.   Salutations have passed with
the master of the house.   The king then looks round
at the furniture, and admires some of the articles.

What now is the matter?   The king catches sight
of a mirror, and, seeing himself in it, smiles in admiration of his own handsome figure.   The others
crowd round, and look in the glass with amazement.
It contains the whole group, and everything that is
in the room.   If they had ever seen a looking-glass
before, it was a small one; they never saw anything
like this.   But presently a marraboo, who is in the
royal train, comes and pulls the king by the sleeve
to draw him away, urging him to leave the house
directly.   Surely there is some magical incantation
in that mirror!   It is a white man's greegree!   It is
a charm which will throw its spells around you, and
make you the white man's servant!

The monarch hesitates for a moment.   But he is
not going away so quickly, without any presents; and
he likes to see himself in the mirror.   He stands
erect; he is a head taller than any of the rest, and
his embroidered tunic and white turban set him off
to advantage.   So the marraboo is quieted, and the
company talk, and smile, and laugh at themselves
and at each other before the mirror.   They are a
singular group!   A little conversation ensues on the

state of the country. The use, also, of a few European articles is explained to the Africans, who cannot help expressing their admiration of everything European, and throwing out some hints which cannot easily be mistaken.

Now a bottle of wine is produced, and his majesty is asked to take a little. He tastes it, and puts down the tumbler. One of his attendants, a blacksmith (who is an important personage in Africa, and is generally one of the royal councillors), intimates that his majesty has a stomach-ache this morning, and that he would prefer some rum. A bottle of this fiery liquor is immediately produced and uncorked. The blacksmith takes it up, fills a large tumbler—which will hold nearly a pint—to the brim, and gives it to the king, who without an instant's hesitation drinks it off. The glass is replenished, and the blacksmith helps himself to a good draught, and gives the remainder to one or two others. He then pockets the bottle, and another takes possession of the tumbler, both for the use of royalty. Some little presents, including tobacco, are now given; the king shakes hands with the Englishman, and takes his leave,—to visit another friend. We suppose that he had a stomach-ache in every house to which he went, for when he set off to return home, he seemed to walk down to the canoe in a serpentine manner. His horses were on the other side of the river; and we hope that a long ride would restore his mental equilibrium before he reached home. But some of these fellows are never quite sober.

Leaving Macarthy's island, we embark in a smaller vessel, laden with those species of merchandise which suit the wants and tastes of the interior tribes; and we again pursue our slow voyage up the noble river. We soon pass the border of a country which was famous, at that time, as the residence of King Kemingtan. This dreaded chieftain kept the whole neighbourhood in a state of trouble, did much damage to trade, and even annoyed the British in a variety of ways. He was a savage, reckless robber, who hesitated not to commit crimes of greatest enormity. He was a specimen of what a bold freebooter can do in such a country as Africa.

Kemingtan usurped the sovereign power, by killing his two elder brothers, to whose dead bodies he denied the rights of sepulture. On one occasion, a messenger brought him tidings of a defeat sustained by his troops, upon which, in his rage, he levelled his musket, and shot the luckless reporter dead upon the spot. On another occasion, being angry at a marraboo, whom it is not lawful to kill, he cut off his hands and feet, and let him bleed to death, saying, "It was God who killed him, not I, for I only maimed him." This was probably spoken in derision of the Mahometan's God, in whom he did not believe, being an infidel. Yet, though denying the existence of a supreme ruler, this chieftain was not exempt from the superstitious fears of his countrymen; but in an emergency had recourse to gree-grees of a dreadful kind. Being afraid of an attack from a powerful neighbour whose country he had pillaged, he adopted the following expedient, suggested by a diviner as cruel as himself. The people were summoned together outside the gate of Dunkaseen, his capital, as if for a religious purpose. Various incantations were performed by his marraboos, and two holes were dug in the ground close to each other. The drums beat, the musical instruments were sounded, and the dance was commenced by the griots. All at once, a girl, who was amongst the bystanders, was pointed out to Kemingtan's men, who seized and pinioned her, and dragged her to the holes. One of her legs was thrust into each hole, which was immediately filled up with earth. As she stood in this helpless condition, a number of men brought large lumps of wet clay, and built round her body, until, in spite of her entreaties and screams, and those of her mother who was present, they covered her head, and made her the tenant of a tomb. This pillar containing a human victim was declared to be a powerful greegree, sufficient to deter any mortal from assaulting the town. And it had the desired effect; for the atrocious deed, which was noised abroad, struck such terror into the enemy, that they dreaded to assail a place guarded by such infernal spells.

At length Kemingtan came in collision with the English. He seized upon a British vessel laden with merchandise, and appropriated the cargo to his own use. A handful of native troops were sent out against him, commanded by a gallant captain, who knew nothing of the art of war, or how to conduct an expedition in such a country as Africa. The soldiers, who were eager enough to fight, were conveyed in boats up a creek towards Dunkaseen. Having landed, they cut their way through a dense forest, dragging with them two or three small pieces of brass cannon. At length they came within sight of the town, and, without waiting to rest or refresh themselves after a fatiguing march, immediately opened fire upon the walls, thinking that these would fall at once, and that they would obtain an easy victory. But it required a great many rounds of shot to make a breach in mud walls; and when this was effected, their allies, commanded by Mantumba king of Woolli, refused to make the assault as they had promised to do. By this time, the British native troops were entirely exhausted, especially from want of water. Then the lion came out of his den, and boldly attacked them. A skirmish ensued, in which some native soldiers were killed, and two Europeans were wounded. A hasty retreat was sounded, and had not their flight been covered by Mantumba with his Mandingoes, they would probably have been all slain. They left their cannon behind them, which Kemingtan took possession of, and mounted on a mud fort in his town. He now defied the world to attack him.

Notwithstanding his victory, the chief of Dunkaseen was very angry with the British for having joined with his enemies; and it is said that he even threatened to attack Macarthy's island, the report of which kept some of its inhabitants in great fear. He intended, however, to make a greegree of the first white man's head that he could get. This terrified

the traders, as their small vessels were not prepared
to withstand an armed force brought against them in
canoes.

It happened that the first white man who ventured
into Kemingtan's presence was a missionary, who
went to ask him to send his sons to an educational
institution for natives on Macarthy's island. The
king seems to have been pleased, both with the boldness of the man who thus ventured into the lion's den,
and with the generosity of the offer. He allowed him
an interview. "His looks were depraved, determined,
and malignant. Whilst I was addressing him, he
scarcely looked towards me, but amused himself by
playing with a double-barrelled gun; and truly I
was not sorry when I saw him lay it down. He
made me no reply, which I am informed he rarely
does until a second interview." In the evening, he
sent the missionary and his interpreter some rice,
goat-mutton, and a mess of milk and kooskoos.
Next morning they were again favoured with an
interview. "He received us very civilly, and even
condescended to look at me. He said that too much
talk was not good, but what he said he meant; he
was glad to see me; that the object I came for was
very good, but it was so new and strange, that he
could not promise me to send his children; however,
he would think of it." He then accepted the presents offered to him, and in return provided the
strangers with horses and guides to Fatatenda.

As the level of this part of the country is considerably above that of the river, it is not overflowed

by the annual rains. Here, as on other dry districts,
you may see those fine species of timber growing
which are so much valued in England; such as the
African oak, mahogany, teak, and lignum vitæ.
These kinds of timber do not crack nor warp with
change of weather. They have been seasoned by long
growth under the rays of a tropical sun, and have
become almost indestructible, except by fire. Hence
they are very valuable for ship furniture and fittings;
and all that can be obtained from Africa finds a ready
market in Europe and America. The difficulty of
carriage down to the rivers, and the effects of a
tropical climate upon British ships and seamen, alone
prevent more being exported. These hard woods
would be of great importance in the country itself if
good houses were built, as they are not destroyed by
the white ant.

This insect, the *Termes bellicosus*, is one of the
plagues and blessings of Africa; and, as one of the
extraordinary phenomena of natural history, we must
not pass it by without observation. We could not
forget it in Africa, for there it obtrudes itself upon
our attention continually, in a variety of ways. It is
an incessant pest to the traveller when he rests for the
night. He cannot lay any of his boxes or traps on
the ground, for fear of their being eaten into, or wholly
devoured by white ants. They are very fond of soft
wood, and will spoil a good plank in one night. They
throw up mould against the object of their attack,
and, under this covered way, they carry on their depredations with extraordinary despatch. Suppose you

have left a box on the earth, or against the side of a
hut for a few days; when you come to look at it, you
find a little mould cleaving to it, and, as it were,
glueing it to the earth or clay wall.   On removing it,
you find all the under part of the wood gone, a thin
surface alone remaining, which falls into dust on
being touched.   The cunning insects do not make
holes quite through the wood, lest their operations
should be discovered.

But this source of annoyance is also a means of
promoting public good.   The *termes* is one of nature's
scavengers.   The immense mass of wood which falls
in the African forests and plains would produce a
pestilence, if left to rot slowly on the surface of the
ground; the routes also would be obstructed.   But
now, as soon as a branch or tree comes down, it is
attacked by the white ants, which soon devour its
pith and fibre, so that the first heavy rain breaks the
thin shell, and mixes its debris with the soil; and
the whole soon disappears.   So do native towns, when
they have been deserted for a short time.   The
rafters of bamboo, which supported the thatch of the
huts, are destroyed by termites; the roofs fall in and
become a prey; the walls of unburned clay are washed
down by pitiless showers, and nothing remains of the
late habitations of men save a few mounds of earth,
which the white ant now occupies.

Look at those earthen cones!   Some of them are
several feet high, and almost as big as a small hut.
If you could examine one of them, by first getting rid
of its inhabitants, you would be surprised at the ac-

curacy and beauty of its internal structure.   It is
composed of arched chambers, galleries, and maga-

WHITE ANT'S NESTS.

zines, all communicating with one another, and with
the royal apartments in the centre.   It has roads,
staircases, and bridges, not excavated, but built in
the most scientific manner.   The skill of the termes
probably exceeds that of any creature except civilised
man.

Each town or colony consists of three distinct
orders of termites.   The highest class, or nobility,
are the only perfect insects, as having wings.   They
are of great size, being equal in bulk to thirty of the
labourers, and seem to enjoy a short life of ease, as
they neither work nor fight.   But their honours are
of brief duration.   As soon as their four wings have
grown to maturity, they either sally forth, or are
driven out to seek and form new settlements.   Then
the air is full of them.   They fly at random, knocking against your face and everything else that comes
in their way.   In a few hours, their aërial flights are

terminated, and all their soaring is gone for ever. They lose their wings, and become the prey of birds, insects, and reptiles; or they fall into the water and perish. They are also captured, roasted, and eaten by the negro. A few pairs, only, out of many millions survive, and, being found by some of the lower class who are out at work, are by them elected kings and queens. One pair founds a new colony. The new sovereigns are immediately enclosed in a large chamber of clay, from which they have no egress, and which protects them from enemies. Their willing subjects begin the work of building about the royal pair, and provide for the future "hope of the nation." The queen soon becomes very big, resembling a large white snail. She is said to reach to 20,000 or 30,000 times the size of an ordinary termes, and to become 1000 times larger than her consort. She then produces eggs with extraordinary rapidity, from 50,000 to 100,000 in 24 hours, which are quickly carried away by the labourers, and placed in the cells and apartments prepared for their reception. We obtained possession of two or three of these queens by storming small colonies. It is dangerous to attack larger ones; and the usual way of destroying their habitations is by blowing them up with gunpowder.

The second class of termites is the military, or fighting order. They do nothing else than act as police and soldiers. They are a much larger and more perfect insect than the lowest class, but inferior to the nobility. They are fierce and vindictive; so that great care must be used in approaching a settlement, especially with hostile purposes. The bulk of the population consists of labourers, which are nearly a hundred times as numerous as the soldiers. They are about a quarter of an inch in length, and resemble our ants. By a wonderful instinct, given by the all-wise Creator, these insects pursue their respective occupations with consummate skill and perfect order, each knowing its own sphere of labour, and actively performing it, as if it were the only work to be done under the sun. It is a wonderful community. Should you ask, why the same insect lays three kinds of eggs at the same time, which will undergo different stages of development, and become labourers, soldiers, or princes? How they elect their sovereigns? Why they treat royalty with so much honour, and yet imprison it more closely than a Chinese emperor? How each comes to know its own functions, and to fill its own place? How they understand architecture; and even the building of arches, which the ancient Egyptians did not know? To these, and all like queries, we can only reply, that they are amongst the mysteries of nature. The facts are so. Let him who thinks that such a marvellous economy could be produced by chance, or developed from inert matter, explain it if ne can. We see in it the work of an Omnipresent Deity.

Do you see that man climbing the lofty palm, which has a stem straight and branchless as a ship's mast? You perceive that he has a hoop of rope or some other material round his waist and the tree, by which means, with the help of hands and legs, he is able to mount with much agility. Yet it is a dangerous

PALM TREE.

business. He is a gatherer of palm-wine. He makes incisions in the bark of the branches at the top; hangs a calabash under them, and leaves the matter to

Nature.   She causes the juice to exude from the palm, and by her own heat ferments the liquid, so that when the man returns, he finds the new wine ready for sale or use.   It is something like our cider; and is very largely drunk by the Negroes in places where this palm grows.

The beautiful tamarind-tree also abounds in this neighbourhood, and in most parts of tropical Africa. The natives understand its value as a medicine, and use it as a cooling and laxative draught in all fevers and inflammatory disorders.

We at length reach Fatatenda, a trading town of some importance.   It is about 500 miles up the Gambia, and the most inland depôt of European merchandise.   The river is here about 100 yards wide, and two fathoms deep when not swollen in the rainy seasons.   The tide rises several feet at this great distance from the sea; but vessels proceed no farther, as a little higher up are the falls or rapids of Barraconda. A good deal of commerce is here transacted by servants of European merchants.   We have said that the process of trading with Negroes is very tedious.   It is impossible to bring them to conclude a bargain, if they expect to gain a farthing by protracting the negotiation, and wearying you out with endless clamour. So we shall proceed, without envying the merchant's vocation, but only wishing we had his patience.

A ride of two days from Fatatenda will bring you to Medina, which may be called the capital of Woolli, since the king resides in this town.   The journey thither is through a deep forest, which can only be safely traversed by a person well acquainted with its intricate and devious ways. If you wish to have an interview with his sable majesty, you can obtain it through his minister, to whom a suitable present must be made. Indeed, everything is done in Africa by means of gifts. Without these, you could achieve nothing. The Frenchman, Caillée, who went into the country empty-handed, was treated like a slave, except when his falsehoods about his early history and conversion to Mahometanism were believed by Moslem zealots. On the contrary, Dr. Barth, who travelled like a gentleman and gave gifts to every one, was treated like a prince.

When you have satisfied the rapacity of the Premier of Woolli, you send through him a present to the king, requesting an audience. If he be pleased with your offering, he will grant an interview; otherwise, you must increase the value of your present. If satisfied, he sends you some food, which costs him nothing. If your company be large, a sheep or goat may be furnished; if small, the supply will probably consist of fowls and kooskoos. The last named dish is universal amongst the Negroes of Western and Interior Africa, so that it has obtained a world-wide fame. Would you like to taste it? Then you may try to make some in the following manner.

Take some flour prepared after the African fashion. It is made from a small kind of grain, called millet or Guinea corn, from which the husk is separated, and it is then pounded into flour in large mortars by the women or slaves. Rice-flour is also used. A kind of

E

mutton broth, either from sheep or goat's flesh, is poured over the meal and well stirred, so that a sort of hasty-pudding is the result. But those who prepare kooskoos in the most approved and delicate way, do not pour broth over the flour, but steam the latter over a pot containing a stew and condiments, so that it imbibes the flavour of the meat and the seasoning. This is a slow process of cooking, but a very successful one. The kooskoos prepared in this manner has been highly commended by Europeans, and is indeed far from unpalatable. Of course, it is eaten after the simple fashion of the East. The food is put into a large bowl, and the guests squat round it. With some fingers of the left hand they steady the bowl, and with those of the right they help themselves to its contents. Sometimes a wooden spoon is used. Flesh or shea-butter is also eaten with the kooskoos. But in whatever way this dish may be prepared, or whatever may be its accompaniments, it forms the staple supper of the Negroes. This is their chief meal. Breakfast generally consists of a gruel, with perhaps a little tamarind in it, to give it an acid taste.

When Mungo Park visited Medina, the existing king was named Jatta. He was a venerable old man, favourably spoken of by Major Houghton. The traveller was forewarned not to presume to shake hands with his majesty, as this was not etiquette. " I found him seated upon a mat before the door of his hut ; a number of men and women were arranged on each side, who were singing and clapping their hands. I saluted him respectfully, and informed him of the purport of my visit. The king graciously replied, that he not only gave me leave to pass through his country, but would offer up his prayers for my safety. On this, one of my attendants, seemingly in return for the king's condescension, began to sing, or rather to roar, an Arabic song, at every pause of which the king himself, and all the people present, struck their hands against their forehead, and exclaimed with devout and affecting solemnity, Amen, Amen." His majesty then promised a guide. Next morning Mr. Park repeated his visit, and found him sitting upon a bullock's hide, warming himself before a large fire. He received the traveller tenderly, and entreated him to desist from trying to penetrate into the interior; for fear he should meet the same fate as Major Houghton.

The Rev. W. Fox, probably the last white man who has visited Medina, describes it as a walled town, containing about twelve hundred inhabitants, most of whom are pagans. "The wall is about eight feet high, and has three entrances or gates, between each of which the ground is excavated several feet deep." The king's name was Mansa Koi. He was rather stout, about sixty years old, and had reigned thirteen years. His residence and apparel differed little from those of his subjects. "We found the old king lounging upon his bed inside his hut, and I was seated beside him, the rest of the company squatted on the floor." His majesty was very complaisant, said "very good" to what was proposed, and gave free permission to "pass on."

At this time, there might have been seen in Bambako, a neighbouring town, two of those singular
beings, called by the Mandingoes "Funne," and by
Spaniards "Albinos," or White Negroes. These are
occasionally met with in tropical Africa. Their
colour evidently proceeds from a disease, probably of
the skin, as they are very sensitive to the stings of
insects. They seldom live long. Those at Bambako
were females; one about twenty-five years of age, the
other about fifteen. They appeared sickly, but were
robust, and said to
enjoy good health.
Their parents had
other children quite
black. Albinoes are
regarded as pheno-
mena, or "wonder-
ful things," by the
natives, but they are
not shunned.

Here is another
strange sight! It is a
singular dress, made
of bark, hanging
upon a tree near
the entrance of the

MUMBO JUMBO.

town. It belongs to Mumbo Jumbo. Who is
he? and when is his dress worn? Let us see. As
the darkness of night is approaching, dismal cries are
heard in the woods. They gradually approach the
town, till by and by a figure, dressed in the habit
above mentioned, comes to the bentang. He is

armed with a rod of public authority, and all the inhabitants assemble around him, women as well as men. Indeed the fair sex are chiefly concerned in the issues of this pantomime. The usual songs and dances commence, and are continued till midnight. But the wonted gaiety and mirth with which these amusements are ordinarily pursued, are absent from many breasts on the present occasion. Conscience is doing its work in female hearts, which are trembling for the results. By and by Mumbo Jumbo points out his victim, who is immediately seized, stripped naked, tied to a post, and severely beaten with his rod. It is Lynch law. There is no resisting —no appeal. The unfortunate woman is thus publicly scourged, amidst the derisive laughter of the whole population; and none mock her more than her own sex, when their own fears have been dissipated about themselves.

What has the woman done? and who is Mumbo Jumbo? He is either her husband, or some friend to whom has been committed the charge of this business; but the mask prevents his being known. And the wife's fault, for which she is thus indecently chastised, is, that she has been a quarrelsome termagant in the house. For, as the Pagan Negroes are not limited in the number of their wives, and some of them have a great many, family broils often arise, as might be expected. Sometimes the women quarrel so violently that they refuse to submit even to their husband's decision. When he finds that his authority is despised, and that he can no longer rule his own household, he

appeals to the town councillors, who have recourse to
Mumbo Jumbo. It is, therefore, a device of the men
reserved for cases of emergency, to uphold their own
dignity, and "tame the shrew" of their large family.
So also the ominous dress is hung up *in terrorem,* in
a place where it is likely to be often seen by the
women; just as a rod is sometimes exhibited on the
master's desk at school, to keep unruly lads in check,
through fear of unpleasant consequences.

Wives are usually purchased in Africa, their price
in the west being commonly reckoned at the value of
two slaves. If, however, the girl be handsome, so
that the man is thought to be in love, her parents
ask a great deal more for her. As the money is professedly given in compensation for the services which
the young woman could render to her parents, the
bargain is struck with them. The girl's consent may,
or may not be asked — it is of no importance; she
must obey, or take the direful consequences. For if
the parents have once testified their consent to the
suitor's proposals, by eating some kola-nuts which
he has given them as a sign of agreement, their
daughter must either take this man or remain a
spinster. If an attempt should be made to give her
to another at any future period, the old sweetheart
could come and take her for his slave.

The day of the wedding is now fixed upon (we
speak of the Mandingoes and their neighbours), and
a few friends are invited to be present. Plenty of
food is prepared for the occasion. At sunset, the
bride is taken by some women into a hut, and arrayed
in a white cotton dress which reaches to her feet.

The poor thing is then seated in the middle of the hut, and the old cronies squat round her, and give her a long lecture about her future behaviour. The monotony of this instruction is happily interrupted by gay girls, who come in occasionally, dancing and singing. The rest of the company have been feasting and eating kola-nuts. When all are satiated, the usual amusements take place, and are continued till dawn of day. But about midnight, the bride is silently led to the hut which she is to occupy in future; and upon a given signal, the bridegroom also steals away from the mirthful company.

Some rich Negroes boast of having a great many wives; but Mahometans are limited to four. As these latter usually pay more for their consorts, they expect even a greater deference and submission to their will than the Pagan Negroes do. Except where a stern Moslemism prevails, in the central regions, Negro wives have much liberty, and are permitted to enjoy all public amusements. Indeed, their cheerful singing and agile dancing form a great part of the usual night's entertainments. The husband's authority is very great, and he has the liberty of administering gentle castigations in case of disobedience or unruliness. If a wife should think that she is treated with undue severity, she may appeal to a public council; but as this is composed of husbands, she has little chance of success. If she should be heard to complain of their decision against her, she will probably be brought to submission by the rod of the redoubtable Mumbo Jumbo.

CHAP. III.

African Fever. — Sand-spouts.— Dreadful Heat. — Cure of Fever.—
The First Shower. — Sowing and Reaping. — A Tornado. — Atmo-
spheric Phenomena.—Bondu.—Boolibany.—Dress.—Teucolars.—
Visits to the King.—Commerce.—Kajaaga.—Serawoollies.—Anec-
dotes of Abdul-kader.—Mahometan Proselytes.—Slave Coffle. —
Poor Nealee. — Hunting Slaves. — Domestic Slavery.—Country of
Kasson.—Hyænas.—Dressing Leather.—Negro Surgery.

LET us suppose that your exposure to the heat during
this journey to Medina has brought on a fever. This
is very likely to be the case. It would, also, be very
convenient to have your "seasoning" attack before
you go farther into the interior, and especially before
the commencement of the rains. Time has been
passing whilst you have been looking about the
country, and the month of May has set in with
terrific heat. The sun is vertical, and the thermo-
meter rises in the forenoon to 104° or 110° of Fahr. in
the shade, where it remains till ten o'clock at night;
it then recedes a few degrees only till morning.
" The grasshopper is a burden," and the least exertion
is irksome during many hours of the day. The
broken and restless slumbers of night afford little
refreshment. Perhaps, also, the " prickly heat "

covers your body with distressing itchiness. In the
evening, if you burn a candle, millions of mosquitoes
assail you, and at length drive you to bed, to hide
yourself under the mosquito-curtains.

The wind is sometimes high, coming from the
desert, blowing in gusts and whirlwinds, with columns
of sand, which are singular to behold, especially if
they cross the river. When one of these sand-spouts
passes a hut, it will probably whirl the roof high into
the air, and leave every corner of the dwelling full of
debris of the desert. The air is scorching hot, as if it
came from a fiery furnace, and it licks up every drop
of water except the river. Wooden articles are cracked
or warped. Drawers refuse to open, boxes and desks
will not shut : everything feels hotter than yourself,
whilst you feel burning. The water is at the temperature of a hot-bath in England : and the sailor says
that a chop could be cooked on the iron of the ship's
anchor.

You feel peculiarly heavy, dull, and restive : next
day you are in a burning fever. The primary object
is to " break " it, or obtain an intermission ; for if
you can change it to an intermittent, you may soon
recover. You take all kinds of sudorific medicines,
apparently without success. A friend says, " Try this
native tea, I am sure it will do you good." So, you
swallow down a basin of it, sorely against your will.
You try another, and another, and now you break out
into a profuse perspiration. Quinine and port wine,
with good nursing, will complete your cure. Quinine
seems to be a specific remedy in intermittents ; it

never fails to cure, if the patient has not previously
sunk too low.

The first shower falls in Senegambia during the
third week of May. For some time previously, the
evenings have been cloudy, and much sheet-light-
ning has been seen in the distance. The days are
still clear, but each succeeding night the sky becomes more lowering and the lightnings more vivid.
The natives are now busily engaged in clearing the
ground for sowing seed. Guinea corn, and other
similar species of grain used in these parts, grow to a
great height; so that when the harvest is ripe, the
natives bend down the tall stalks, and cut off the
bunches of ears with a knife. The stubble is left on
the ground, where it does not rot, but remains dry on
the surface until the approach of the rainy season,
when it is burned. It is a grand sight, on a dark
evening, to see the country all in a blaze. But the
operation of burning requires some caution, lest this
fire should spread too far, or catch the trees and consume valuable timber.

After the first showers have fallen, a person, generally a woman, goes out with a hoe, and makes small
holes in the earth. Another woman or child follows,
and drops a few corn-seeds into the hole, and covers
them over with the foot. Thus the grain grows in
small clumps or clusters of plants, and is not scattered
over the soil, as is the case with rice. The young
corn requires to be cleaned with the hoe, as weeds
also grow most luxuriantly. The whole period which
elapses between clearing the ground and gathering

the harvest, is from four to five months; but the process is attended with very little labour. When the blade appears, some of the natives, particularly the Foolas, sow cotton seeds among the corn, which spring up about the time of corn harvest. In this case, the stubble is removed to make room for the cotton plants. Thus two valuable crops are obtained from the same ground in one year, the cotton being gathered in March.

In Senegambia, the first tornado blows near the end of May, and these terrific storms last for a month. Then two months of "rain" follow, which are succeeded by another month of tornadoes. The drying month, October, is the most unhealthy of the whole year, as the air is then saturated with the effluvia of decayed vegetable matter.

No one will forget the phenomena of the first tornado which he has witnessed. Dark clouds begin to rise from every part of the horizon. They gradually creep up to the zenith, the blue of which becomes smaller and smaller, until it disappears, and the whole heaven is covered with a mantle of thick darkness. It becomes gloomy even at mid-day. Distant rumbling has been heard for some time, and faint flashes of electric fluid have been seen playing in the firmament. When the last speck of blue has left the heavens, the storm may be immediately expected. It is preceded by a death-like stillness of nature. Not a breath of wind moves; not a sound is heard, except the bleating of goats, or the cry of the feathered tribe, as they hurry away in fright to their

wonted places of shelter. Then, in a moment, comes
a terrific blast, which almost seems as if it would
sweep the earth with the besom of destruction. All
fences fall before it; huts are unroofed, trees are uprooted, and boats are hurried down the river with
frightful rapidity. The blast passes; then rain falls.
It is rain indeed! It does not drop, it pours like
water from the rose of a watering-can. The ground
is deluged in a few minutes, and vapour ascends from
the heated soil like a thick mist. Then comes a flash,
and a crash of thunder, as if it would rend both
heaven and earth. It roars with deafening noise,
and nothing else can be heard. The lightning increases in vividness, and the artillery of heaven plays
incessantly. Lightning bursts from every point of
the compass, though the storm comes from the east.
The electricity is so brilliant, that the smallest objects can be discerned at midnight, and no shutters
can keep out the lurid glare. After the sheet-light-
ning has thus flashed, there is a momentary darkness,
and then the forked-lightning plays on the dense
clouds with dazzling brightness, and finally darts into
the earth. Woe to any creature, man or beast, who
is near the spot where the electric fluid falls! It
even scorches trees, sets fire to huts, and tears up the
ground.

The tornado is one of the sublimest displays of
nature's powers, as all its phenomena are exhibited
on the grandest scale. A man then truly feels that
he is a weak and insignificant creature. He is in the
midst of mighty elements in great commotion, any

one of which could annihilate him in an instant,
and he is helpless as an insect. This terrific storm
sometimes lasts for two or three hours. At first, it is
repeated after an interval of several days; afterwards
it occurs almost daily. It merges into the proper
rainy season. Yet, from this appellation, you must
not suppose that it rains incessantly for two months,
every day and all day long. This would soon produce a flood that would overwhelm all the plains.
It pours down for half a day at a time. It literally
" pours," as we have said, not drops, for as great a
depth of water has been known to fall in one day in
Africa, as during a whole year in England.

Proceeding eastward from Woolli, we next come to
Bondu. The royal residence has been removed from
Fatteconda, where the king lived during Mungo
Park's time, to Boolibany. This is one of the
strongest towns of Western Africa. It is situated in
a large plain, where it is surrounded by a number of
small towns or villages. Its walls are constructed of
solid clay, ten feet in height, of a zigzag form, with
strong bastions, and pierced with loopholes. The
gateways are also surmounted by small turrets, furnished with holes to shoot through. It has wells of
water inside as well as outside the town.

The sovereign of Bondu is called an Almami,
which probably expresses the same thing as a caliph
or religious king, for he is a Mussulman and receives
sacred honours. His residence or palace resembles a
castle. It is built of mud walls of great thickness,
which are intersected with partitions of clay, sup-

ported by strong timbers. These divide it into
several courts and chambers, which communicate
with each other by intricate passages. Some of the
rooms are for domestic use, some for store-places,
some serve for an arsenal, containing fire-arms and
ammunition, and are guarded by sentries. The flat
roof is very strong, surrounded by a thick parapet,
on which three small cannons are mounted : the
whole is encompassed by a strong outer wall.

Artillery in Africa! This is a new idea. We suppose these pieces of ordnance once belonged to some
slaver condemned on the coast, and sold to a merchant. Useless to a European, who would not dare
to fire them, these old cannon are highly vaunted by
a native prince, who supposes they will last for ever.
If an enemy should appear, the same thing would
probably occur at Boolibany as happened to a negro
neighbour of ours. His black gunners crammed an
old field-piece full of powder and shot of all kinds,
filling it up to the muzzle. A train of gunpowder
was laid to the touch-hole. It is fired. Bang! The
enemy are safe enough, for the piece has burst and
killed some of the artillery novitiates.

Boolibany has a large mosque, where prayers are
read or chanted in Mahometan style five times a day.
The priest or marraboo wears a white turban, red or
blue crown, and long white robe with large sleeves,
like a surplice. Sometimes he uses a low hat made
of rushes, with a tremendous brim, to serve as a parasol. The respectable inhabitants have their smocks
embroidered with coloured worsteds. Some of this

class live in square houses with flat roofs, but the
common people dwell in the ordinary African hut.
The female gentry are distinguished by a broad
bandage worn round the forehead, adorned with beads
of gold, silver, amber, coral, or coloured glass. They
have also large gold ear-rings, which reach nearly to
the shoulder, and are supported by a string of red
leather passing over the head. Both sexes wear
sandals.

In the best African houses you would find little
worth stealing, except articles of dress and female ornaments, as above mentioned. The sheep-skin mat, or
bullock's hide, elevated on a platfrom of clay or canes,
forms the Negro's best bedstead; and a wrapper, his
bed-clothes. Two or three low stools, earthen jars,
pots, calabashes, and the all-important pestle and
mortar, constitute the furniture of the wealthiest individuals. They do not " live " in the house.

The inhabitants of Bondu are principally Teucolars; but Boolibany, as a place of much trade, has a
mixed population. Being now a Mahometan country
it ought to be more civilised than its Pagan neighbours, and it is so in some respects. But the Moslem
faith has always a baneful influence upon the temper
of the Negro, which is naturally mild and hospitable.
In Bondu there is a regular code of laws, and a
court for the trial of offenders. The principal laws
refer to assaults, manslaughter, theft, adultery, murder, and high treason. Only the last two crimes are
punished with death, which is inflicted by strangula-
tion. Assaults are punished by fines or lashes; man-

slaughter by the price of six slaves; theft by amputation of the right hand, or in confirmed cases by starvation. For adultery, the male offender is visited with loss of property, or if he be poor, with a severe flogging: but the woman generally escapes punishment from her husband, or is even rewarded by him for entrapping a victim, from whom he gets "heavy damages."

Mr. Park's account of his interview with the Almami of Bondu exhibits some of the characteristics of African princes in a humorous way. The traveller had concealed some valuables in the roof of his hut; expecting his luggage to be searched during his absence at court. He put on his best blue coat, in order to preserve it; and he took with him a present of gunpowder, amber, tobacco, and his umbrella. It was a state visit, as he had in the morning seen the king privately under a tree.

" We found the monarch sitting upon a mat (in the court) and two attendants with him. I repeated what I had before told him concerning the object of my journey, and my reasons for passing through his country. He seemed, however, but half satisfied. The notion of travelling for curiosity was quite new to him. He thought it impossible, he said, that any man in his senses would undertake so dangerous a journey, merely to look at the country and its inhabitants. However, when I offered to show him the contents of my portmanteau, and everything belonging to me, he was convinced; and it was evident that this suspicion had arisen from a belief,

that every white man must of necessity be a trader.
When I had delivered my presents, he seemed well
pleased, and was particularly delighted with the
umbrella, which he repeatedly furled and unfurled,
to the great admiration of himself and his two attendants, who could not for some time comprehend the
use of this wonderful machine." Being desired to
remain, Mr. Park says, " he proceeded to an eulogium
on my blue coat, of which the yellow buttons seemed
particularly to catch his fancy; and he concluded
by entreating me to present him with it; that he
would wear it on all public occasions, and inform
every one who saw it of my great liberality toward
him." The traveller knew what this humble request
meant; and taking off his coat, laid it at the monarch's feet.

In the morning, Mr. Park was again sent for to
the palace by the king, who asked to be bled. But
as soon as he saw the lancet, his heart failed him; so
he proposed to postpone the operation, "as he felt
himself much better;" and requested the stranger to
favour his wives with a visit. "I had no sooner
entered the court appropriated to the ladies, than the
whole seraglio surrounded me; some begging for
physic, some for amber; and all of them desirous of
trying that great African specific, *blood-letting*. They
were ten or twelve in number, most of them young
and handsome, wearing on their heads ornaments of
gold and beads of amber.

" They rallied me with a good deal of gaiety on
different subjects; particularly upon the whiteness of

my skin, and the prominency of my nose. They insisted that both were artificial. The first, they said,
was produced when I was an infant, by dipping me
in milk: and they insisted that my nose had been
pinched every day, till it had acquired its present
unsightly and unnatural conformation. On my part,
without disputing my own deformity, I paid them
many compliments upon African beauty. I praised
the glossy jet of their skin, and the lovely depression
of their noses. But they said that flattery, or (as
they emphatically termed it) 'honey-mouth,' was not
esteemed in Bondu." However, they presently sent
him a jar of honey and some fish. Simple creatures!
What man or woman does not really like "honey-
mouth," however much he or she may rail against
it?

There are many merchants in Boolibany and other
towns of Bondu, on account of its central situation.
They trade with Gedumah and other Moorish countries
on the north; bartering corn and blue cotton cloths
for the salt of the desert and sweet-smelling gums.
They carry the salt to Dentila and more southern
states, where they exchange it for shea-butter, iron,
and gold-dust. The customs or duties levied on merchandise in transit are very heavy, and sometimes
consist of muskets and gunpowder or Indian baft.

Beyond Bondu is the petty kingdom of Kajaaga,
inhabited by Serawoolies. They are jet black, like
the Jollofs, and are also an active and commercial
people. They make long journeys in the pursuit of
trade. Their language is very guttural. It was in

this country that Mungo Park's hardships first began, as he was here pillaged of much of his property by the king's servants, on the pretext that he had not paid the usual transit dues for his goods, nor sent a present to the sovereign. He was delivered from his precarious situation by a nephew of the King of Kasson (on the eastern border of Kaarta), who came to arrange some disputes which threatened a rupture between the two countries.

The inhabitants of Kasson were converted to the Moslem faith after the most approved fashion. An embassy came to Teesee from the redoutable monarch Almami Abdulkader, King of Foota Torra, a country on the west of Bondu. They demanded a public audience of Tiggity Sego, King of Kasson. It was granted; and the ambassadors then declared it to be the will of their august sovereign, that the King and all the people of Kasson should embrace the Mahometan faith, otherwise he would join his arms to those of Kajaaga, with whom there was then a variance; for he could not stand neutral, and see an infidel nation attack the "faithful" people of Kajaaga. Abdulkader had seized upon this critical moment to carry out his schemes of proselyting Kasson, which he probably would not have ventured to do at another time. As the case was urgent, and nothing but destruction seemed to await their refusal, the people of Teesee agreed to submit. They offered up eleven prayers out of the Koran, which was the recognised sign of their conversion, and the whole country became nominally Mahometan.

But Abdulkader was not always so successful in
his religious expeditions. He made a similar attempt
to convert Damel, a king of the Jollofs. On this
occasion, the ambassador was accompanied by two
chief Bushreens, or Moslem teachers, who carried
each a large knife fixed on the top of a long pole.
" As soon as he had procured admission into the presence of Damel, and announced the pleasure of his
sovereign, he ordered the Bushreens to present the
emblems of his mission. The two knives were accordingly laid before Damel, and the ambassador
explained himself as follows : ' With this knife Abdulkader will condescend to shave the head of Damel,
if Damel will embrace the Mahometan faith ; and
with this other knife, Abdulkader will cut the throat
of Damel, if Damel refuses to embrace it—take your
choice.' Damel coolly told the ambassador that he
had no choice to make ; he neither chose to have his
head shaved, nor his throat cut ; and with this answer the ambassador was civilly dismissed."

To fulfil his threats, Abdulkader raised a powerful
army and invaded the Jollof country. By their
king's command, the people retired before the advancing foe, filling up the wells, and destroying what
provisions and effects they could not carry off. The
assailants pressed onward till they were exhausted
from hunger and thirst. Having at length found a
watering-place in the woods, they sat down to rest
and fell asleep. Before morning, they were suddenly
attacked by Damel's army, which was fresh and vigorous ; by whom the invaders were completely routed

and almost annihilated, being pursued and cut down
by the Jollof horsemen. Amongst the prisoners was
Abdulkader himself, the ambitious and vain-glorious
fanatic.

"When his royal prisoner was brought before him
in irons, and thrown upon the ground, the magnani-
mous Damel, instead of setting his foot upon his
neck, and stabbing him with his spear, according to
custom in such cases, addressed him as follows: ' Abdulkader, answer me this question! If the chance
of war had placed me in your situation, and you in
mine, how would you have treated me?' ' I would
have thrust my spear into your heart,' returned Abdulkader, with great firmness; 'and I know that a
similar fate awaits me.' ' Not so,' said Damel; ' my
spear is indeed red with the blood of your subjects
killed in battle, and I could now give it a deeper
stain by dipping it in your own; but this would not
build up my towns, nor bring to life the thousands
who fell in the woods. I will not, therefore, kill you
in cold blood, but I will retain you as my slave, until
I perceive that your presence in your own kingdom
will be no longer dangerous to your neighbours, and
then I will consider of the proper way of disposing of
you.'"

The events of this war soon became a favourite
topic of conversation throughout all that region of
Africa, and Damel obtained a great reputation. The
singing men joined in his praises, and spread his
fame far and wide. Mr. Park declares that, strange
as this history may appear, he heard it from so many

quarters that he could not doubt of its truth ; and it was afterwards confirmed by nine men, who were taken in the wood along with Abdulkader, and having been sold as slaves, sailed in the same ship with himself (Park) to the West Indies. Damel liberated his royal prisoner at the end of three months' "penal servitude," in compliance with the earnest request of the people of Foota Torra. We presume that he was cured of his propensity to proselyte men by the knife and sword.

Nobody could suppose that much religion would ensue from this summary and wholesale method of conversion pursued by Moslem kings. The faith of the proselytes is at first quite nominal. Soon, however, Bushreens come amongst them, teach them a few prayers or verses of the Koran, narrate the legends of their faith and the exploits of Mahomet, and institute the daily prayers. They thus obtain a few staunch disciples; but the greater part of the people know little and care less about these things. So that even in nominally Mahometan states, there are a great many professed pagans, and the bulk of the rest are heathens in their heart. It is somewhat different, as we shall see, in towns situated on the Niger.

Here is a little noisy company! Who can they be? What are they doing? A venerable sort of man is sitting on the ground, with a number of urchins in a circle about him. Some of them are naked, some have a rag about their loins, and a few have a shirt. The Bushreen is repeating some lines from the Koran, wagging his head, and intoning his words in the most ceremonial fashion. The little fellows, squatting around, repeat his words, with similar intonations and waggings of the head, so that the whole scene is most ludicrous. This is their education; and it is in Arabic, of which few understand a single word, except the name of Allah. We have found some of the Bushreens themselves to be as innocent of comprehending the Koran as any of their followers. But a few literati from the interior are pretty good Arabic scholars. When these settle in the west, they are treated with great respect; and under Moslem princes they obtain much distinction and legislative power, since they explain the laws of the Koran by which a people ought to be governed.

Our mention of slavery in connection with Abdul-kader's defeat, introduces us to this sad subject. It is as common in Africa as kooskoos or white ants. It meets you everywhere. It often obtrudes upon your view in a painful manner, and presents sights of tearful woe and sad desolation.

Here is a coffle or slave-caravan entering the town of which some of the travellers are natives! They have been long absent from home, and now return in a sort of triumph. Some singing men come first. The other free people follow. Then come the poor slaves, four abreast, fastened to one another by a twisted thong passed round each of their necks; a spear-man walking between each four. These are followed by the domestic slaves, the free women, and baggage. On their march, the slaves are also secured with fetters on their legs which must be held up with

a string.   At night, an additional pair of fetters is put
on their hands : and sometimes also a light chain of
iron is passed round their necks.   The poor creatures
are dreadfully afraid of approaching the coast, lest
they should be carried over the sea, where they expect to be eaten by white cannibals.   If any of them
show evident signs of refractoriness, farther means
are taken to secure them from running away.

THE SLAVE CHAIN AT THE COAST.

The slaves suffer much in travelling through the
forests, especially those that are weak.   They must
keep up with the coffle, or else they would be lost or
devoured by wild beasts.   When they lag behind,
from sheer fatigue, they are beaten and dragged along

by their neck-rope; nor are any means of cruelty or
violence spared to force them onwards. To-night,
their irons will be examined, the hand-fetters put on,
and they will be stowed away in huts guarded by men.
In the morning, they will be led under the shade of
a tree, and encouraged to play at amusing games and
to sing songs, in order to cheer them up. Some of
them will abandon themselves to their fate, and try
to enjoy the present hour: but others will sit de-
murely on the ground, plunged in melancholy, brood-
ing over the past and imagining the dark future.
These slaves are going to Morocco, over the Great
Desert, where their sufferings will probably be intense,
and perhaps most of them will perish amid the sands.

This is no fiction. The truth of the account can be
substantiated by any amount of native testimony that
may be desired. It was witnessed for several months
by Mungo Park, who travelled with a coffle from the
interior to the coast. He gives a mournful account
of the fate of a female slave belonging to Karfa, under
whose kind protection he journeyed. Poor Nealee
complained of pains in her legs, lagged behind, and
refused her victuals. She was ordered to the front of
the coffle, and relieved of her load. The party were
endeavouring to rob a hive in a tree of its honey,
when they were assailed by myriads of bees, and
scattered in all directions. Their bundles were only
recovered by firing the grass, and rushing through
the smoke which had scared the bees. After a search,
poor Nealee was found lying near a brook, stung in a
dreadful manner. She was washed, and her wounds

anointed with certain bruised leaves: but she refused
to proceed further. The whip was applied, and at
length she started up and walked for four or five
hours longer: she then fell on the grass, utterly exhausted. The whip was again applied without effect.
She was tied upon an ass, but could not sit up; and
the beast proved so refractory under this burden,
that Nealee was obliged to be taken off. A sort of
litter was made of bamboo canes, and being tied on
it with slips of bark, she was carried on the heads of
two slaves. At night, the whole coffle were so much
fatigued and discouraged, that some of them *snapt
their fingers*, which is a sign of desperation. They
were all put in strong irons. After a night's rest
they were much recovered.

But poor Nealee's limbs were so stiff and painful,
that she could not walk or even stand. She was once
more tied, like a corpse, on the ass, which again became
so unruly that she was thrown down and had one of
her legs injured. Then the cry of the whole coffle
was *kang-tegi, kang-tegi!* " Cut her throat, cut her
throat!" On hearing this, Mungo Park hurried to
the front of the coffle, that he might not see the
death of the poor woman. In a short time one of
Karfa's domestic slaves came up to him " with poor
Nealee's garment on the end of his bow, and exclaimed *Neallee affeeleeta!* (Nealee is lost.) I asked
him whether the slatees had given him the garment
as a reward for cutting her throat. He replied
that Karfa and the schoolmaster would not consent
to that measure, but had left her on the road." This

was cruel pity! The knife would have ended her
woes quickly: but now she was left to linger a while,
till some wild beast or bird should tear her in pieces.
The coffle were deeply impressed with this tragedy,
and hasted on in mournful silence. But the whole
company had to endure great privation and suffering
before they reached a town where they could rest.

Who are these slaves? and what has been their
crime, that they are held in bondage, and sold as
cattle? Gentle reader! their only offence has been
that they were the weaker party in war, or were unable to defend themselves against the sudden attack
of an enemy. All prisoners taken in battle, and in
the pillage resulting from a defeat, become slaves.
But there are more wicked and atrocious ways of
procuring them. While on M'Carthy's island, we
were one day thrown into much excitement by the
flight of many natives to this place of refuge. Their
towns, not many miles off, were attacked in the night
by a marauding foe and destroyed in the usual way.
Some miscreants band together to steal the bodies of
men. They approach stealthily in the dark, and
rushing through the stockade of the town, set fire to
the thatch of the huts. The inmates, startled by the
noise and the flames, rush out; when most of the
men are massacred: the women, young persons, and
children are caught and taken for slaves. This
slave-hunting goes on continually. Every night
witnesses these bloody horrors: and every morning
sees villages or towns newly destroyed and deserted.

Kidnapping is another mode of obtaining slaves.

A strong man will lurk armed near some place of resort in the neighbourhood of a village : and when he sees a child, woman, or young person passing by, will spring upon his victim like a tiger, drag his prey into the thicket, and carry it off at night.

This slave-catching is the bane of Africa. It sets town against town, and man against man ; rouses the worst passions of the human breast ; and often turns the gentle Negro into a raging wild beast. Excuses for attacking a weak neighbour are easily found by a strong nation ; the real object being, not to avenge an affront or injury received, but to catch human beings and sell them for slaves. Of course, retaliation often follows ; and thus the murderous flame is kept alive by the pouring on of oil, till the country is desolated, or at least minished of its inhabitants. Many fall, to procure one slave.

A large part of the population are domestic slaves or serfs. Their condition is not usually bad. They cannot (we speak of the western parts) be sold except for a crime committed by themselves, or from the bankruptcy of their masters : and there are laws for their protection against hard usage. Still, it is a bad system. And as the domestic slaves form the foot soldiers in war, and are generally armed only with spears, they are the most easily taken prisoners, when their condition is entirely changed. They are also sometimes furtively sold by their owners, or exchanged for others. Alas ! " might overcomes right " all over the world ; and no where more than in Africa!

In passing through the kingdom of Kasson, we

NEGRO TOWN IN THE INTERIOR.

shall find it a populous country, full of towns and villages and cultivated plains, surrounded by woods and rocky hills. The last-mentioned districts have their own inhabitants, as they abound in wolves and hyænas. When pressed by hunger, these wild beasts do not hesitate to form into companies and assault the dwellings of man. "Some of these animals paid us a visit in the evening. Their approach was discovered by the dogs of the village, which did not bark, but howl in the most dismal manner. The inhabitants no sooner heard them, than, knowing the cause, they armed themselves: and providing bunches of dry grass, went in a body to the inclosure in the middle of the village where the cattle were kept. Here they lighted the bunches of grass, and waving them to and fro, ran hooping and hallooing towards the hills. This manœuvre had the desired effect of frightening the wolves away from the village: but on examination, we found that they had killed five of the cattle, and torn and wounded many others." One could almost imagine that these beasts had learned a lesson from the slave-hunters. Poor Africa! there is no security within thy borders! Thy villagers dwell in a state of alarm by day, and in a state of siege by night!

In Kasson, there are some good manufacturers of *leather;* which is one of the regular *trades* of Africa. It is learned and pursued by a class of mechanics called karankeeas. These men tan the hides by steeping them in a mixture of wood-ashes and water till they lose the hair; and afterwards in a decoction of the leaves of the *goo* tree, which is a powerful astringent. They rub and beat the hides frequently, to make the leather soft and pliable; in which they succeed admirably. Bullock-leather is used principally for sandals: sheep-skin and goat-skin are converted into belts, sheathes, and bags; into coverings of greegrees, saddles, and other articles; and into ornaments of various kinds. They are first dyed red or yellow; by means of certain plants known to the natives, whose workmanship in leather is far from despicable.

SANDAL.

The Negroes are bad physicians, seeming only to know the use of some sudorifics, bitters, and purgatives; though this amount of knowledge is of no little importance in a land of fevers. They also suffer much from dysentery, for which they have no successful remedies. They are pretty good at reducing dislocations and binding up fractures. They also perform bleeding and cupping, especially where they can obtain European lancets. The cupping operation is very simple. When plenty of incisions have been made on the inflamed part, a bullock's horn is applied over the place, having a small hole in the end. The operator takes a piece of bees'-wax

in his mouth, and having sucked out the air from
the horn, manages to stop up the hole with the wax
by a dexterous movement of his tongue. This plan
is generally successful in taking away a large quantity of blood, and reducing a local inflammation.

We have thus described most of the things worthy
of observation amongst the Negroes of the fertile
regions of Senegambia. Eastward from Kasson the
route into the interior lies through the wildernesses
of Kaarta and Bambarra, until you reach Sego on
the Niger. We shall glance at a few things worthy
of observation in this vast wilderness, after we have
looked at a very different race of people who dwell
on the southern border of the Great Desert, or on
the northern side of the countries which we have
now visited. Here is the kingdom of Ludamar, possessed by the far-famed and much-dreaded Moors of
the desert. We must not pass them by without
notice.

CHAP. IV.

Ludamar and the Moors.—Their Encampments.—Ferocity.—Treatment of Christians.—Ladies.—Beauties.—Horsemanship.—Life in
the Desert. — A Whirlwind. — Oases. — Gum.—Description of a
Gum Fair.

WHEN we speak of the Moorish kingdom of Ludamar,
we do not mean that all its inhabitants are Moors.
The majority, in fact, are Negroes, who have been
brought into subjection by their Moslem conquerors,
and obey their rule with abject submission. These
Moors crossed the Great Desert from the northern
coast of Africa, and subjugated some of the border
tribes. They still wage frequent wars with other
Negro countries for the sake of pillage, not of settlement. They like the confines of the desert, into
which they repair whenever it is convenient. But
their merchants trade with the inland towns, in
which many of them are located, and where they
exercise great influence.

Having traversed a sandy and barren district, in
which you would probably suffer much from heat
and thirst, you would arrive at the residence of the
Moorish prince. It is a camp of tents, covering a
large space of ground, on which they are erected

without any regard to order. A wild people, indeed, are these swarthy sons of the desert. Indolent and energetic by turns, they love to lounge in their tents, or to scour the plains on their swift horses. The heat is sometimes so excessive that it is painful to touch the sand; and even Negroes will not run over it with bare feet. The Moors seem to deserve the character which they have received, of being the most ferocious, hard-hearted, and bigoted people under heaven. They are ready for any acts of violence or rapine, and they show no pity. Their slaves are treated in the most imperious manner, or put to death without mercy. They are always in the extremes of gluttony or abstinence. They can, like their dromedaries, endure hunger and thirst for a long time with great patience; but when they have opportunity, they will eat as much at one meal as would satisfy three or four ordinary men. They have a ferocious appearance, with wild staring eyes, as if they were lunatics.

DROMEDARY.

Here is the king's tent. It is larger than the others, and has a white cloth over it. But the chief

G

is only distinguished by the fineness of his dress.
Though he is possessed of absolute authority, he
indulges in free intercourse with his subjects; and
sometimes, when travelling, will eat out of the same
bowl with his camel-driver, or recline on the same
couch.   We must let Mungo Park describe an interview with Ali and his ladies; as he is probably the
only European who has had much communication
with them, and escaped from their savage hands to
tell the tale.   Poor Mungo had, with many mis-
givings, sent to Ludamar, to ask permission to pass
through the Moorish territory.   The answer was an
invitation to go and see the prince, whose prisoner
he soon discovered himself to be made.

"We reached at length the king's tent, where we
found a great number of people, men and women
assembled.   Ali was sitting upon a black leather
cushion, clipping a few hairs from his upper lip; a
female attendant holding up a looking glass before
him.   He appeared to be an old man, of the Arab
cast, with a long white beard; and he had a sullen
and indignant aspect.   He surveyed me with attention, and inquired of the Moors if I could speak
Arabic: being answered in the negative, he appeared
much surprised, and continued silent.   The surrounding attendants, and especially the ladies, were
abundantly more inquisitive: they asked a thousand
questions; inspected every part of my apparel,
searched my pockets, and obliged me to unbutton
my waistcoat, and display the whiteness of my skin.
They even counted my toes and fingers, as if they

doubted whether I was in truth a human being."
The Moors afterwards tormented him with a hog,
which they wished him to kill and eat: and on his
refusal, tied it in derision to the door of the hut
which was assigned for his use. They again assembled around him, and made him dress and undress,
button and unbutton, show them his stockings and
everything about his person. At night Ali sent him
some kooskoos and salt and water.

During the night, a constant watch was kept over
the traveller; and a Moor even entered his hut
stealthily, and laid his hand on his shoulder. "I
sprang up the moment he laid his hand upon me; and
the Moor in his haste to get off, stumbled over my
boy, and fell with his face upon the wild hog, which
returned the attack by biting the Moor's arm. The
screams of this man alarmed the people in the king's
tent, who immediately conjectured that I had made
my escape, and a number of them mounted their
horses and prepared to pursue me." On understanding the reason of the outcry, they went away, and
left him in quiet till morning.

This little incident was the means of farther un-
folding the Moorish character. For amongst others,
the king came galloping on a white horse, not from
his own proper dwelling, but from a tent at a considerable distance. Such was the tyranny of his
usual conduct, and such the jealousy with which he
regarded everybody, that his own family and slaves
did not know in what tent he would sleep on any
particular night. He was afraid of assassination, and

would not let his place of rest be known. For the
same reason, he never eat of any dish that was not
cooked under his own immediate inspection; from a
fear of being poisoned. When he was going on a
journey, he provided his food beforehand, by slaugh-
tering a bullock and drying some thin slices of its
flesh in the sun. This, and bags of dry kooskoos,
were carried by him for provision on the road.

"With the returning day, commenced the same
round of insult and irritation: the boys assembled to
beat the hog, and the men and women to plague the
Christian. It is impossible for me to describe the
behaviour of a people who study mischief as a science,
and exult in the miseries and misfortunes of their
fellow-creatures. Anxious, however, to conciliate
favour, and if possible, to afford the Moors no pretence for ill-treating me, I readily complied with
every command, and patiently bore every insult.
But never did any period of my life pass away so
heavily: from sunrise to sunset, was I obliged to
suffer, with an unruffled countenance, the insults of
the rudest savages on earth." They soon stripped
him of all his property, except the clothes which he
had on.

Wishing to make him useful to them in some way,
they devised various expedients of employing him.
At length they hit upon the office of a *barber*: and
Mr. Park was ordered to try his hand in shaving the
young prince's head. "A small razor about three
inches long was put into my hand, and I was ordered
to proceed. But whether from my own want of skill,

or the improper shape of the instrument, I unfortunately made a slight incision in the boy's head, at
the very commencement of the operation.   And the
king, observing the very awkward manner in which
I held the razor, concluded that his son's head was in
very improper hands, and ordered me to resign the
razor and walk out of the tent.   This I considered as
a very fortunate circumstance: for I had ·laid it
down as a rule, to make myself as useless and insignificant as possible, as the only means of recovering
my liberty."

Mungo Park had to endure annoyances, insult,
and persecution of various kinds, renewed from day
to day; till life became an intolerable burden, and
he envied the lot of the poor slaves.   A council of
war was repeatedly held concerning him; some
advising to put him immediately to death, some to
put out his eyes, which they said resembled those of
a cat.   But the king would not injure him, until
his principal wife Fatima, who was then absent,
should have seen him; since such was her desire.

The Moorish ladies were very troublesome, im-
pelled by an ungovernable curiosity.   One day a
party of them came to his hut, and gave him dis-
tinctly to understand that they wished to inspect
every part of his person, in order to satisfy themselves
on some points which were rather indelicate.   Filled
with surprise, the traveller determined to treat the
matter jocularly, and informed them that it was not
customary in his country to strip before so many
beautiful women; but that if all of them would

retire except the young lady to whom he pointed
(selecting the youngest and handsomest), he would
satisfy her curiosity. The ladies enjoyed the jest,
and went away laughing heartily: and the young
damsel was so flattered by his compliment to her
superior beauty, as she rightly understood it, that she
sent him some meal and milk for supper. Since
several of Ali's own women wished to see the white
man, he was conducted round the tents of four of his
ladies, having first dressed in his loose cloak, as his
nankeen trowsers were said to be not only inelegant,
but also very indecent. The ladies were very inquisitive about his person, but feigned to be shocked
with the whiteness of his skin. They each presented
him with a bowl of milk and water.

As a war with a neighbouring state was now
imminent, Ali and his warriors moved off to another
camp, whither Mungo Park followed with the rest of
the people. On his arrival, he immediately waited
on the king, in order to pay his respects to Queen
Fatima who had now joined him. "He seemed
much pleased with my coming, shook hands with me,
and informed his wife that I was a Christian. She
was a woman of the Arab cast, with long black hair,
and remarkably corpulent. She appeared at first
rather shocked at the thought of having a Christian
so near her: but when I had (by means of a negro
boy, who spoke the Mandingo and Arabic tongues)
answered a great many questions, which her curiosity
suggested, respecting the country of the Christians,
she seemed more at ease, and presented me with a

bowl of milk, which I considered a very favourable omen."

If these Moorish women were curious, (and who can blame them for being so, shut out as they are from the rest of the world?) they were nevertheless far kinder than the men. Fatima supplied the captive with a larger quantity of provisions than he had formerly received, gave him water which had become a great scarcity, and procured him permission to accompany Ali to Jarra, whence he hoped to make his escape; in which he was not disappointed. Fatima sent for his bundle of clothes, and required him to explain the method of putting on stockings, boots, and other articles of European apparel.

Notwithstanding her kindness, he was often in great distress for water; since, when there was any in the wells, the men refused to let his boy draw it in order to supply a Christian dog. "I frequently passed the night in the situation of *Tantalus*. No sooner had I shut my eyes, than fancy would convey me to the streams and rivers of my native land. There, as I wandered along the verdant brink, I surveyed the clear stream with transport, and hastened to swallow the delightful draught: but, alas! disappointment awakened me; and I found myself a lonely captive, perishing of thirst amidst the wilds of Africa!"

Here is a Moorish school! The priest is also schoolmaster. He has assembled his pupils in the evening on an open spot before his tent; and there by the light of a large fire, he teaches them some

verses of the Koran, which they write upon their
boards, like slates. When they have succeeded in
acquiring a few prayers in this manner, their education is completed, and they are very proud of their
proficiency.

The training of girls is wholly neglected, except in
the art of making them beautiful. Women are regarded by the Moors as inferior creatures, made for
the pleasure of man, to whom they must yield a
slavish subjection. So, they have singular ideas of
female beauty. It is measured almost entirely by
size and corpulence. "A woman of even moderate
pretensions, must be one who cannot walk without a
slave under each arm to support her: and a perfect
beauty is a load for a camel." All Ali's wives were
very fat. In consequence of this prevalent taste for
unwieldiness of bulk, the Moorish ladies take great
pains to increase their size. Mothers compel their
young daughters to drink a large bowl of camel's milk,
and swallow a great quantity of kooskoos every morning. If the girl has no appetite or feels sick, it does
not matter: she must take the prescribed quantity,
that she may become fat and get a husband. "I
have seen a poor girl sit crying, with a bowl at her
lips, for more than an hour; and her mother, with a
stick in her hand, watching her all the while, and
using the stick without mercy, whenever she observed
that her daughter was not swallowing. This singular
practice, instead of producing indigestion and disease,
soon covers the young lady with that degree of

plumpness, which in the eye of a Moor is perfection itself."

The ladies of rank, therefore, do nothing but gossip or look at themselves in a glass: indeed, they are physically incapacitated for any exertion. But they are humoursome, and vent their anger upon their poor female slaves. Their dress is scanty; consisting of a broad piece of cloth wrapped round the waist, and hanging nearly to the ground; to the upper part of which, two square pieces are sewed, one before, and the other behind, which are fastened together over the shoulders. A bandage of cotton cloth surrounds the head, so arranged as partially to screen the face from the sun. Many of them veil themselves from head to foot when they go abroad. This economy in dress is the result of their indolence; since they do not manufacture cloth, and are compelled to purchase it from the Negroes. Some of the men are good workers in leather.

The Moors are splendid horsemen. This is their pride and their security. See, how they gallop at full speed over the dusty plain, and rein up their fiery steeds in a moment! You would think that both horse and man must come down together, or that the rider must be thrown far over his charger's head. Sometimes, indeed, the animal is pulled down upon his haunches by a jerk of the strong bit: but it is rare for a Moor to lose his seat. He sticks to the saddle as if it were a part of himself; which its peculiar shape enables him to do. It is high both before and behind. This form renders it very uncomfortable to a European, at least for a while: but we can easily imagine how constant practice removes this difficulty: after which, a skilful rider feels as safe in his Moorish saddle as a child fastened into his chair. For ourselves, we never attained the aptitude of yielding to the motions of the horse; but always pronounced the native saddle to be a bore. And the same with the stirrups. But " Habit is second nature."

The Moors procure and breed the best horses, which are sometimes valued at twenty slaves. They are very fleet, and some of them truly valuable. "Ali always rode upon a milk-white horse, with its tail dyed red. He never walked, unless when he went to say his prayers. And, even in the night, two or three horses were always kept ready saddled at a little distance from his own tent." These horses are fed three or four times a day; and in the evening receive a large quantity of milk, which they relish much.

Their boldness and the swiftness of their steeds make the Moors a terror to the Negro. Two or three of them will come suddenly upon a herd of cattle; and before the keepers can collect in their defence, will drive a large part of them away ; which they can do at a gallop with consummate skill. One bold horseman has been known to accomplish the feat of carrying off several bullocks from under the walls of a town, in sight of the Negroes, whose arrows fell harmlessly around him. They use their spear on horseback with great skill: and some of them are said to be equally expert with the musket. Though, therefore, they are no match for the Negroes in numbers, and

"MODERN HORSEMEN."

are often worsted by them in a pitched battle; yet
they are generally successful in a marauding expedition. When the native kings combine against them,
they strike their tents and retire into the desert,
where they are safe.

Contrary to the habits of the Negro, the Moors
live a good deal on the flesh and milk of their cattle.
They procure arms, ammunition, and other articles, by
the sale of the slaves which they take in their predatory excursions. This commerce is carried on by the
caravans which cross the desert to Barbary. They
also exchange salt for corn and cloth from the Negroes:
and those tribes who own the gum oases trade with
the French on the Senegal. Their women spin goat's
hair into a strong thread, of which they weave
coverings for their tents. They make saddles, bridles,
and pouches, out of the skins of their cattle, which
they know how to tan.

This desert life would be intolerable to any but an
Arab or a Moor. It would be so painfully monotonous. As their slaves perform all the drudgery of
getting wood and water, and watering the cattle; the
people themselves have literally nothing to do. No
wonder they indulge so much in sensual pleasures at
home, and love to pick up a quarrel with their
neighbours. No wonder they have seized upon the
border lands, where they may enjoy a little variety
of foliage and pleasant fields.

There are some oases in the desert; beautiful spots
of verdure in the midst of a wild of barren sand.
Here there are perennial springs of water, lofty palms

and other trees, with small patches of pasturage.
These have their respective owners, who occasionally
frequent them to gather the fruits and feed their
cattle. The chief oases, in this part of Africa, are
those in which the gum-tree grows. The principal
gum-forests are Sahel, El Hiebar, and El Fatech.
The acacia grows to the height of twenty feet, and
is two or three feet in circumference; a stunted,
crooked, ragged-looking tree, with leaves of dirty
green. The gum-tree swells with the moisture of
the rainy season, and its bark cracks with the super-
vening heat. Then the juice flows out and dries on
the surface, in small lumps or large drops, of the size
of a partridge's egg. In a month's time nature has
completed her work, without the aid of human
gardener or husbandman.

The tribe to which the gum-oasis belongs then
assemble in a tumultuous manner, to gather the
harvest. It occupies them about six weeks to pick
it off the trees and stow it away in large sacks made
of tanned hides. Having slung their merchandise
over the backs of cattle, the whole multitude proceed
to the gum-fair which is held on the banks of the
Senegal. The princes and chief men are mounted
on their fleet horses or dromedaries, which are gaily
caparisoned. Armed horsemen ride about, to act as
police in keeping some kind of order, and defend the
caravan from an attack of enemies. The chief
women are seated in large baskets fastened on the
backs of camels, and covered with an awning.
Crowds of foot passengers, mixed with cattle, goats,

beasts of burden, and slaves, form a promiscuous
assembly, filling the air with shrill and discordant
sounds.

Thus they journey to a desolate plain on the bank
of the river. It is a dreary spot, in a sea of glistening
sand, unrelieved by a single tree or plant. Here the
French merchants await the coming of the caravan,
which takes a long time to compose itself and encamp
in peace. On a given signal, the fair commences;
and an attempt is made to transact business. What
wrangling, disputations, high words, and threatenings
ensue! The price has to be fixed: but the Moors
find a hundred reasons for delay. The Franks are
urgent; for their time is precious. The Moors care
nothing about time, and spin out the negotiation as
long as possible, hoping that their customers will be
obliged to give in. The Moors wish to overreach in
the price of the gum; the Franks cheat in the size of
the measure. At length the gum changes hands;
cottons, blue caps, and other goods are received in
barter. The fair ends; the tumultuous parties retire;
and the desert resumes its wonted silence and soli-
tude.

CHAP. V.

Wilderness of Kaarta.—A Traveller lost.—Kindness of Women.—
Corn-Spirit.—Wild Beasts abroad.—Hunting Elephants.—"White
Man's Lies."—Woods of Tenda.—Wolves.—Lions.—How to catch
a live Lion!—Discomfiture by Bees.—Gold District.—Iron.—
Native Lawsuits.—The beginning of Troubles.—Failure of British
Expeditions.—Crossing Rivers.—Fight with an Alligator.—
Palavers.—A difficult Choice.—Negro Philosophy.—The Jalonka
Wilderness and People.—Nitta-Tree.—Soap-making.—Manding.
—Park's deliverer.

RETURNING from our excursion to the Moors of
Ludamar and the desert, we travel into the heart
of Africa through the vast wilderness of Kaarta and
Bambarra. We call it a wilderness, because it is
neither a champagne country nor a desert. Many
portions of the soil are barren: but the greater part
consists of woodland, sometimes thinly and sometimes
thickly covered with trees. Here and there you
meet with a solitary town or village, and its surrounding patch of culture. The human inhabitants are
principally Foolas, who can here find pasture for their
cattle. But it is chiefly the abode of wild beasts and
birds of the largest species.

It was in this wilderness that Mungo Park
wandered for three weeks, after effecting his escape

from the Moors; suffering many privations from
hunger, thirst, and fatigue.   He was frequently
taken for a Moor, and laughed at by the Negroes on
account of his sad plight; at other times he was
rejected as a white man.   As he had been robbed of
everything but his clothes and pocket compass, he
had no means of procuring a guide or of buying food.
Ashamed and repulsed by the male sex, he found
mercy at the hands of women.   They pitied his distress, and frequently gave him something to eat, unknown to their lords.

" At the door of one of these huts an old motherly
woman sat, spinning cotton : I made signs to her
that I was hungry, and inquired if she had any
victuals with her in the hut.   She immediately laid
down her distaff, and desired me, in Arabic, to come
in.   When I had seated myself on the floor, she set
before me a dish of kooskoos, that had been left the
preceding night, of which I made a tolerable meal ;
and in return for this kindness I gave her one of my
pockethandkerchiefs; begging at the same time a
little corn for my horse, which she readily brought
me."

Again he says, " In the morning, I endeavoured,
both by entreaties and threats, to procure some
victuals from the Dooty, but in vain.   I even begged
some corn from one of his female slaves, as she was
washing it at the well; and had the mortification to
be refused.   However when the Dooty was gone to
the fields, his wife sent me a handful of meal, which
I mixed with water, and drank for breakfast."

" I set off for the village; where I found to my
great mortification, that no person would admit me
into his house.   I was regarded with astonishment
and fear, and was obliged to sit all day without
victuals, in the shade of a tree.   The night threatened to be very uncomfortable, for the wind rose,
and there was great appearance of heavy rain: and
the wild beasts are so very numerous in the neighbourhood, that I should have been under the necessity of
climbing up the tree, and resting among the branches.
About sunset, however, as I was preparing to pass
the night in this manner, and had turned my horse
loose that he might graze at liberty; a woman, returning from the labours of the field, stopped to
observe me: and perceiving that I was weary and
dejected, inquired into my situation, which I briefly
explained to her.   Whereupon, with looks of great
compassion, she took up my saddle and bridle, and
told me to follow her.   Having conducted me into
her hut, she lighted up a lamp, spread a mat on the
floor, and told me I might remain there for the
night.   Finding that I was very hungry, she said she
would procure me something to eat.   She accordingly went out, and returned in a short time with a
very fine fish; which having caused to be half broiled
upon some embers, she gave me for supper."

The good woman then called to the female part of
her family, who were gazing upon the stranger, to
resume their task of spinning; in which they were
employed a great part of the night.   "They lightened
their labours by songs, one of which was composed

extempore; for I was myself the subject of it. It was sung by one of the young women, the rest joining in a sort of chorus. The air was sweet and plaintive; and the words literally translated were these: —

'The winds roared and the rains fell,—
The poor white man, faint and weary, came and sat under our tree;
He has no mother to bring him milk, no wife to grind his corn.
    Chorus. Let us pity the white man;
No mother has he to bring him milk, no wife to grind his corn, &c.'

Trifling as this recital may appear to the reader, to a person in my situation, the circumstance was affecting in the highest degree: I was oppressed by such unexpected kindness; and sleep fled from my eyes."

Perhaps, one reason why the *men* were so suspicious and unfeeling to Mungo Park, was, that he could give them no satisfactory reason for passing through their country. The idea of travelling from curiosity is so utterly repugnant to an African's mind, that he cannot possibly believe it. Had the white man been a trader or a pilgrim to Mecca, he might have fared better. But who was he? What was he doing here? were questions which it sorely puzzled them to solve. The same reason would militate against the convenience and safety of any other European traveller. When Dr. Barth went, on a kind of embassy, with the avowed purpose of making a treaty of trade with the native kings; his reception amongst them was very different. They could understand this reason: it commended itself to their heart and judgment.

Yet Mr. Park testifies, " I do not recollect a single

H

instance of hard-heartedness towards me in the women. In all my wanderings and wretchedness, I found them uniformly kind and compassionate. And I can truly say, as my predecessor Mr. Ledyard has eloquently said before me, 'To a woman, I never addressed myself in the language of decency and friendship, without receiving a decent and friendly answer. If I was hungry or thirsty, wet, or sick, they did not hesitate to perform a generous action. In so free and so kind a manner did they contribute to my relief; that if I was dry, I drank the sweetest draught, and if hungry, I ate the coarsest morsel with a double relish.'"

Still, the traveller was sometimes kindly entertained by the men, especially when he journeyed in company with natives; who were thus a kind of voucher for his respectability. On one occasion, he observes, " In the morning, when I was about to depart, my landlord, with a great deal of diffidence, begged me to give him a lock of my hair. He had been told, he said, that white men's hair made a saphie, that would give to the possessor all the knowledge of white men. I had never before heard of so simple a mode of education; but instantly complied with the request: and my landlord's thirst for learning was such, that with cutting and pulling, he cropped one side of my head pretty closely; and would have done the same with the other, had I not signified my disapprobation by putting on my hat, and assuring him, that I wished to reserve some of this precious merchandise for a future occasion."

In the midst of this wilderness you would find "beer-shops," where the Pagans enjoy themselves as much as the more civilised people of Europe. A number of Negroes collect in one of these houses, and sit round large vessels of " corn-spirit " (as they call it), drinking of it plentifully until some of them at least are inebriated. This intoxicating liquor is not the palm-wine, formerly mentioned; it is brewed from corn. They also make use of a kind of mead. They have thus three kinds of exhilarating drink; from which devout Mahometans abstain. The latter take their revenge in a large consumption of tobacco and snuff, of which all Africans are very fond.

YOUNG AFRICAN ELEPHANT.

This vast wilderness is a favourite haunt of elephants. Here they are comparatively undisturbed. The African species seems, from the shape of its grinder, to be different from the Asiatic. It is generally very wild; and modern Africans do not try to tame them, like the Carthaginians of old. In fact,

whenever any one comes near the habitations of men,
it is pursued till it is either killed or frightened away
from the human presence. At some seasons of the
year, elephants roam over the country in large herds,
seeking food and water. When the pools are dried
up, they frequent the rivers: and it is at this time
that the hunters are chiefly on the look out. With
these men, the occupation is a matter of business,
not of pleasure. The hunt has nothing of the chivalry
and *éclat* with which it is pursued in India. It has
no semblance of *sport*. Here is the description of
one, of course as given by a native.

"Wishing to see the way in which elephants are
killed, I joined a party of four hunters, who were
armed with long guns, and each furnished with a bag
of dry provisions, that would serve him for five or
six days. We started for one of the loneliest parts
of the forest, when my companions began to search
for the usual marks of the elephants' whereabouts.
These consisted of the prints of feet, fallen dung, and
broken branches of trees. At length we discovered
these unequivocal marks of a small herd having
recently passed. On a careful examination, the
hunters declared that the beasts must have been
there on the previous day, and would probably now
be not far off. We followed the track till night-fall,
and then slept in the trees.

"Next morning, we continued the pursuit, assured
that we were approaching our prey. Occasionally
stopping to listen, at last we heard a crashing of
boughs in the distance, caused by the marching of

these bulky creatures through underwood and small trees. We became very excited, but proceeded in silence, as stealthily as cats. The herd is now in sight, and we follow them, dodging behind trees, so as not to be seen; but keeping an eye upon their movements. Our guns are all ready, loaded with ball, and primed. At last we see what we desired, one of the younger animals wandering a little from its companions. We press forward, and intercept its return to the herd. Drawing nearer and nearer to it unperceived, we select a moment when it is passing in front; and on a given signal, we all fire from our lurking places, and then fall flat on the ground. The elephant has received two or three of our balls; but on looking round, he can see no enemy; for the long grass quite conceals us from his view. He applies his trunk to the wounds, but cannot extract the balls; and then runs about frantically, to seek his foe. Approaching us, he affords an excellent opportunity for a second volley, under most favourable circumstances. We can scarcely miss him: every ball from our long guns enters his body or head; and he falls dead before us. The rest of the troop are scared away by the noise, not knowing the calamity which has befallen one of their number.

"We immediately run up to our victim, whose teeth we strike out with light hatchets. Taking off the skin, we extend it on the ground to dry. Then cutting out the most delicate parts of the flesh, we cook, and feast upon a portion, and dry thin slices for future provision. The lions and hyænas would afterwards dispute for our leavings with the birds of prey, which were hovering around, and which would come in for the first share. We killed three more elephants before returning home, having been absent for nearly a month. During this time, we lived on flesh, wild-honey, and the meal which we carried with us. We became rich by our expedition."

The desire of Europeans for ivory, and the price which they pay for it, is another subject of wonder to the Negroes. True, they are told that it is used for handles to knives and similar purposes; but this does not explain the matter in a satisfactory way. For why will not common bone or wood do for handles? Ivory does not make the blade cut better; nor is it more easily handled. They generally doubt this account of its use; and put it down as one of the "white man's lies." The bundle of these "lies" is supposed to be very large. They naturally give us credit for no more veracity than is current amongst themselves: and the strange things which we tell about our country, though all true, utterly stagger their belief.

The return of some of their own countrymen from sojourning in England, is beginning to enlighten them a little on foreign subjects. Still, many listen to the accounts of what these Negroes have seen, as to the "Arabian Nights' Entertainments." When we have told them about white rain (snow), and the water becoming so hard that men can walk upon it; they have asked, "Do you think me fool enough to believe that?" Many of them still suppose that we dwell upon the water, and that there is no other *terra firma* in the world than their own. Those who live near the coast, or who come in contact with Barbary merchants, know better; and the appearance of steam-boats in some of their own rivers, is beginning both to instruct and to confound them. But if we have plenty of land of our own, why do we want African timber, and rice, and hides, and ground-nuts, and bees'-wax, and palm oil, and spices, and gold? What fools we are to give good cloth and ammunition for useless ivory? And, then, to take away slaves (probably to eat them)! There is some mystery about all this; as much as about the knotty question, " who was Moses' mother?"

If we had taken you straight eastward from the Gambia, without veering to the north in order to visit Kasson and Ludamar, we should have led you through a number of petty kingdoms, which lie about the upper parts of the great African rivers. The chief of these countries, in the direct route, are Tenda, Fooladu, and Manding. They, with several others, may all be said to be included in a vast wilderness, which finally unites with that of Kaarta; but they are more thickly peopled than most of the kingdom of Bambarra. It is high land, forming the commencement of the mountains which bound Senegambia on the south; and there is much rocky and sandy ground interspersed with the forests. As the length of this wilderness includes ten or twelve degrees of longitude, we may glance at a few of its phenomena.

One of the things of which you would be most painfully sensible in traversing this region, is the presence of wild beasts, of large size and ferocious character. They literally swarm here; so that you would have to keep a constant look out, by day and by night. Think of the impudence of the wolves by the following accounts. "The wolves killed one of our best asses within twenty yards of the place where we slept." "We had not time to cook, and the rain prevented the watch-fire from burning; owing to which, one of our asses was killed by the wolves. It was only sixteen feet distant from a bush under which one of the men was sleeping. —Watched with the sentries all night, as the wolves kept constantly howling around us. During the night, the wolves carried away two large cloth bundles from the tent door to a considerable distance; where they eat off the skins with which they were covered, and left them." The poor things must have been very hungry!

The lion is quite as bold as the wolf, and rather more dangerous to the human species. "We heard a particular sort of roaring or growling, not unlike the noise of a wild boar; there seemed to be more than one of them, and they went all round our cattle. Fired two muskets to make them keep at a distance; but as they still kept prowling round us, we collected a bunch of withered grass, and went in search of the animals, suspecting them to be wild boars. We got near one of them, and fired several shots into the bush, and one at him as he went off among the long grass." The travellers then found out that the intruders were nobler animals than boars, and kept a good watch. "About midnight, these young lions attempted to seize one of the asses, which so much alarmed the rest, that they broke their ropes, and came at full gallop in amongst the tent ropes. Two of the lions followed them, and came so close to us, that the sentry cut at one of them with his sword, but did not dare to fire for fear of killing the asses."

"We had not proceeded a hundred yards farther, when, coming to an opening in the bushes, I was not a little surprised to see three lions coming towards us. They were not so red as the lion I formerly saw in Bambarra, but of a dusky colour, like the colour of an ass. They were very large, and came bounding over the long grass, not one after another, but all abreast of each other. I was afraid, if I allowed them to come too near us, and my piece should miss fire, that we should be all devoured by them. I therefore let go the bridle, and walked forwards to meet them. As soon as they were within a long shot of me, I fired at the centre one. I do not think I hit him; but they all stopped, looked at each other, and then bounded away a few paces, when one of them stopped and looked back at me. I was too busy in loading my piece to observe their motions as they went away, and was very happy to see the last of them march slowly off amongst the bushes." The lions again approached them in the forest, when the travellers, with a loud call, whistle, and other noises, scared them away.

The account of an attempt to catch a live lion

used to be told by the Negroes of these parts, as a
joke against the people of Doomasansa, amongst
whom the following ludicrous but fatal incident
occurred. Being much annoyed by a lion which
committed frequent depredations on their cattle,
they determined to go and hunt him out. They
found him concealed in a neighbouring thicket,
where they managed to approach him near enough
to get a good shot at him. They fired and wounded
the royal beast in the leg. He immediately sprang
at them, but fell down among the grass and was
unable to rise. Finding that he could not move, and
was therefore completely within their power, they
held a council of war as to what should be done. It
was easy to dispatch him by another volley; but they
wished, if possible, to take him alive. This would be
an undeniable proof of their bravery; and if they
should convey him to the coast, they might sell him
to the Europeans for a good sum of money. But
how was it to be done? No one durst approach
him, to fasten a rope round his neck. Various
schemes were proposed, amongst which was the following; to strip the roof of a hut of its thatch, and
carry the bamboo frame to where the lion was, and
throw it over him. He would then be in a cage;
and could be tamed at leisure. If, however, he
should attempt to spring upon the men who carried
the roof, they would only require to let it down upon
themselves, and fire at the lion through the rafters.

This plan met with general approbation. The
men, each armed with a gun in his right hand, and

supporting the roof with the left shoulder, boldly
approached the enemy. But as they drew near,·
they were so frightened by the horid fierceness of his
looks, that they stopped short, and consulted for their
own safety by covering themselves with the roof. At
this critical moment, the lion, who had recovered
strength, and was in a dreadful rage, exerted all his
energy, and made a spring at them. He was too
quick for the men, and got amongst them before the
roof reached the ground; so that he was caught with
them in the same cage; and as they could not escape,
he tore them in pieces, and devoured them at leisure.
It is said, that nothing will enrage 'an inhabitant of·
Doomasansa more than to bid him "catch a live ·
lion."

If the traveller escapes harm from the larger
denizens of the forest, such as wolves, lions, elephants, hyenas, and wild boars; he may still suffer
much inconvenience from a smaller animal, to which
allusion has already been made. The number of
bees which hive in the trees is enormous. Their
rich stores of honey are a great temptation to parched
and hungry mortals. Surely a little can be spared for
the use of man! The bees think differently; calcu-
lating that they have a right to all that they gather
by their own labour: and they are prepared to
defend their property with their lives. It requires
persons of experience and tact to get honey and bees'-
wax out of the woods of Africa; but large quantities
are obtained and are purchased by foreign merchants.

A native who was travelling with a caravan, incautiously went to rob a hive near the place of encampment; thinking that he could easily defend himself against a few bees. He miscalculated the number and spirit of the enemy. As soon as they found their precincts disturbed, they came out in such multitudes, and assailed him with such fury, that he instantly took to flight, and ran for refuge to the coffle. The bees pursued, and attacked the caravan, which they completely routed. Horses and asses broke away and dispersed; men and women followed helter skelter; and the bees took possession of the camp. It was a long time before the people could find courage to collect, and return to the baggage, with large firebrands. Having set fire to the grass, the flames spread more widely than they anticipated, and they could with difficulty save their effects from being burnt.

We have heard of the defeat of a large army by bees, which took place farther eastward. A wood through which the troops were marching happened to be full of hives: and some of the horsemen having committed a trespass on the honey, they were assailed by myriads of insects, which hung over them like a cloud. The stung horses became unmanageable, and broke in amongst the footmen; these in turn became panic-stricken, and the whole army consisting of ten or twelve thousand men were put to flight. The wounds which the soldiers received from their aerial foes were not mortal; but their march was impeded for that day.

In the hilly parts of this wilderness, many streams arise, which constitute the bulk of the great rivers of Western Africa, the sources of which are situated a little higher up in the mountains. This region forms also the principal gold district of Africa. The precious metal used to be obtained by washing the sand and gravel which form the beds of streams; and this plan is still sometimes resorted to. But as these sands have been often searched, little gold can now be found in them; unless when heavy rains have caused the water to deviate from its usual channel. Then, gold is found in large grains, quite pure.

The usual mode pursued by the gold seekers is that of digging. This process also is very simple. Pits are sunk, first by way of trial. A deep hole is made, and several calabashes of sand taken out of it are carefully washed, to see if the soil contains any precious dust. When the presence of gold has been ascertained, the diggers proceed to their work in earnest. It has been described as follows.

We saw a large field containing a number of pits of two kinds. The one sort, out of which the metal was obtained, were about twice as deep as a man. The other kind were shallow, and lined with clay, for the purpose of holding water. When a man in the pit had thrown out some of the gravel, a woman took up a portion and put it in a large calabash with a little water. She crumbled it as much as possible, and then threw out the large pebbles. Mixing up the rest, she whirled the calabash quickly round, so that some water with the coarser part of the sand

flew out. She added more water, and continued the
process, till there was little left but a quantity of
dark earthy matter, which is called gold rust. In
looking through this rust, two or three grains of
yellow metal were found. (These grains differ much
in size; some being very small, and others of considerable magnitude.) The woman put what she
found into a quill, which she stopped with cotton,
and then fastened it in her hair.

The average value of gold obtained by one digger
during the dry season is the price of two slaves. The
greater portion of what is obtained is bartered with
the Moors for salt. Another part finds its way to
the coast and it is sold to European traders. The
rest is manufactured by the natives themselves into
ornaments for their women, such as rings, ear-rings,
bracelets, and chains. Some ladies in full dress have
more than fifty pounds' worth about their persons.
The articles which African goldsmiths make would be
esteemed heavy and clumsy by Europeans; but it is
wonderful how neat they are, considering the simple
and coarse tools which the Negroes are obliged to
employ. We have seen rings that were far from
inelegant.

The smith puts the native gold, without any flux,
into a crucible of clay dried in the sun. This he
places in a heap of charcoal, which he lights, and
blows with a common double bellows, until the gold
is fused. He pours the metal into a mould, to form
it into a thin bar; and then works and draws it out
with pincers, heating it again if necessary, till he gets

it into the desired shape. As it is unalloyed, it is
very soft, and of a deep yellow colour. The natives
are very jealous about foreigners inquiring after the
sources of their rivers; as they suppose it to be connected with the finding of gold: having no idea
whatever, as we have said, of geographical curiosity.

Manding and other countries also contain iron-
stone, which the natives know how to smelt, and
manufacture into different instruments and utensils.
As European articles are cheaper and better made,
Negroes on the coast supply themselves from
abroad: but those in the interior are obliged to
manufacture for themselves. The blacksmith, who
is also goldsmith, is an important man, and ranks as
an artizan along with the worker in leather.

SMELTING IRON.

The furnace is a tunnel of clay, about three feet
wide, and eight or ten feet high; the bottom of it
being lower than the ground. "A little higher up,

we make holes, into each of which we insert a tube
of clay.   Air is admitted by these tubes, which we
open or stop up at pleasure.   We put some dry wood
into the furnace, and cover it with charcoal.   Over
this, we lay a course of iron-stone broken into pieces.
Then we put more charcoal, and more iron-stone;
and so on, till the furnace is filled.   We blow
up the fire with our bellows, through one of
the tubes, till a flame appears above the top; after
which it burns violently.   It is frequently supplied
with new charcoal; but after the first day, is not suffered to burn so fiercely.   At the end of three days,
all the tubes are taken out, and it is allowed to cool.
This requires several days more: after which, part of
the furnace is taken down, and the iron is found in
a large cake.   Part of this lump is useless; the rest
is worked by means of a forge and anvil.   We have
a double bellows, made from two goats' skins, with
separate tubes, which unite before entering the forge.
We can make many things out of this iron; but it is
harder and more brittle than yours."   (It is in fact
steel.)

Many were the sufferings of Mungo Park in this
vast wilderness, both on his return from his first
journey, and in performing his second expedition.
On the latter occasion, he wisely chose this route in
preference to a more northerly one.   It was far more
direct.   The kingdoms through which he had to pass
were weak, with a widely-scattered population;' so
that he trusted to be able to overcome any resistance
that might be offered.   He had three companions,

along with a lieutenant and thirty-five soldiers, from a regiment which had been serving at Goree. They *appeared* to be dashing men; but were found in the sequel to be of shattered constitution, and far from up to the mark as useful soldiers. However, he was delayed too long in his preparations; and the rainy season came on before he could reach the Niger. His men began to droop and die in this wilderness, until, out of a company of forty-two, he was left with Mr. Martyn and three others to perform the voyage. They had all died of fever or dysentery.

It was a fatal mistake to travel during the rains. Had he remained in one of the most healthy parts of the Gambia till the rains were over, he would have gone forward with seasoned men, though their number might have been reduced; and he would have travelled during the most favourable part of the year. He pressed forwards, and lost all.

Other expeditions into West Africa have failed from the same reason. Some persons have thought that by going in the dry season, Europeans may escape fever altogether. Their spirits have been buoyed up with this hope; and they have been led to expect, that with care and temperance they would avoid this African pest. When the reverse has happened, and they have all been "laid down," they have become panic-stricken, and the consequences have been unusually disastrous. This proved fatal to the grand Niger expedition, which was arranged and conducted with so much skill and prudence in other respects. It is a general, and we may say, invariable rule, that

I

every European who stays for any length of time in
tropical Africa, will have an attack of fever. This is
his "seasoning." If he have it in the dry season, so
much the better; as his recovery is likely to be more
rapid and perfect. If he do not have it till the rainy
season has set in, he is likely to have frequent relapses,
unless he take a voyage. It is hard to recover strength
during this humid and debilitating period of the
year: and many who have weathered it out till the
drying month, have sunk at last from mere exhaustion. After his "seasoning," the European need not
fear much, if he be careful and temperate. Future
attacks of fever, which he must expect to have occasionally, will cause no more inconvenience than an
English influenza.

Hence, it is manifest, that none but seasoned men
should penetrate into the interior. An expedition
cannot afford to wait for the recovery of every sick
person: and the first attack of fever is always a
critical one. Many die of it at once. What the
average of recoveries is, we should hesitate to say:
but it will be very small, unless great care, more
than skill, is employed. In this respect, a steam-
boat expedition has great advantages over a land
journey. But the vessel should not penetrate far,
until the men have had their first fever; and when
this happens, it should be ready to run out to sea,
and remain there, well off the coast, until they are
quite recovered. Some would probably die; others
would have to be sent home; the vigorous remainder
would return to their enterprise, with the best hopes

of success. A journey inland, of only a few weeks,
undertaken during the early part of the dry season, is
quite another thing. But even then, the party must
be prepared for the consequences of any undue exposure or exertion; and must be content to wait with
their sick, and nurse them until they recover. Our
own "seasoning" took place in very hot but dry
weather; but we had not a second attack.

In passing through this part of Africa, there are
many rivers to cross. When these cannot be forded,
and the natives have baggage to convey, they have
recourse to the expedient of a temporary bridge. This
is easily made; trees are cut down or uprooted on either
side, and their tops firmly fastened together in mid-
stream. Against these, forked sticks rest, whose tops
support poles, about a foot above the water. Two rows
of these are made, and bamboos laid across them for
a platform. One of these suspension bridges is constructed in a few hours over a rapid stream, so that a
whole caravan can pass in safety. Where there is a
village near the bank, there will generally be canoes,
in which case, the people are ferried across, and the
beasts are made to swim over.

If you are fording, you must beware of alligators,
which in most parts are large and fierce. We can
furnish an authentic account of a battle between a
native and one of these huge reptiles. The man was
actively employed in driving some asses of the coffle
across the water, where it was shallower; the rest of
the company being engaged with the canoes a little

higher up. When he reached the middle of the
stream, being wholly intent on the beasts before him,
he did not perceive the approach of an alligator.
The monster seized him by the thigh and was
dragging him under water. He did not lose his
presence of mind in this critical situation; but, not
being furnished with any weapon of offence, he
thrust his finger into the eye of his enemy. Stung
with pain, the creature let go its hold, and the
Negro cried out to his companions for a knife.
Before they could come to his aid, the alligator
returned to the charge, and seized him by the other
leg. In despair, the man thrust his hands into both
its eyes with such force, that it was evidently stupi-
fied. It quitted him, floundered about, and then
made off, before it could be attacked with weapons.
The Negro was much lacerated, having a large wound
in either thigh, besides several marks of the reptile's
teeth in other places. The reader will now know
what to do, if he should ever find himself in such a
predicament. A cool head, and ready hand will save
out of many difficulties and deaths.

Before leaving this part of the country, we must
refer to the *palavers* or law-suits of the natives.
Blackie is a capital talker, an accomplishment which
is not confined to the female sex. The practised
pleaders amongst them would split a hair with a
chancery barrister, and would certainly win the cause,
if success depended upon much speaking. Mungo
Park was detained with the coffle of his protector,
for a period of no less than four days, in order to

settle a dispute which was publicly litigated. The circumstances were as follows.

Modi Lemina, one of the Slatees belonging to the coffle, had formerly married a woman of Tambacunda, in which the party were now resting. It was a walled town, of some little importance in those parts; so that a proper assembly could be called to hear the suit. The fruit of the marriage was two children. But the husband subsequently went to Manding, and remained there for eight years, without sending any account of himself to his dear wife. She, supposing herself deserted, and seeing no prospect of her husband's return, prudently waited for three years in her desolate condition; and then united herself to another man, by whom also she had two children. Lemina, now passing through the town, found out and claimed his former spouse. The second husband refused to deliver her up: insisting, that by the laws of Africa, when a man has been absent from his wife for three years, without giving her notice of his being alive, she is at liberty to marry again. Such was the subject of litigation between the two husbands. However, it does not appear to have been asserted, that the fair one was really ignorant of her first spouse being alive: but he certainly had not intimated it to her, so that the point of law seemed to be in favour of the second husband.

" After all the circumstances had been fully investigated in an assembly of the chief men, it was determined that the wife should make her choice; and be set at liberty either to return to the first husband,

or continue with the second, as she alone should think
proper. Favourable as this determination was to the
lady, she found it a difficult matter to make up her
mind, and requested time for consideration : but I
think I could perceive that *first love* would carry the
day. Lemina was indeed somewhat older than his
rival, but he was also much richer. What weight
this circumstance had in the scale of his wife's affections, I pretend not to say."

Negro philosophy is very simple and meagre.
They do not presume to pry into the knowledge of
things remote or unseen. They form no conjectures
about astronomy : but take it for granted that every
new moon is a new creation. They know nothing
about years, as such ; but count time by rainy seasons,
moons, and suns or days. The Pagans generally
believe in a God, but would consider it idle or pre-
sumptuous to form any opinion of his character or
ways. Yet custom has induced them to offer a short
prayer on the appearance of the new moon. Having
said it in a whisper, they spit upon their hands and rub
them over their faces. Many of them think there
will be a future world, better than the present ; but
"no man knows anything about it." They believe that
spirits or demons, and consequently witchcraft, have
great influence over human affairs. Hence their use
of greegrees, offerings, and magical ceremonies.

The Jallonka wilderness lies between Tenda and
Manding. It is a very barren country. The villages
are wretchedly poor ; and all the inhabitants are
thieves. Perhaps there is no place on earth, where

the people are more determined and barefaced robbers. They prowl about a coffle by day and by night, ready to steal anything on which they can lay hands, be it large or small. If one of the company loiter a little behind, he will probably be pounced upon by men lurking among trees, who will strip him of everything, including his clothes, and send him forward in a state of complete nudity, if they dare not keep him. On other occasions, when they have sufficient notice, they will form into a band, to attack and plunder the coffle. If they succeed in overcoming it, they make slaves of all the people who do not belong to the neighbourhood.

During part of the year, the people live much on the fruit of the *nitta* tree, a species of mimosa which abounds in this district. The long, but thin, pods of the tree contain a yellow powder, enveloping a few black seeds. This meal has a sweet gummy taste, which is not unpalatable when mixed with milk or with flour and water. The seeds of the bamboo, also, are pounded and dressed for food, having a taste somewhat similar to rice.

Their only articles of commerce, besides a little gold, are iron and soap, which they manufacture and barter at Bondu. The soap is prepared by boiling down ground nuts, and adding a ley of wood ashes. The article produced by this means is far from despicable.

Manding, to which we have already referred as the chief gold-country of Africa, is better peopled than the regions through which we have recently conducted

the traveller. Yet it is by no means populous. The
inhabitants are partly Mahometan, partly Pagan; an
industrious race, and not inhospitable. It was here,
in Kamalia, that Mungo Park fell in with Karfa
Taura, whose brother had been kind to him at
Kinyeto. This Slatee proved the warm friend and
preserver of the white man. He gave him a hut to
live in, supplied him with provisions, nursed him
during an alarming and tedious fever; and afterwards
conducted him with his coffle, in a journey of 600
miles to the Gambia; where he delivered him in
safety to his friends, who had long given him up for
dead. It is true that Mr. Park had agreed to give
Karfa a recompense for his trouble, viz., the price of
one prime slave: but it must have appeared doubtful
whether this would be realised in case of the traveller's
death.

When Karfa reached Pisania on the Gambia, and
saw a schooner lying there at anchor, he was almost
overwhelmed. Its build and size, its masts and sails,
and the contrivance of propelling it by the force of
wind, were quite new to him. "I found that the
schooner with her cable and anchor kept Karfa in
deep meditation the greater part of the day." "This
good creature had continued to manifest towards me
so much kindness that I thought I made him but an
inadequate recompense, when I told him that he was
now to receive double the sum I had originally promised." Other instances of kindness were shown
towards Karfa, upon whom they were not lost. "He
would often say to me, 'my journey has indeed been

prosperous.' Then, when he saw the superiority of European arts, he would become pensive, and say with a sigh, 'Black men are nothing.'" At other times, he asked Mr. Park with great seriousness, what could possibly have induced him to think of exploring so miserable a country as Africa?

CHAP. VI.

The Niger at Bambaku.—Rapids.—Sego.—The King.—Shea, or Butter-tree.—Sansanding.—Moorish Intolerance.—White Man's Saphie.—Jenné.—Negro Umbrella.—Burial of the Dead.—To Koromé.—Foolbé—Their stern Bigotry.—Rascality of Arabs.—The Servant is Master.—Disorderly state of Timbuctu.—Sidi Alawaté.—A candid Robber.—Rags on a Tree.—Devil Worship.—Reception of a Stranger.—Sheik el Bakay—His noble Conduct—His Camp in the Desert.—What is Timbuctu?—Caravans.—The Great Desert.—Storms of Sand.—Thirst.—Serpents.—Districts South of the Niger.—The Reformer of Masina.—A Village Market.—Buying Money.

WE now arrive at the Niger. It becomes navigable just after it bends eastward, to pursue its long course through the heart of Africa. Previously it has been flowing southward, down from the mountains in which it takes its rise, and where it is joined by other streams which increase its magnitude. The great bend takes place where the kingdom of Manding joins that of Bambarra. Here is the town of Bambaku; at a village near which you may embark in a canoe, and sail down some rapids to Marrabu. Three rapids have to be passed, which are navigable when the river is swollen with rain.

The first regular port on the Niger, to which

canoes come from the east, is Marrabu, in N.
lat. 12° 48′, and about 4° 20′ of W. long. From
hence, sailing is easy to Sego, the capital of Bambarra, situated at the south-eastern extremity of this
country. The banks of the river are marshy, with
much woodland.

Sego is an important town, and ranks high in the
estimation of the natives. It is built on the south
side of the Niger, though there is a suburb on the
north side, in which the king formerly dwelt. It is
said to be composed of several towns joined together;
which probably means a town divided into different
quarters, after the Arab fashion. This is the first city,
as you come from the west, which has been wholly
revolutionised by the Moors and Arabs. It can, therefore, scarcely be called a native town, though Mandingoes form the bulk of the population. Moorish residents have great influence, both socially and politically.
They have improved upon the native plan of building
houses; making them square, with flat roofs, many of
them with upper stories. Of these habitations we shall
speak more at large, when we get nearer Timbuctu.
Sego contains many mosques; and the forms of Islamism are strictly kept up by the Moors and native
Mahometans. The whole population of the capital
and suburbs is said to amount to 30,000; which is
a large number for an African town. Indeed, it is
described as a place of considerable civilisation and
magnificence. But the influence of the Moors would
prevent any European from entering it; and they
hindered Mungo Park from so doing.

There is a ferry across the river, which brings in a considerable revenue to the king. The canoes are formed of the trunks of two large trees, excavated and joined together, but only placed side by side for half their length. They are, therefore, very long and narrow, and have an awkward appearance, but are large and roomy. Sego is a place of considerable merchandise, for which it is well situated, and has good markets.

The King Mansong seems to have been well disposed towards Mungo Park, when he came to this part of the river during his first journey; but prejudiced councillors forbade the traveller's having an interview with him. The Moors were doubtless jealous of Europeans, lest they should share in their own lucrative trade; and it was easy for them to arouse the suspicions of the natives. "What did the stranger want? To see the river! What nonsense! Were there no rivers in his own country that he could look at? And is not one river like another?" So Mansong sent a message, that he could not possibly see Mungo Park, until he knew what really brought him into the country. Afterwards, finding that he was destitute, he sent him a bag of 5000 cowries, and told him to leave the neighbourhood.

On his second expedition, Mr. Park sent forward his guide Isaaco, with a handsome present to the king, requesting a safe passage through his country; declaring that his object was to open up a passage for trade between the white and black men; but that this must be kept secret from the Moors. In reply,

SCENE ON THE NIGER.

Mansong sent Modibinne, his prime minister, and four of his friends, to converse with Mr. Park : and they said, " We have heard what you have spoken. Your journey is a good one, and may God prosper you in it : Mansong will protect you. We will carry your words to Mansong this afternoon; and to-morrow we will bring you his answer." This answer was a promise of protection, as far as his power extended. " If you wish to go to the East, no man shall harm you from Sego till you pass Timbuctu. If you wish to go to the West, you may travel through Fooladu and Manding, through Kasson and Bondu : the name of Mansong's stranger will be a sufficient protection for you. If you wish to build your boats at Samee, or Sego, at Sansanding, or Jennie, name the town, and Mansong will convey you thither."

This was a kingly declaration. In consequence, Mungo Park chose Sansanding as the place of his boat-building; and there he continued in peace till he embarked on his fatal voyage. When, after a time, Isaaco returned from the Gambia to seek tidings of the unfortunate traveller, he found Dacha occupying his father's place as King of Bambarra: from whom he requested to be farthered on his journey of search. " On my entrance in the first yard, I found a guard of forty men, young, strong, and without beards. On entering another yard, I met another guard, well armed and very numerous, lying in the shade. A little farther on, I found the king sitting. There were four broadswords stuck in the ground, on each side and behind him, which had been given to him by Mr. Park. He had on his military coat, which he is obliged to wear when he sends out an army, and cannot leave off until the army returns. He commonly wears dresses of white or blue cotton or silk, with a great many greegrees, covered with plates of gold or silver, sewed about his dresses." Dacha promised and gave the assistance required.

Sego Somma used to be the residence of the Bambarra princes: and before the king proceeds to war, he goes to this suburb, to have greegrees made, and to see that all things are ready. For, when a king or noble is taken prisoner, they keep him until the fasting moon is come. He is then brought to this village; and being laid down in a house reserved for this purpose, his throat is cut. When the blood has all flowed out, the body is carried into the fields and left as a prey for wild beasts. The blood is an offering to some imaginary spirit, and is supposed to have a magic spell about it. The place of sacrifice is sacred for eight days; and no man is allowed to pass by it, without taking off his cap or shoes. This shows how little influence Mahometanism has upon the hearts of the Negroes. Another bloody custom is, that when a male child is born of one of the king's wives on a Friday, its throat is instantly cut. Poor Friday seems to be an unlucky day all the world over!

This neighbourhood abounds with the celebrated Shea or butter-tree, which is found in many parts of tropical Africa, and is highly prized by the natives. For butter grows on trees in Africa, as well as oysters.

The Shea is something like a pear tree. Its leaves, which are six inches in length, grow in tufts, supported by a short foot-stalk. Its blossoms proceed from the extremities of its branches, are small, and grow in clusters. The petals are white and the stamina numerous. The fruit is oval, of the size of a Guinea-hen's egg, and of agreeable flavour. Under a thin rind, is found a dark kernel covered with a sweet pulp. This kernel is dried in the sun, then pounded, and kneaded to the consistence of dough, when it is mixed with hot water, till the butter is separated and rises to the surface. It is then boiled and skimmed, and wrapped up in leaves. It will keep well for two years, without being salted; and is as palatable as butter made from milk; having the additional recommendation of being firmer. A great deal of this butter is made in Bambarra, where the tree grows in the woods without culture; and furnishes a valuable article both of food and commerce.

The character of the Moors may be farther seen from an incident which took place on Mr. Park's first visit to Sansanding, when he was alone and unprotected. He had himself been at first taken for a Moor; but this mistake was unhappily discovered. The Moors assembled in numbers around him and questioned him about his religion. They "insisted that like the Jews, I must conform so far as to repeat the Mahometan prayers: and when I attempted to waive the subject, by telling them I could not speak Arabic, one of them, a shereef from Tuat in the Great Desert, started up and swore by the Prophet,

that if I refused to go to the mosque, he would be
one that would assist in carrying me thither. And
there is no doubt but this threat would have been
immediately executed, had not my landlord interposed
on my behalf. He told them that I was the king's
stranger, and that he could not see me ill-treated
whilst I was under his protection. He therefore
advised them to let me alone for that night; assuring
them, that in the morning, I should be sent about
my business."

In the evening, however, the Moors renewed their
annoyances. "They climbed over the top of the
mud wall (of the yard), and came in crowds into
the court, in order, they said, to see me *perform my
evening devotions and eat eggs*. The former of
these ceremonies I did not think proper to comply
with ; but I told them I had no objection to eat eggs,
provided they would bring me eggs to eat. My landlord immediately brought me seven hens' eggs, and
was much surprised to find that I could not eat them
raw : for it seems to be a prevalent opinion among
the inhabitants of the interior, that Europeans subsist
almost entirely on this diet. When I had succeeded
in persuading my landlord that this opinion was
without foundation, and that I would gladly partake
of any victuals which he might think proper to send
me ; he ordered a sheep to be killed, and part of it
to be dressed for my supper."

" About midnight when the Moors had left me, he
paid me a visit, and with much earnestness desired
me to write him a saphie. ' If a Moor's saphie is good

(said this hospitable old man), a white man's must needs be better.' I readily furnished him with one, possessed of all the virtues I could concentrate; for it contained the Lord's Prayer. The pen with which it was written was made of a reed: a little charcoal and gum-water made very tolerable ink, and a thin board answered the purpose of paper." What strange and crude ideas these Negroes must have! What perplexing notions of the white men!

Sansanding contains about 11,000 inhabitants, and has two large and not inelegant mosques. It can boast of a good market crowded with buyers and sellers. Here, in a large open square, are a number of stalls, shaded from the sun with mats. Some contain nothing but beads; others are supplied with balls of indigo; others have cloth from Howssa and Jenné. One has bits of antimony, another has sulphur, a third has rings and bracelets made of copper and silver. In the opposite houses, you may purchase amber, silks, and tobacco. Near this, is the salt-mart, and in the centre are the shambles where good meat can be bought. Not far off, is the depot for beer, of which 200 gallons are often sold in a day. The leather-market is in an adjoining space. The profits on foreign articles are very large: as an example of which it may be sufficient to state that a dollar will fetch from six to twelve thousand cowries, or from twenty-five to fifty shillings! European arms, beads, and cloths, of certain descriptions, meet with a ready sale.

Lions of large size, and other wild beasts, infest

K

this neighbourhood. Small green islands, of an enchanting kind, are inhabited by Foolas, whose herds are here secure from beasts of prey. The broad river abounds with excellent fish, which are caught with nets made of cotton, after the European mode. Lower down the river is Silla, and still farther, the large town of Jenné. It is two miles and a half in circumference, and contains 10,000 inhabitants; but its government is entirely in the hands of the Moors, who have a governor of their own creed, though appointed by the King of Bambarra. It has some good houses made of sun-dried bricks; and contains shops well stocked with European commodities. Thirty or forty Moorish merchants reside in this place, and, with their usual intolerance, do not allow infidels to enter the town, which is situated on an island.

After Jenné, the Niger contracts to about half a mile, and becomes deep. It is navigated by many trading canoes, which often unite into flotillas. The river boats, made of planks fastened together by ropes, are nearly 100 feet long, twelve or fourteen feet broad at midships, and drawing six or seven feet of water. There are rocks in the river, and some villages on its banks which are low; and much of the country is overflowed during the rainy season. We must not forget to mention a very simple umbrella used by the natives, consisting of a large ciboa leaf placed on the head; which completely protects the body from a pelting shower.

Finally, in taking leave of the Negroes of this part of Africa, we may advert to the last office that is per-

formed for a man by his friends, — his burial. When
death takes place, the relatives and neighbours assemble, and testify their sorrow by loud dismal howl-
ings. Food is provided for these mourners: and in
the evening, the corpse is dressed in white cotton,
wrapped up in a mat, and buried under the floor of
the deceased's hut, or under a favourite tree. In the
latter case, prickly bushes are laid over the grave, in
order to prevent the wolves or hyenas from digging
up the body.

Sailing down the Niger the traveller will at length
reach Koromé, a village on the bank of this noble
stream, insignificant in itself, but important as being
the outer harbour of Timbuctu. The Koromé lends
its name to a branch or creek of the river which runs
up some miles to Kabara, the proper harbour of that
far-famed city. Mungo Park, on his second expedition, did not attempt to penetrate to Timbuctu,
but kept in the main stream, repelling several armed
canoes which came from the shore to stop his passage.
M. Caillé, in 1827, accomplished the task of ascending to Timbuctu: but his information is meagre
compared with that of Dr. Barth, who reached this
place in September 1853. The journal of this last
traveller is very circumstantial, and seems in every
way worthy of credit; so that we shall implicitly con-
fide in the account which he has furnished of these
strange regions.

Proceeding from Koromé, you would sail to Kabara,
the channel being at first about 200 yards wide, then
narrowing till it becomes a mere canal. This is also

dry during a part of the year; so that Timbuctu cannot
be always approached by water.   Kabara is built on
a mound of earth, to preserve it from being washed
away by the annual overflowing of the Niger.   The
house in which Dr. Barth lodged was of oblong shape
and built with massive clay walls.   It had ante-rooms,
an inner court-yard leading to a number of small
chambers, and an upper story.   This introduces us
to a new description of African houses, bespeaking
a higher grade of civilisation.   And, in reality, we
must now take leave for a time of the semi-savage
Negro, living in a state of simplicity and rudeness,
and contemplate him in a more civilised condition.

This change is doubtless owing to the spread of
Mussulman tenets and customs in these parts of central
Africa.   The whole of the country along the Niger,
from Howssa (or Haussa) on the east to Jenné on
the west, has for many centuries been under the
dominion of a strict Mahometanism.   The bigotry
of this religion has greatly increased the ferocity of
the native population, but has also saved them from
sundry pagan vices, and has materially added to their
social comforts.   These subjects will be amply illus-
trated in the details of our narrative.   Meanwhile,
we confine our observations to the houses of the respectable inhabitants, which are built on the eastern
idea of seclusion, especially of the females.   You
enter through one or two ante-rooms for servants or
slaves, and pass into a court which has chambers for
the men; and then through another ante-room and
court with apartments for the women.   Sometimes,

a flight of stairs leads from one of the ante-rooms to
the chambers of an upper story.   But these spacious
edifices seldom contain much furniture.

The principal inhabitants of this more civilised
region, according to Dr. Barth, are Foolbé (or Fulbe)
or Fellani, a branch of the warlike Foolas whom we
have already noticed.   These enterprising people have
here embraced the Mahometan religion in all its
severity, so as to outdo Mahomet himself.   Especially
in Timbuctu, which is reckoned a sacred city, they
have carried their fanaticism to the utmost pitch of
rigour.   Few of its inhabitants have more than one
wife, though the Koran allows four : and not only is
strong drink utterly prohibited, but smoking is dis-
allowed.   The very presence of a Christian or infidel in
their city is deemed a sacrilege.   Their daily prayers
and periodical fasts are most scrupulously observed.

It is this vaunted sacredness of Timbuctu which
has given it so much renown amongst the natives,
and has kept it so secret from Europeans.   The town
is well situated as a mart of trade, being in the route
of several caravans ; but Timbuctu has never been the
head or centre of a great kingdom, as we have usually
thought.   It has "never acted more than a secondary
part: and now it is only the chief town of a province of
the Songhay empire."   The reader of African travels is
often puzzled with finding so many kingdoms in this
district, and so many kings, sultans, or emirs.   But
these names are given to the chiefs of all provinces,
and even of principal towns.   In reality, when we
have left Bambarra, we enter into the Foolbé and

Songhay empires, containing a number of provinces or kingdoms, tributary to the great sultans or sheiks, whose present residences are Masina and Wurno. The Songhay empire was formed at the commencement of the present century by Othman, a celebrated Mussulman saint. He inspired his followers with a religious zeal which overcame all obstacles, till it placed him on the throne of an extensive dominion. He died as he had lived, " in a sort of fanatical ecstasy or madness."

Dr. Barth had learned the character of the people before he journeyed to Timbuctu. He, therefore, wished to appear amongst them as an eastern sheik; and, although he did not conform to Mahometan usages, he hoped that he might be able to conceal his own religious tenets, at least until he could place himself under the protection of the liberal Sheik El Bakay, to whom he was recommended. Yet he did not wholly succeed in keeping his secret, of which one or two persons were cognizant. The principal of these was his Arab guide, named El Walati, a thorough rogue and deceiver. This crafty man practised all kinds of deception on his employer, who became aware of his rascality, but could not free himself from his trammels. Had it been known that he was a Christian, he would not have been allowed to go near Timbuctu; but would have been sent back from one of the distant towns. El Walati, therefore, was really master, as he had the traveller completely in his power. He constantly extorted from him new gifts in addition to his pay as guide, and made him give presents to his own friends and to whomsoever he pleased. He seems to have sometimes appropriated part of the goods to his own use; and at other times, to have sent Dr. Barth's presents to a chief as if they came from himself. He stayed as long as he pleased in the towns through which they passed, and disposed of horses and camels furnished for the journey; making a lucrative trade all the way through. So that he must have become rich at the Doctor's expense.

But a traveller must have a guide and servants, if he travels as a gentleman: and though he assuredly knows that they are fleecing him, he can do no better than submit, and be as much on his guard as possible. Major Laing was killed by his treacherous guide, for the sake of his property; and Dr. Barth had to be constantly on the watch lest he should meet a similar fate.

Now for the far-famed mysteries of Timbuctu! The Sheik El Bakay was absent on an expedition at the time of Dr. Barth's arrival at Kabara. El Walati was prevailed upon, by new gifts to himself and friends, to carry a message to the city; and about midnight, Sidi Alawaté, brother of the sheik, arrived with a party of followers. After supper, he had an interview with the traveller, concerning whom he had been privately informed by the messengers that he was a Christian, but under the special protection of the Sultan of Stambool or Constantinople. Dr. Barth required to use all the dexterity of which he was master, to parry the close interrogatories of Sidi Alawaté on this important point. A letter from the

Turkish Sultan, the acknowledged head of Islamism, would have made his way clear: but this had not been sent after him, as he had desired. However he managed so far to satisfy the young chief that he promised him protection: whilst the others of the party still thought him to be a Mahometan. Next morning they all set out for Timbuctu.

The city and neighbourhood were in a very distracted and unsettled condition. It had been conquered by the Foolbé, (or Foollan) of Masina in 1826: but they ruled over the inhabitants and occasional residents with such oppression, that the neighbours induced the powerful Sheik El Mukhtar, elder brother of El Bakay, to remove from his residence in Azawad to the city itself, in order to restrain the overbearing power of the Foolbé. Afterwards, the Tawarek Arabs, who inhabit the adjoining deserts, got possession of Timbuctu, about the year 1844. The Foolbé were conquered in battle and driven out of the town. In return, they cut off the usual supply of provisions, and reduced the city to great distress. Then a compromise was effected, by the mediation of the Sheik El Bakay, and the place was given up to the Foolbé, under Songhay officers or emirs. Thus there were four different and often contending powers at work, the Foolbé, the Tawareks, the Songhay emirs, and the Sheik El Bakay. The result of such divided interests may easily be guessed.

The cavalcade is now passing through the desert which intervenes between Kabara and Timbuctu! The path is beset with thorny bushes and underwood,

where roving Tawareks lurk, to attack and plunder
unprotected travellers. One spot, about midway of
the distance, bears the omnious name of " He does
not hear ; " because it is too distant from either place
for the cry of an assaulted person to be heard. One
of the *gentlemen* who frequent this road, had called
on Dr. Barth at Kabara, and tried to extort a present
from him, by giving him the comfortable information
that he was a " great evil-doer," " and might do him
much harm." But this flattering account of himself
failed to gain its desired object ; as the traveller and
his servants were well armed, and they journeyed to
Timbuctu in the company of Alawaté and his
followers.

The next object of curiosity on the route was the
Talha tree of the Weli Salah. It is dedicated to a
Mahometan saint, by whom his devotees expect to be
recompensed, if they pay due honour to his memory.
So, for some reason or other, they suppose that if they
hang a rag on one of the boughs, the saint will not
fail to reward their kind attention with a new shirt !
This present is not sent down from heaven, but is
furnished in the ordinary dealings of Providence.
Though, therefore, it can never be known that a new
shirt is more the reward of piety than of industry ;
yet superstition hopes the best, and the tree is actually
covered with rags. It is regarded as a cheap lottery.
How hard is it to get rid of superstition ! This
seems to be a mere relict of the pagan Devil-worship,
transformed to Mahometanism. For, we remember,
when sailing up the Gambia, that we passed a spot

deemed sacred to the Prince of Darkness. He is
thought to have an invisible seat or temple in that
locality, and to have the power of levying black-mail
upon all passers-by. So the natives offer him a small
portion of every part of the cargo of their vessel, by
throwing it into the stream in the name of the Devil.
Otherwise, they suppose that Satan would brand them
with a mark of his displeasure, which would issue in
their speedy death.

News had reached the city that a stranger of importance, a sheik from the East, was coming to pay
it a visit. A number of people issued forth to meet
him, to pay their compliments, and to invoke his
blessing. For a holy man has power to bless; and
Dr. Barth had previously been obliged to go through
this ceremony, by laying his hand on a knot of kneel-
ing expectants, and muttering a benediction in Arabic.
This might do when passing through a village which
he would not revisit after his real religion had been
discovered: but he dared not attempt it at Timbuctu. The rage of a Mussulman would know no
bounds, if he found that he had been blessed by a
Christian, instead of by a veritable sheik. What was
to be done on this emergency? An Arab is seldom
at a loss for a trick or subterfuge. Alawaté advised
the traveller to gallop forward, gun in hand, and
meet the strangers with a flourish. This ruse succeeded. He was received with many salaams, which
were easily returned by a flying horseman, who hastened to get under cover.

Passing the ruins of the clay wall with which the

town was formerly surrounded, Dr. Barth's cavalcade
traversed some narrow streets, where two horses could
scarcely proceed abreast, till he reached the house
provided for him, nearly opposite that of the Sheik
El Bakay. As he was the professed guest of the
sheik, it was arranged that his house should be locked
up and no visitors allowed, till that prince returned
home. How mortifying to be in the midst of Timbuctu, and yet unable to see the place, except from
the roof of his house!

It was soon rumoured that a Christian had entered
the town, and that the Foolbé were determined to
kill him. These news were far from pleasant to Dr.
Barth. Besides, Sidi Alawaté, who had promised
protection, took advantage of this untoward circumstance, to extort a large present from the helpless
traveller, who was now a kind of state prisoner. The
crafty Arab took care to make hay whilst the sun
shone, by getting all that he could from his guest
before his brother's arrival. He tried to rouse his
fears by giving him to understand that the house
would be attacked, and yet promising to defend him ;
— at the same time asking for more gifts. At length,
the sheik himself returned, a fine, generous, and
noble-spirited man, who immediately assured his
guest of personal safety, and entered into long con-
versations with him about arts and politics. An
order which soon came from the capital to drive the
Christian out of the town, roused the spirit of the
sheik, who, in order to show his own importance,
determined to keep him there. At length, however,

they were obliged to retire to the sheik's camp, about
seven miles distant from the city.

Tent-life in the desert has irresistible charms for
an Arab, until his tastes are changed by a long residence in a town, where his manners become sophisti-
cated. He loves the pure air and free country of
Nature; for his wants are few, and his habits are
simple. Look at the camp of Sheik El Bakay! Two
large tents of white cotton cloth, with top coverings
of chequered design, mark the residence of the chief
and his family. The interior is furnished with
woollen curtains of various colours, wrought by the
women. These divide the dwelling into two apartments, the outer for the men, the inner for their
wives and children. The same chamber serves for
parlour, bedroom, and storehouse; and sometimes
contains a strange medley of articles heaped together.
A number of smaller tents, formed on the same
simple model, but made of skins, are grouped round
those of the chieftan.

Morning and evening afford busy scenes, when the
cattle, goats, and camels are being driven out to
pasturage, or are being brought home for the night.
Then the whole camp is animated. The slaves are
bringing water on the backs of asses; the women are
preparing a frugal repast: and the men are performing their devotions in a sanctuary of nature fenced
with thorny bushes. In the evening, they form into
groups around blazing fires, to chant the Koran with
their deep voices, or engage in conversation on various
topics, till a late hour of the night. For the Arabs

CAMP OF SHEIK EL BAKAY.

are great talkers and story-tellers. Some of them
are adepts in inventing tales of fiction, which they
deliver impromptu without the least hesitation, to
the great delight of their hearers. The Negro
dancing and music are not allowed by good Mussulmen. Thus the life of these mixed Arabs runs on
very tranquilly, except when they are engaged in
predatory excursions, or in war: for they never miss
a good occasion or pretext for plunder.

The sheik himself and most of his followers had only
one wife, and were very domesticated persons. The
women of the Tawareks are said to possess much
more personal liberty than those of the Moors and
Arabs; and to go about freely unveiled, which is
never the case with the latter.

The country around, though called a desert, is not
altogether devoid of herbage. Small acacias and
thorny bushes abound, affording good browsing for
the goats: and camels can always manage to find
sustenance in such broken grounds, when the proper
pastures fail. During part of the year, there are even
"streams in the desert," owing to the rise of the
river, which then shoots out liquid branches in all
directions.

We need not narrate the quarrels and manœuvres
of the different factions who sought to have the pre-
eminence in Timbuctu, whilst Dr. Barth was among
them; nor the intrigues that were used by the Foolbé
to get him into their own hands; nor the noble conduct of his host in shielding him from harm, at the
risk of coming into open collision with powerful rivals.

The traveller was preserved; but he was never allowed
to perambulate the city. ˙ In riding to and from the
sheik's quarters, he ·necessarily. passed through a few
streets; and he once visited one of the outskirts, and
surveyed the outside of the "great mosque" situated
in that neighbourhood.   He also had a good view of
the north quarter of the town from the terrace of his
house.   For the rest of his information about the
place, he was necessarily indebted to others, with
whom he casually conversed, or whom he employed
to make proper surveys.

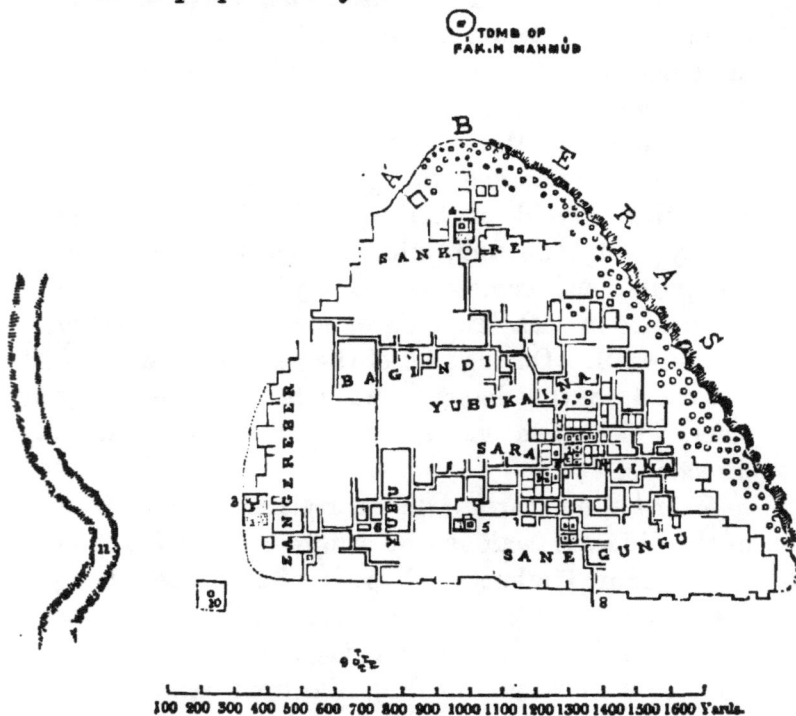

PLAN OF TIMBUCTU.

What then is Timbuctu? It is a town of triangular form, with its base pointing to the river, from which it is about six miles distant; situated in a plain, rising not many feet above the average level of the stream. Its entire circumference is three miles. The streets are partly straight, partly winding, paved with hard sand and gravel; some of them having a gutter in the middle. There are nearly 1000 clay houses, generally in good repair; with about 200 conical huts, chiefly in the outskirts. The houses resemble that which we have already described; only that the inferior ones have but one court-yard and no rooms on the terrace. In true Mahometan fashion, there are no public buildings of any consequence, except mosques; for the old palace has been removed. There is a large and a small market, and a few open areas. The northern angle of the town, where the mosque of Sankore is situated, is considerably elevated by large accumulations of rubbish, through the repeated ruins which have taken place. The "Great Mosque," is a noble building, 262 French feet in length, by 194 in width; having a large open yard which encloses the principal tower. It has nine naves and seven gates.

Timbuctu has no resources of its own, and no produce either agricultural or mechanical, except leather-work, which is of a superior description. It depends entirely on trade by the transit of caravans, and on being the residence of some wealthy merchants and powerful chiefs. Its importance has therefore declined in proportion as other towns, like Jenné and

Sego have enlarged, and as the river navigation has increased. But the serious obstacles which occur lower down the stream prevent much river-traffic

LEATHERN BAG.

from the east; so that the merchandise brought from that direction must pass through Timbuctu, until such time as the districts south of the Niger shall be

made peaceful and secure. Meanwhile, most of the
foreign goods that come to this part of the interior

LEATHERN ORNAMENTS.

are brought from Morocco or Tripoli across the
desert, for which the peculiar situation of Timbuctu
is very advantageous as an advanced station.

The caravans generally consist of two or three
thousand camels to carry men and merchandise.
The slaves are obliged to walk, and they form a
considerable part of the exports of central Africa to
the northern coasts. A large caravan is under no
absolute commander, being an assemblage of persons
who travel together for mutual defence against the
lawless tribes of the desert. Smaller parties place
themselves under the protection of one of these
tribes, whom they pay for the trouble of escorting
them in safety. Yet these may be attacked by a
powerful rival.

L

In crossing the Great Desert, there are convenient
stations for nearly a hundred and fifty miles, from
Timbuctu as far as El Arouan or Arawan, a town
inhabited by Moors, a mere place of trade, dependent upon strangers for its supplies. Afterwards,
the desert becomes frightfully arid, and the daily
heat is excessive. M. Caillié describes the thirst as
awfully tormenting. The water of the caravan, which
is carried in skins, is doled out twice a day with the
utmost care, that it may last until they reach a well
or station, which is not for many days. Of course,
the travellers who have plenty of good camels to
carry skins of water, are better supplied than others.
M. Caillié literally went about begging a few drops
from his neighbours, as his guide and protector (so
called) would not give him enough. The east wind
brings mountains of sand which threaten to overwhelm a caravan. Occasionally pillars of sand, like
waterspouts at sea, come across their track, whirl
them about like straws, and throw them upon one
another in the utmost confusion. The sand wraps
them up in darkness, as in a dense fog, confounding
earth and heaven, and blending them into one: so
that the travellers know not where they are, and
can scarcely distinguish anything at the distance of a
foot. It is surprising that they ever perform such a
journey in safety.

But the poorer class and the slaves suffer much
from thirst, and many of them as well as of the
camels succumb to exhaustion, and perish. "When
I had drunk, I had an unpleasant sensation all over

me, which was quickly succeeded by fresh thirst."
Sometimes the expected wells are dry; and the
fainting caravan must push forward to the next
station.   Here the wells may be filled up and require
to be cleared out; during which operation, the camels
will literally fight for the first draught of water.   The
poor beasts suffer dreadfully, finding only a few
thorny plants (*hedysarum alhagi*) to feed upon.
This plant is a, merciful provision of Providence, without which the desert could hardly be
traversed.   It grows to the height of about eighteen
inches, and is *green all the year*.   Its roots are thick,
and serve the travellers for fuel.   When a camel
appears to be failing, it is slaughtered, that it may be
fed upon by the company.   In great emergencies,
these animals are killed, in order to get the few drops
of water which may be in their stomach.

Enormous serpents frequent the desert, lurking
amongst the brushwood, and sometimes darting upon
a traveller, and inflicting a poisonous wound.   One
is described as nearly five feet in length, whilst its
body did not exceed an inch and a half in thickness.
It is strange how people can be found willing to traverse this desert repeatedly, or to live encamped in
its environs, like the Moors.

In the interior regions of the Niger, there is a
short rainy season in the spring.   A couple of showers,
not of long duration, fall during the day, and are repeated about seven times, though not on successive
days.   At Timbuctu it commences near the end of
March.   This atmospheric phenomenon does not

prevail at the coast, nor in the more southerly parts
of Negroland. It is perhaps a provision for the skirts
of the desert. But along with the benefits which it
confers, it helps the production of flies and mosquitoes,
which are enough to drive a stranger almost to
despair. Horses, also, are nearly maddened by the
stings of these insects.

The country south of the Niger belongs to the
empires of Masina on the west and Gando on the
east. Between these people there is no amity.
The Reformer of Masina wished to force his neighbours to reduce the number of their wives to two, to
change their wide dresses, and conform to other modes
of asceticism. The others resisted such an interference
with their liberties : so that a religious enmity has
sprung up between the Foolbe and Songhay, who form
the strongest parts of the population. The country
is, therefore, in a state of anarchy. Otherwise, the
best route from Timbuctu to the great towns of the
east would be across the angle which is formed by a
great bend of the Niger southward, about three
degrees east of Timbuctu. This short cut meets the
river at Say.

The people of this district are various in appearance
and manners. In one town, you may meet with men
of slender shape, sharp features, and expressive countenance, dressed in white. In the next village, you
may find a race of sturdy negroes, with rotund face,
black curly hair, and robust limbs, clad in light blue
shirts, and armed with muskets.

The country is generally fertile and thickly peopled.

It is mostly a vast plain, with swampy forests, intersected by numerous streams, abounding in grain and
cattle. Farther south, is the mountainous district
which bounds the valley of the Niger, still unexplored,
but said to be peopled by rude savages, even by some
cannibals.

The towns and villages of this district are composed
of clay huts, which differ a little from any that we
have hitherto seen. Let us look at one, in the little
town of Sebba. It is a circle, twenty feet in diameter,
having the walls ten feet high. They are made of
matting coated with clay, which is well polished: and
the roof is supported by a pole in the centre. It
has a number of clay benches, to serve for seats,
sideboard, and other conveniences. The fireplace
consists of four lumps of clay, near the middle of the
hut, with a slight wall between it and the door, to
protect it against gusts of wind. Several large jars
of clay, for holding corn, serve for furniture. As ants
abound in the place, a basket for containing small
articles is suspended from the roof.

Here is a village market, where a good deal of
business is transacted. The people attending it
number from two to five hundred. It is held in an
open space on the border of the village. For the
convenience of strangers, there is plenty of ready-
cooked pudding, tiggera or cold paste, and sour
milk, offered for sale. The merchandise consists of
corn, nuts, salt, kola nuts, cotton-strips, dyed cloth,
copper drinking-vessels, and asses. Many of the
people have copper ornaments; and some of the

young girls wear in the plaits of their hair a copper
device, representing a warrior on horseback, having
a sword in his hand and a pipe in his mouth. This
ornament is probably emblematical of the kind of
husband which the damsels wish to get. It is also
perhaps a demonstration that the Songhay will fight
for their pipe and dancing, the chief pleasures of
their life, against the fanatical followers of the Reformer.

But if you would wish to buy anything in this
market, you must first buy the money. The currency is one of the difficulties of an African traveller:
for it varies in different places, even in adjoining
towns. Cowrie shells are the most common medium
of exchange: but in some markets, it is shirts; in
others, as in this village, it is cotton cloth. A number of narrow strips, such as they weave in Africa,
are sewn together, to form a certain breadth and
length of material; and this is the standard coin of
the place. If you wish to purchase food or anything
sold in public, you must furnish yourself with some
of these " farawel " or " feruwal." To get these,
you will generally have to part with your goods at
a loss: and you may sustain several losses before
you have obtained the right medium of exchange.
Such are some of the inconveniences resulting from
a want of standard money. Sometimes Dr. Barth
could not procure food or fodder, because he had
not the money of a particular village. We may
meet with other difficulties on this matter.

Before leaving this district, we should notice a

beautiful tree which grows in these forests. It is a species of acacia, of large size, conspicuous amongst other trees, growing to the height of eighty feet, with a wide-spreading crown. The inhabitants call it " mur ; " other natives call it " korgum." Out of its trunk and largest branches they manufacture their canoes ; and from its pith, they make a kind of vegetable butter. A small bush, called " kirche," produces a small, white, sweet fruit, a little of which is not unpalatable.

CHAP. VII.

LET us now take a glance at the far-famed Niger,
in its course from Timbuctu towards the sea. This
course is, like most earthly things, uneven and not
to be depended upon. A few miles below Koromé,
the low and marshy banks are exchanged for a stony
district, which commences with a small island entirely surrounded by large rocks of granite. The
stream is now broken by a number of islets and
cliffs, its banks are steep, and its general aspect wild.
Soon, an immense ledge of granite projects into the
middle of the river, leaving a channel not more than
350 yards wide. This place is called Tinalshiden.
It is ascertained that Mungo Park passed these defiles in safety.

A large and well-built town, Tin-sherifen, is next

reached. It is inhabited by the Sook tribe, distinguished amongst their quarrelsome neighbours for
their peaceful character and literary pursuits. A
young lady, daughter of one of the chiefs, visited
Dr. Barth in this town. She was very handsome,
with soft and regular features, and inclined to cor-
pulency; clothed in a becoming upper garment of
red and black silk, in alternate stripes, which she
sometimes drew over her head. Perceiving that
the traveller was interested in her appearance, she,
half-jokingly, proposed a matrimonial union: to which
the other laughingly consented, provided one of his
weak camels could bear her weight.

East of Koromé, the Niger flows through a barren
region, in which are a number of encampments of

TAWAREK CAMP IN MOTION.

the Tawarek Arabs, who move about according to
their taste and necessities.

These wild tribes infest all the desert country on
the north of the river, and thus prevent a free intercourse between the negroes of the Niger and those of
the east.

Farther down, the river is shut in by two masses
of rock, which obstruct it like an iron gate, making
the navigation very difficult. Still lower, the stream
is confined by steep banks to the breadth of about
150 yards, but of great depth. Then it is divided
into several small channels : then begins to widen
and assume its former noble appearance.

In this changeable way, the Niger flows to Gogo,
once the capital of the Songhay empire, and six
miles in circumference; now consisting of some 300
mud huts, amidst heaps of ruins, and only able to
muster one good canoe. A large mosque still remains, having seven terraces, which gradually di-
minish in diameter, the lowest being forty to fifty
feet on a side, the upper about fifteen. Below
Gogo, the Proteus Niger becomes studded with sand-
banks : and again, grand masses of rock start up
from its bed to a height of seventy or eighty feet.
Afterwards, an unbroken sheet of water appears,
encompassed with beautiful scenery. A short distance lower, it is divided by ledges of rocks ; and
below this, it surrounds a large and verdant island,
containing a village of 200 huts. Once more, it
stretches out into a breadth of several miles, studded
with numerous and pretty islets. But it would be
tedious to describe all its turnings and changes, as

it progresses southward, passing by Say, toward the ocean.

Yet we must advert to the most difficult part of the navigation of the "Father of Rivers," as the Niger is termed by the natives. This is between Yaoori and Boossa, where the intrepid Mungo Park met his fate. His pilot was discharged at Yaoori; and himself, Mr. Martyn, and three white boys continued their voyage, without having any person to point out the safest channel, or warn them of coming danger. His oarmen, who were slaves, are said to have been chained to the canoe, to prevent their running away. We shall presently revert to this melancholy incident: but let us now take a glance at Yaoori.

The city is of great extent, and is said to be as populous as any other in central Africa. The wall is from twenty to thirty miles in circuit, and though made of clay, is strong and high. It has eight gates, which are fortified. The inhabitants make neat saddles and good cloth: and they cultivate indigo and tobacco, besides various kinds of grain and onions. They also manufacture a coarse gunpowder. The sultan's residence, as well as the houses of the chief inhabitants, are two stories high, having thick stairs of clay leading to the upper apartments. A few are square, but most are of a circular form; and they have good door-ways. The palace consists of a group of buildings inclosed within a high wall. On passing through the gate, a visitor is conducted through a low avenue formed by pillars, and perfectly dark; which leads to a large square yard, frequented by the domestics, a number of naked girls and boys. Advancing into another yard, you would find the sultan sitting alone in the centre of the square, on a piece of carpet, with a pillow on either side. He assumes much consequence, and exacts from his visitors the most humiliating forms of address; so that even the Arabs must speak to him on their knees.

Yet the Messrs. Landers found some of His Majesty's daughters to be most troublesome acquaintances; and it was with great difficulty that they could get rid of them at any time. The monarch himself had recourse to all kinds of meanness, to obtain possession of everything belonging to the travellers that he happened to fancy; expressing his admiration of one article, offering to purchase another, and wishing to examine another more minutely. These were only different modes of begging. He seemed to try and keep his guests in the town, under a variety of excuses, until he should fleece them of all their property, as he had done to other unfortunate travellers.

Near Yaoori, the Niger presents a very noble appearance, flowing in one large continuous stream, unbroken by rocks or sand-banks. A little lower down, two beautiful islands clothed with verdure render the scenery still more picturesque. But soon afterwards, the navigation becomes very difficult. A range of black rocks runs directly across the channel; and the water has only one narrow passage,

through which it rushes with great impetuosity.   In
ascending the stream, it is said that the natives require
to lift the canoes over this dangerous pass, planting
themselves on the rocks on either side.   Still farther
down, the river is divided into branches; but each
channel is filled with rocks, sand-banks, and low
islands covered with tall rank grass.   Again the
stream widens to a breadth of two miles; and again
it is divided by a number of inhabited islands.   Once
more, it appears as smooth as a lake, and the country
about it like a park, adorned with lofty trees, waving
corn, and grazing cattle.   Now its width has
diminished to half a mile, and again it spreads forth
into a large expanse, obstructed by islands and
shoals: till, near Boossa, it is not more than a stone's
throw across, and black rugged rocks rise up in the
centre of the stream.   Here Mr. Park is said to have
perished.   He had repeatedly driven off the canoes
of natives who approached with hostile purposes, and
in one instance had killed a number of them.   The
chief of a village to whom he committed some property, to be conveyed to the king, as a present from
the white man, failed in doing so, appropriating the
articles to himself: and the king being angry that
the travellers passed by without seeing him or for-
warding a gift, sent armed men to intercept the
boat when it was passing by the black rocks above
mentioned.   They attacked the Englishmen with
lances, pikes, arrows and stones.   Mr. Park and his
companion defended themselves for a long time;
but some of the men were killed, and the boat got

aground. Overpowered by numbers and fatigue, and
unable to move the boat off the shoal on which it
stuck fast, they jumped into the water, as the last
hope of escaping, but were carried away by the
violent current and drowned. There is little doubt
that it was the King of Yaoori who perpetrated this
act of violence.

The islands in the river are inhabited by a peculiar
race of people, who are also scattered in villages
along the banks. Look at their strange dwellings!

ELEVATED SLEEPING HUT.

They are nearly circular, seven or eight feet in
diameter; having clay walls, two or three inches in
thickness, and thatched with the palm leaf. These
nests are raised on a platform supported by thin
pillars of clay; and instead of a doorway, they are
furnished with a small aperture near the roof, to
which the owners climb and squeeze themselves

through, closing the entrance with a mat suspended
inside. This mode of hut is adopted in order to
protect them from the wet ground, and from the
attacks of ants, snakes, and alligators. They have,
also, a common hut for culinary and other purposes,
during the day; but they always sleep in their nests.

The Cumbri men are expert fishers and good
agriculturists; but they are very dirty and slovenly
in their persons and habits. The women daub their
hair with red clay; and when they wish to appear
uncommonly smart, they insert a crocodile's tooth
through their lips, so as to project upwards as far as
the nose. Well may it be said, that, " there is no
accounting for taste." The people are industrious,
mild in manners, kind, and hospitable. They themselves feel the effects of oppression, and can sympa-
thise with the sufferings of others. From their
timid and unwarlike nature, they easily fall a prey
to surrounding freebooters; and great numbers of
them are carried off into slavery. They pay a tribute
to the Sultan of Yaoori, who is more careful to
exact from them his due, than to defend them from
external foes. If the tribute or rent be not forthcoming at the proper time, he despatches a troop of
horsemen to the villages, to bring away as many of
the people as may be deemed equivalent to his
dues. These exactions have sometimes roused their
lethargic spirit and made " cowards brave; " so that,
in desperation, they have resisted his power with
effect. Yet notwithstanding their depressed situation,
the Cumbri are far from being a melancholy race.

They seem to have little feeling about the past, the
present, or the future.　They are now contented and
pleased, if they can have their favourite pastimes of
dancing, singing and music.　During moonlight,
both sexes continue all night in these sports, skipping
and dancing in the wildest manner, clapping hands,
shouting and screaming with delight, in the full hey-
day of animal and muscular enjoyment.

The town of Boossa consists of a great many
groups of huts, near to each other; bounded on one
side by the river, and on the other sides by a semi-
circular wall, with turrets and a moat.　Some years
ago, when it was assailed and taken by the Felattas,
the people fled to the islands of the river; and then
uniting with their neighbours, attacked their common
enemy and retook the town.

" Our hostess is an agreeable and good-natured
woman, but she is excessively vain of her person; so
much so, that she employs several hours a day in
dressing her hair, which hangs down below the face
in three plaited cues, one from the forehead, and one
from each side of the head: after which, she affixes
ornaments on different parts of her body, and stains
her lips and teeth a shining red colour with *henna*
(a species of myrtle).　When all this is done, she
admires herself in a broken looking-glass which we
have given her.　This is the most whimsical and
diverting part of the ceremony.　She approaches the
glass and retreats from it again; smiles when she
fancies that she looks pretty; and distorts her features and throws her body into all manner of comical

attitudes, to ascertain which is the most engaging. Although only a drummer's wife, our hostess is considered a person of respectability; for her husband's situation is one of the most important in the kingdom."

A woman of very different character was the widow Zuma, sister of the king. She was a warrior princess, of light copper colour, good features, matronly appearance, excessively corpulent, and plainly attired. She delighted to relate her quarrels with her own prince, the ruler of Wowow, and how she escaped from his resentment by climbing over the wall at night, and travelling on foot to Boossa. She complained that having fought with the Yarribeans against Alorie, she had received no recompense for her valour, though she had lost some of her slaves in the engagement; which neglect so disgusted her with the military profession, that she abandoned it and retired into private life. But she had gained a name of renown.

It is a holiday at Boossa; and the people assemble to witness some public sports. The queen is present, dressed in a negligé of rich English silks; behind her are other wives of the king, and her female slaves. The rest of the spectators are standing, sitting in groups on the grass, or lolling against trees. The men are generally dressed in a tobe, trousers, and cap. Most of the women are clad in country cloths; but some wear Manchester cottons of a large and showy pattern. Eight drummers and a fifer are animating the dancers. A man starts forward from

M

the crowd, flourishing a bundle of rushes over his head; and after moving about according to the music, is joined by two women who imitate his actions, and dance together till they are tired. Another party instantly take their place, and are succeeded by others. The king now appears with a guard of honour, and seems to take great delight in the entertainment. Then a tall, awkward woman dances alone before his majesty, using such extraordinary motions of the body as to gain universal applause. The king is fired with noble emulation; and when the tall lady has ceased, he steps forward to display his own proficiency in the dance. All the company rise out of respect to the sovereign, and uproariously applaud, as is meet, his slow and stately movements, which are far from graceful. When this dance is ended, his majesty commences a second, in which he imitates the canter of a horse going into battle; and then retires, amidst the acclamations of his admiring subjects.

The people await his return, when he comes from his hut, followed by a boy carrying two calabashes of cowries; some of which are distributed amongst the musicians and dancers, and the rest scattered by the royal hand among the crowd for a scramble; which produces its usual ludicrous effects. The kind king gives his people a parting treat, by dancing sideways till he reaches his residence. This gracious act fills them with joy and gratitude; and they return home delighted with the day's sport.

Lo! the popular mirth is suddenly turned into sad-

NEGRO DANCERS,

ness, and a cry is raised throughout the town! "The sun is dragging the moon across the heavens." Some great calamity is at hand, and perhaps the end of the world is come. The Mahometan priests tell the king that the moon was displeased with her appointed path through the heavens, because it was thorny and difficult: and she had to-night slipped out of her own orbit, and got into the track of the sun: whereupon he, in just indignation, is forcing her back, and clothing her with darkness, that she may not shine upon the earth. This is their theory of an eclipse. King, queen, and people believe the story; and they endeavour to avert the threatened catastrophe of an extinguished moon, by shouting and making all kinds of noises, to frighten away the sun from injuring the luminary of the night. Their cries, bodily contortions, blowing of trumpets, clashing of cymbals, shaking of empty calabashes, beating of drums, blowing on bullock's horns, clinking of chains, and every other sort of din possible,—produce one of the most extraordinary scenes that can be imagined. A stranger, ignorant of the cause, and suddenly placed amongst these people, might suppose himself to be amongst a legion of bedlamites or devils holding a grand revelry; so outrageously wild and horrifying is the appearance of the company. The Negroes continue their efforts until they are supposed to be crowned with success; and the sun having let go the terrified moon, she has returned to her proper course, and regained her privilege of enlightening the earth.

Below Boossa, the Niger again becomes a noble

stream, flowing down in placid grandeur. Its banks
are covered with dense forests, having a few scattered
villages, but chiefly peopled with wild beasts of the
largest description. The natives here have adopted
a simple way of destroying the elephants. They fix
a large harpoon firmly in the midst of a path which
these animals frequent in their nightly visits to the
water, inclining the point of the weapon so as to come
in contact with their huge breasts, and then covering it with stubble. When an elephant comes
hastily against it, it enters his flesh; and not knowing
the cause, he presses forward and forces it deeper
into his body. The natives then attack and destroy
him with ease.

Farther down the Niger is Wowow, a place of considerable importance in river navigation. The king
comes to the gate to receive his visitors. He is preceded by a number of Mallams, and followed by a
man bearing a heavy sword; behind whom is a train
of his royal wives and children. In the town wall,
on each side of the gateway, is a large niche, one of
which the king enters and there stands like a statue,
until the interview takes place. In the other is a
pole, which a naked youth has mounted, entwining
his legs around it, and continuing perfectly motionless, like his sovereign. This scene continues until
a royal messenger from the last town which the
travellers have visited introduces them to His
Majesty. If he tarry, all the company must wait
in their present position; the king and boy in their
niches, the queens and their children squatting in

the entrance, the visitors in front, the Mallams
sprawling between them and the king, and groups of
people sitting at a respectful distance. The ceremony of introduction is completed in a few moments;
as the monarch thinks it more dignified not to look
on his guests, or raise his head above a certain height.
On holidays, they have horse-races in the vicinity.

The customs of this people resemble those of most
Negro towns. But it seems that the marriage tie is
not here considered to be very binding. When a man
dislikes or gets tired of a wife, he treats her with dis-
respect and unkindness, the meaning of which she
understands, and returns to her friends. They then
come to the husband's dwelling, and formally ask him
if it be his wish that his wife should remain away.
If he answer in the affirmative, the marriage is regarded as dissolved, and the woman is free to enter
into a new union.

A characteristic incident, showing the way in which
these Negro kings ask for presents, is given by Mr.
Lander. The latter had sent an old latten tinder-
box to his majesty, requesting him to fill it with a
little pure salt; as that sold in the market was very
bad. But both king and queen coveted the salt-
cellar, and spoke in rapturous terms of its form and
lustre. "He exclaimed, 'Alla, how wonderful! even
the most trifling articles belonging to the white men
are fit for the use of mightiest kings. Alas! Alla
has given them all the riches and glory of the world,
and its knowledge; and left none whatever for black
men.' The king was affected. He thrust the vessel

into the pocket of his tobe, smoothed it down with
his hand, looked melancholy, and said, 'How nicely
it fits! what a beautiful thing! how convenient it
would be in travelling!' He then took it out again,
turned it round and round, opened and shut it repeatedly, and then bestowing on it a last commenda-
tion, as outrageous as any of the former, it was
returned to us filled with genuine salt." The meaning of all this was obvious. The tinder-box was immediately sent as a present to his Majesty, who
handsomely rewarded the bearer, and sent his best
thanks to the donor. It must, however, be understood, that if this way of obtaining what they covet
by *hints* does not succeed, the chiefs find some other
means of accomplishing their object.

Though a species of Mahometanism prevails in
Wowow, the old religion is not abolished; and the
fetish is still worshipped by many of the people.
See, here is a long procession of female devotees,
walking and dancing through the town, with large
branches in their hands! The priestess has just
swallowed the fetish-water, and is now supposed to
be inspired by a demon. She is convulsed all over,
her features terribly distorted, and her eyes widely
fixed on vacuity. She is carried on the shoulders of
one woman and supported by two others. They all
appear to be out of their senses, fantastic and frantic
in all their movements; singing or shrieking to the
music of drums and fifes, and brandishing their
weapons in the air. Now the priestess enters the
traveller's hut to bless its inmates. She is singularly

dressed in man's apparel, and rolling her distorted eyes, utters a yell more dismal than a dog's at midnight. She falls down on her knees before the stranger, gazes at him with a look of tenderness, holds out a friendly hand, and blesses him. A native receives her benediction in a rougher style. The female places him in a stooping posture, and twists his left arm behind his back: then letting this go, to his great relief, she presses down his shoulders with both her hands, muttering the blessing which he desired. It is supposed to be given by a spirit, and he is satisfied. The followers of "the ancient faith" believe in a God and spirits, in a future state of bliss, and also in a purgatory.

We go down the Niger to Rabba. The river varies in width from one to three miles, sometimes flowing in an undivided stream, sometimes dotted with islands, sometimes divided into branches by a large island. The banks are very verdant, studded with mean and dirty villages, interspersed amongst mighty trees and luxuriant foliage. In your passage, you would meet many canoes, formed out of a single trunk, built up with planks, and having a cabin in which the voyagers dwell.

Now a vast rock appears in mid-stream, rising to a height of 300 feet. It is very steep, and forms an object of much observation. It is called Mount Kesa, and is supposed to be the residence of a benevolent *genius*, who supplies the wants of the needy, restores the wearied traveller, and alleviates the sorrows of the oppressed.

We need not tarry at Rabba, except to mention its being an extensive and populous town, supplied with abundance of provisions, and all kinds of African produce and manufactures. It has large flocks and herds, and excellent horses. The little town of Zagozhi, on the opposite bank of the Niger, is famous for canoes, of which the chief has about 600. Their chief is styled "king of the dark water." He can furnish you with means of conveyance down the river. If you proceed, you will find that the width of the stream increases, though it is still very variable; and that the banks are mere marshes and morasses, so that it is impossible to land for a great many miles. Hippopotami abound in prodigious numbers; and it is unsafe to be near the shore at night for fear of enormous crocodiles. The Coodiana, the Chadda or Sharry, and other rivers join the Niger and swell its waters. The towns and their inhabitants become more rude and inhospitable. Some of the pagan tribes are very savage, and have become river-pirates, to the great annoyance and loss of merchants. So great is their mutual distrust, that when the crew of a canoe stops to purchase a few yams, both buyers and sellers are armed, and the goods are laid down on a spot mid-way between them; since neither party can trust the other. This little affair may require several hours for its completion.

Such an increased demoralisation of the natives towards the sea-coast proceeds from their slave-trade with Europeans, which has been carried on in the outlets of the Niger for hundreds of years. These

Negroes have imbibed the worst vices of foreigners,
and joined them with their own. They seem lost to
pity and every spark of righteousness; intent only on
gain and selfish gratifications, without any consideration for their fellow-creatures. The Messrs. Lander
had ample experience of the brutality of these pagan
tribes. They describe the Kirri people as a savage-
looking race, strong, and well-proportioned. Their
clothing is the skin of a tiger or leopard fastened
round the waist. Their hair is plaited and plastered
with red clay; and their face full of deep incisions so
as to resemble furrows, and dyed with indigo. The
Eboes have the same ferocious look, and are said to
be cannibals.

A mixture of savage childishness and pride in
European ornaments was seen in the king of Eboe.
On his head was a cap, shaped like a sugar-loaf,
covered with strings of coral and bits of looking-
glass. His neck was also encircled with several
necklaces of coral; and long strings of it hung
down to his knees. He wore a short Spanish sur-
tout of red cloth, much too small for him, ornamented with gold lace, epaulettes, and coral beads.
On each wrist were thirteen or fourteen bracelets
fastened with old copper buttons. His trousers, of
the same material as his coat, reached only to the
middle of his legs; the lower parts of them being
adorned with coral. A string of little brass bells
ornamented his ankles, and his feet were naked.
He was amazingly proud of this finery.

Other inhabitants of the outlets of the Niger re-

semble those now described. They are well armed
with guns and small cannon, delight in drinking
rum, are slave-catchers and slave-dealers, plunder
and extort from all who come within their reach,
— greater rogues and villains than can be well
imagined.

In tracing the course of the Niger downward, we
made mention of Boossa, which was visited both by
Clapperton and the Landers. If instead of following
the river, we had taken the shortest route to the Gold
Coast, we should have been in the track of all these
travellers. Let us just glance at two or three of the
towns and other curiosities which they saw in their
journeys.

Kiama is a town of huts, built after the Negro
fashion. The king's habitation is erected in an enclosure, with a number of huts for his several wives,
having such small doors or apertures that it is necessary to creep in order to enter them. In the outer
apartment of King Yarro's dwelling, there were
several sacred figures, or fetishes, which were supposed to guard the sovereign, and to which the
people applied for protection from various dangers.
In an inner apartment, the travellers found Yarro
sitting alone on buffalo hides. The walls were
adorned with objects which one would not have expected to see in the heart of Africa. There were
prints of King George the Fourth, the Duke of
York, Lord Nelson, the Duke of Wellington, an
officer of dragoons, and a smart English lady. On
the floor was a confused heap of muskets, lances, and

other weapons of war. The royal wives were very
curious, and they were afterwards heard scolding his
Majesty severely for not giving them part of a bottle
of rum presented to him by his guests. This shows
how loosely these people hold their Mahometan precepts.

How did these barbarians learn to have horse-
racing? It would almost seem as if they wished to
mimic the English. A race is held once a year on
the anniversary of the Bebun Salah : and no "Derby
day " can be looked forward to with greater impa-
tience. All the townsfolk are out upon this occasion,
dressed in their best attire. One distinguished group
consists of the king's wives and children. Manchester
cloths of the most showy patterns, and dresses made
of our common bed-furniture, are fastened round the
waist of sooty maidens. All the women have adorned
their necks with strings of beads, and their wrists
with a variety of bracelets made of glass beads,
brass, and copper. Rings of different materials
ornament their ankles. No efforts have been spared
in order to set themselves off to advantage, and
to draw the eyes of others to admire their charms
and finery. The veils and mufflers which prevail
in the latitudes of Timbuctu and Howssa are here
unknown, and personal liberty is the order of the
day.*

Now the royal cavalcade appears. Four horse-

* This is seen in the young virgins, who have no dress but beads
and wild flowers, and seem perfectly unconscious of any shame in
nakedness.

men lead the way. They are followed by several
men carrying on their heads a great quantity of ·
arrows in quivers of leopard's skin. Then come two
buffoons, throwing up and catching sticks, and performing other antics. Next are a number of little
boys, nearly naked, flourishing cows' tails over their
heads and dancing along merrily. These precede the
king himself, who is on horseback, followed by a
number of fine men on handsome steeds. When he
draws up in front of his house, where the royal group
are assembled, two or three soldiers fire a salute from
muskets of the sixteenth century.

The race-horses now appear, caparisoned with bright
cloths, silk tassels, little brass bells, and greegrees.
Their riders are dressed in caps, loose tobes, and
trousers of different colours, red morocco boots, and
white or blue turbans. Upon a given signal, the
eager steeds bound forward and gallop along the
course. All are excited. The riders brandish their
spears, the little boys flourish their cows' tails, the
musketeers discharge their pieces, the buffoons per- ·
form their antics, and the king is watching the race
with earnest delight. The sun shines on a variety of
dresses of brilliant colours, crimson, green, white,
yellow, blue, which flutter in the breeze; a host of
spears glitter in the sunbeams; the horses prance and
their bells tingle. It is an animated and extraordinary sight. Honour and fame are the only reward of
the victors in the course. A second race is run by
some naked boys, on ponies without saddles. Another race, like the first, closes the entertainment.

But dancing and singing will be kept up throughout
the night.

Katunga is the capital of Yarriba. It lies at no
great distance from Rabba on the Niger, and is a
town of considerable importance in this locality. The
vast plains in which it stands are beautiful and fruitful: but they do not seem to be well cultivated, as
provisions are dear, and the people seldom eat animal
food except that of the lowest kind, as reptiles, vermin,
and insects. The British travellers were received by
King Mansola in a very cordial and familiar manner.
He was dressed in robes of state. Instead of a turban, he wore a headpiece like a bishop's mitre,
adorned with strings of coral. He had a tobe of
patchwork, made of green silk, crimson silk damask,
and green velvet. His legs were covered with English stockings, and his feet with native sandals. A
large piece of light blue cloth, given by the late
Captain Clapperton, served for a carpet. His eunuchs
and others prostrated themselves before him, and
rubbed their heads with earth two separate times;
they kissed the ground before him, and placed each
cheek on it reverently. Some rolled about on the
ground, like porpoises in the water, till Ebo their
chief desired them to rise: for these black eunuchs
are very fat and unwieldy.

On a more private occasion, his majesty wore
only the ordinary costume of the country, consisting
of tobe, trousers, sandals, and antiquated cap. On his
right, some eunuchs and old people were reposing on
the ground; on his left was a circle of his young

wives; and behind them sat some widows of his
royal predecessors. The only musician present was
a whistler, who occasionally treated the company
with a few of his performances. After a while, there
seemed to be something important going on; for a
great deal of whispering took place between the
monarch and his wives; and both parties left the
yard two or three times. At length the secret came
out. Mansola presented 2000 cowries, equal to
about three shillings and sixpence, to the guides who
had accompanied the travellers, that they might purchase provisions on their way home. As his majesty
could not or would not afford this contemptible
present, he had required his wives to contribute it
among them, each paying her portion. It seems
that these queens are obliged to work for their own
food and clothing, and to furnish a quota towards the
king's expenses. They do this chiefly by trading,
which sometimes compels them to take long journeys.
Such is royal life at Katunga.

The king is quite despotic, and seems to make
little of the lives of his subjects; since he issued an
order that if any of them annoyed the strangers by
impertinent curiosity, Ebo should take off their
heads. This mandate insured to the travellers a
greater degree of quiet than they had ordinarily
enjoyed in Negro towns.

Bohu was the old capital of Yarriba, and is of
large extent, fortified with a triple wall and moats.
The governor was very complaisant to the strangers,
sending them a bullock, yams, bananas, and a huge

calabash of milk containing at least six gallons. His chief minister is appointed by the king, and seems to act as a kind of spy on the governor.

The former governor of Jenna, near the coast, had recently died, and the king of Yarriba put one of his meanest slaves into the vacant office. This was done from motives of jealousy; lest if a person of any influence were made governor, he might rebel and become independent. When the governor received his present from the travellers, he expressed his gratitude and satisfaction; but said sorrowfully that he must send some of it to the king, who would not allow him to wear red cloth till he had been longer in his situation.

Who is this that comes dancing and yelling into your hut, pretending to be possessed of an evil spirit? It is the fetish priest; and you had better take no notice of his fooleries, but give him a few cowries and let him go. He imposes upon some of the people, but others call him a knave and a devil. On his shoulders he has a large club, on which a human head is carved. To this weapon strings of cowries are suspended, with bells, broken combs, sea-shells, bits of iron and brass, nut-shells, and bits of wood having a rude face imprinted on them. This club is an ominous weapon. It is sometimes used on melancholy occasions. For instance, when a governor dies, two of his favourite wives are obliged to quit the world with him, to bear him company, as it is called, in the future state. They may either die by this fetish club, or drink poison. The real reason for this

sacrifice probably is, that they may try to keep their
lord alive as long as possible, and pay all manner of
attention to his health and comfort, knowing that
their own fate is involved in his. At the death of
the last governor, the two ladies in question, not being
tired of life, hid themselves; but one of them was
found whilst the Landers were in the town. The old
woman on receiving her choice of deaths, preferred
the poison; but was putting off the evil hour from
time to time, hoping to escape; and was bribing the
chief inhabitants to pass over the circumstance. Other
people were clamouring for the fulfilment of her duty.
Notwithstanding the representations and remon-
strances of the priest, and her own prayers for forti-
tude to drink the fatal cup, she could not find
resolution to accomplish the deed. " She has entered
our yard twice, to expire in the arms of her women;
and twice has she laid aside the fatal poison, in order
to take another walk, and gaze once more on the
splendour of the sun and the glory of the heavens;
for she cannot bear, the idea of losing sight of them
for ever." Her friends and slaves condoled with her
at her approaching death; her grave was dug in her
hut; and preparations were made for a "wake" at
her funeral; but the lady clung to life. Spies were
set over her that she might not leave the yard, and
she would probably soon require to submit to her
fate. The governor of Jenna himself must die when
news arrive of his royal master's decease; and then
some of *his* wives must bear him company. Such is
the bloody custom of heathenism.

There are here strolling musicians, with drums, whistles and horns; who perform much to their own satisfaction, if not to that of strangers. The drum is of peculiar construction, and its top is encircled with brass bells. It is held under the left arm, and is played with one hand, the other being engaged with the bells. It is also pressed with the arm and utters a shrill sound; so that it serves at once for drum, tambourine and bagpipe. The musicians are supported by voluntary contributions of the public, who require their services on all festive occasions.

CHAP. VIII.

BEFORE we leave the western parts of Africa, we shall
go a little further on our present route, to look at
the interior of Guinea. Yet the country between
us and Dahomey is wasted by wars and is very in-
secure, so that travelling to it would be difficult,
though the distance is not great. Nor could we
easily reach it from Senegambia, from which it is
separated by very high mountains, inhabited by
Foolas of different tribes. For the people of these
hilly districts are rude and inhospitable; as will be
manifest to any one who reads the adventures of
M. Mollien, in his journey to discover the sources
of the Gambia and Senegal, or the wanderings of

M. Caillée in his attempt to reach Timbuctu by this way. Many of these Foolas are Mahometans; and the mountains of Kong are steep and rocky, intersected by numerous streams, torrents, and dense forests. Near them, are the pagans of Wassulo and other petty kingdoms, living in a state of primitive simplicity. Farther east, is a tribe of Cannibals.

It is easy to enter Guinea from the Gold or Slave Coast, on account of the British colonies planted there. We may enter Dahomey by Whydah, its only seaport, and we can reach Ashantee from Cape Coast Castle. These are two principal kingdoms of Guinea. For the Fantis (or Fantees) who live on the coast, though a numerous people, are divided into small independent kingdoms or districts; the chief of whom, called the Braffo or nominal Lord paramount, resides in Abrah; and another lives in Cape Coast beside the British. But the two powerful kingdoms which we have mentioned are, in some respects, unique in their circumstances and national customs. It is barbarism on a grand scale. Every feature of savagism, except cannibalism, is here exhibited in a striking manner; united with attempted grandeur in a gorgeous display of gold, and of finery obtained from Europeans.

We suppose ourselves in Dahomey, by stepping over the intervening district. Here is a country which has been increasing in dominion, and diminishing in population. Its proper inhabitants are nearly extinct, and it has become a kingdom of united freebooters. It exists by war and plunder, to which

all the men and women are addicted. Of 200,000
inhabitants, not more than 20,000 are free people;
yet its standing army consists of about 12,000, of
whom 5000 are women. The latter is a strange
institution.

These female soldiers are dressed in a uniform
like the men, and are regularly armed with muskets,

FEMALE SOLDIER OF DAHOMEY.

which they know how to use. The uniform for both
sexes is a tunic, short trowsers, and skull cap. The
female officers wear a coral necklace and garments

of richer material than the privates. These Amazons
are highly esteemed by the king, whose guard they
form on public occasions. They have peculiar prerogatives; they may not be gazed at by men; they
are sometimes called the king's wives, though they
bear no connubial relationship to him. They are
single ladies, who have renounced the uses of their
sex, often declaring, "We are men, not women."
They are, like the male army, under a commander
who is also head executioner; which two functionaries
hold the first place of authority under the king.

Imagine, then, a band of these women, dressed in
a short tunic of blue-striped cotton reaching below the
thighs, and wide trowsers which reach a little lower;
their arms bare from the top of the shoulder, and
legs bare from above the knee; with a close white
cap variegated with blue, and a belt in which a short
sword and club are stuck; grasping in one hand a
long bright-burnished musket, and in the other a
grizzly human head,—surrounding the royal throne,
clamouring to be sent forth to battle, and protesting
that their valour is greater than that of the men, —
and you have some notion of these African Amazons.
In fact, the nation goes to war every year; easily
finding a pretence, often of the most frivolous kind,
for attacking a neighbouring tribe, to whom they
are formidable on account of their weapons and the
bravery of their female army. Before each campaign, a "custom" of a month is made, with feasting,
dancing, and human sacrifices. The chiefs or cabooceers bring their own men to the war; for which

they receive no pay, except booty, and presents from the sovereign.

When we consider that the king has thousands of wives, that each of his nobles has hundreds, that 5000 women are warrior celibates, and that war and royal jealousy constantly demand their victims; we do not wonder that the Dahomans are decreasing in number, and that the population is only preserved by mixing with the female slaves taken in the annual forages.

The power of the monarch is absolute in the fullest sense of the term. People of all ranks prostrate themselves before him, throwing dust over their heads. When the king's stick is shown, all who are present bow down and kiss the dust. A king's daughter and two officers reside in each of his minister's houses as spies, and to exact tribute according to his success in trade. No man can say that his head is safe on his shoulders for the next twenty-four hours. For an accusation is easily made where it is desired; and the laws are as bloody as those of Draco, every crime being punishable with instant death.

Savages they are, and savages they are resolved to continue. It is forbidden, under penalty of imprisonment or slavery, to alter the construction of a house, to sit on a chair, to be carried on a hammock, or to drink out of a glass. Only the king, who is above law, may do these things. His revenue is maintained by taxes, custom duties, toll gates, and a tithe of palm oil, which is the principal article of

exportation besides slaves.   Cowries are the circu-
lating medium, but dollars have also been introduced.
The dress and dwellings of the people resemble those
of other Africans.

Would you look at Abomey, the capital of this
robber kingdom?   It has no walls, but a ditch and
hedge of prickly acacia, about eight miles in circuit.

THE GATES OF ABOMEY.

You must enter, however, through one of its six
gates or blocked passes.   But take care! each of
these passes consists of two openings, one for the
king, the other for his subjects.   Take the proper
one!   As you enter, you see a fit emblem of the
kingdom, a human skull on each side of you: it is a
wholesome warning.   Inside, is a pile of skulls of

men and beasts: but there is no announcement of
what this means. You find no regular streets; and
the houses are surrounded with high walls of red
clay: so that you would scarcely suppose yourself in
a town of 30,000 inhabitants. You see no shops,
but some stalls in the smaller market-places; beside
which there are two large markets for occasional
use.

You wish to be presented to the king, as a
stranger of importance, perhaps as Commander
Forbes was presented in 1849 and 1850! Some
cabooceers and their followers come and pay homage
to you and conduct you to the palace. Its walls are
surmounted with human skulls: the buildings
within are like those of other Dahomans. The
square is full of musqueteers, with plenty of the
banners and umbrellas of cabooceers. Women-
soldiers stand on each side of his majesty, who sits
under a thatched gateway, dressed in a loose robe of
yellow silk adorned with spangles, and a Spanish
hat trimmed with gold lace. A gold chain of European manufacture is his only ornament. The
cabooceers pass before him three times, kissing the
dust each time. He rises. Forty bands of music
strike up their discordant notes, and all the ministers
and officers prostrate themselves, whilst royalty
shakes hands with his welcome guests. After the
usual compliments and gossip, his sable majesty asks
if you would like to see a review of his Amazons.
Certainly! And they perform various evolutions,
which you do not understand ; but you can see that

OIL PALM TREE

they know how to fire and handle a musket,—these brazen-faced wenches,—and that their officers know how to use a small whip with which they are furnished.

The favourite wife, at least for the present time, sits behind her royal husband, under a large parasol of crimson and gold, decked in silks and gold ornaments. The king asks if you will drink with him? Yes. He rises : and as you touch glasses, a salute is fired (a salute seems to be fired whenever the king does anything); and eunuchs and ladies hastily hold up clothes before his person; — for his subjects must not see him drink.

Your presents have been received ; and the king sends you some in return; — a bullock to each guest, with cloths, cowries, rum, oil, flour, pepper, and soap : so that you can feast yourself well, wash yourself, and buy what other things you need. A small gift is also made to each of your attendants. Every day you remain in Abomey, you receive oil, soap, and provisions. The people use much palm oil mixed with their corn, beans, and meat. Palm oil is now the staple article of export from Guinea to England and other countries which have renounced the slave trade. The quantity brought to Liverpool alone is very large.

Once a year the king makes a public display of his wealth : — for what is the use of it, unless it can be seen ? All his goods and chattels, including carriages and sofas, are borne along the street by six or seven thousand people. Amongst them is a drum orna-

mented with skulls and jaw-bones, and a princess's
umbrella decorated with 148 human jaw-bones. In
the procession are twelve canoe-shaped baskets, each
containing a human victim, his hands and feet tied,
dressed in white; who is presented, at the foot of the
throne, with a head of cowries, of the king's royal
bounty, to purchase a good last meal, as he is
destined to die on the morrow. Next day, a scramble
is given by the king from the platform, of cowries,
cloth, tobacco, &c. Rum is largely given to the
élite on the platform. On the occasion above referred
to, when the victims were brought forward, the
Englishmen offered a hundred dollars for several
of them; and the lives of three were thus spared.
The others were stripped, and the baskets containing
them were severally placed on the parapet, whence
by a royal kick, they fell into the pit, where the
men's heads were instantly cut off; and after their
bodies had been clubbed, they were thrown out to
be devoured by vultures and dogs. On the following day, presents were made to the ministers and
officers, crawling in the dust before the royal
monster.

Victims are still permitted by the king to be
offered on the death of a person of note; but not as
in Ashantee, or as formerly used to be in Dahomey.
These people worship the fetish of the leopard, which
is held sacred, and to which sacrifices of blood are
made. The knowledge of their religious mysteries
is confined to the priests and the initiated.

You would find no particular difficulty in getting

into Ashantee from Cape Coast. The danger would
be in reference to your getting out of it again.
Passing through the forest land of Fantee, you cross
the river Prah, and reach Quisah, the frontier town
of Ashantee. You must obtain permission to proceed,
from the chief of Adansi, who lives in Fomuna, a
neat town about a mile farther. You would be introduced to him, sitting in front of his house, under
a large umbrella, with his principal men on either
side. If this chief approves of your journey, he will
keep you at Fomuna, till he has received a message
from the king at Coomassie, to whom your arrival
is immediately reported. You may be detained for
some time at this place : for the king has to consult
his fetish, and find a lucky day, or omen, for everything that he does or allows to be done.

Let us suppose ourselves in the company of the
Rev. Mr. Freeman, on his first visit to Coomassie.
The king is dreadfully alarmed at his coming. He
is also afraid to refuse him, lest the white fetishman,
as he calls him, should injure him by magic spells.
Yet his own fetishmen are adverse to allowing the
religious stranger to come to the capital. At length
permission is given. We arrive at Esargu, about
nine miles from Coomassie, where we have again to
wait for another summons. We now advance, and
are met by another royal messenger, who invites us
forward : and immediately afterwards, three officers
make their appearance, wearing gold-hilted swords.
A number of soldiers also arrive and precede us to
the suburbs of the town.

Here we again wait under a large tree for another
invitation from the king. Presently, the royal
linguist, who is one of his chief men, comes in a
palanquin, over which a large umbrella is held. He
is attended by other officers bearing gold-headed
canes. These take care of our baggage. Another
messenger, attended by troops and umbrella-men,
requests us to meet the king in the market-place;
and we proceed in his company. But what are
these two heaps of earth, newly made, on each side
of our road? They are the graves of two unhappy
men, who have just been buried alive, as fetish
victims, to prevent any evil happening to the king
or country through our visit. Nothing can be done
by the sovereign of Ashantee without a sacrifice of
human life, in order to propitiate the unknown
powers of the air. This is a land of bloodshed.

The king sits to receive us, surrounded by his
nobles, officers, and captains, a large body of military, and thousands of unarmed attendants. A
narrow path is opened for us to the royal presence,
but we must salute all the cabooceers as we pass
along. This will occupy some time. At last we are
graciously received by his majesty. According to
the etiquette of the country, it is now our turn to be
saluted; so, the king retires to a little distance with
his people. His cabooceers now advance and greet
us as we are seated; the cavalcade being mixed up
with bands of music, umbrellas, and all kinds of
fantastic ornaments. At length, the king passes with
his suite, who are nearly covered with gold; and the

procession is closed by the war-captains and their troops. It requires an hour and a half for this gorgeous pageant to pass by our station. The number of persons present cannot be less than 40,000. One poor drummer has lost an ear because of this exhibition. He was walking a little behind the king, as he passed by us; and his performance on the drum not being deemed satisfactory, the king snatched a sabre from one of his attendants and aimed a blow at his head. The poor fellow avoided the cut, and threw himself upon the protection of a powerful cabooceer, who interceded for his life. This was spared; but he was condemned to lose an ear, for his carelessness in drumming badly before the king's stranger.

A stay in Coomassie is very unpleasant to a humanised mind. We cannot be there many days without witnessing bloodshed, or at least hearing the death-drum. When any relative of the king, or of a chief dies, a sacrifice is made, that the deceased may not go unattended into the other world. On ordinary occasions, the victims are principally slaves : but one respectable freeman at least is also sacrificed. When a person of distinction expires, all the slaves rush out of the house, and hide themselves in the bush : as one or two are instantly slain to accompany the deceased. The relatives and friends of the family then send presents of gold, cloth, rum, and powder, to be used at the funeral. The king sends the largest contribution. The worst cruelty takes place at the interment.

Think of the funeral of a woman of quality, when a
" custom" or sacrifice is made! Companies of females,
daubed with red earth, in imitation of blood, dance
along, screaming and bewailing the deceased. Other
women carry rich cloths and other articles which
belonged to her. A tumultuous crowd rush forward
with a confused noise of drums, horns, musketry,
yells, groans, and cries. Chiefs and captains assemble
with flourishes of trumpets and firing of muskets.
These all wend their way to the market, where the
king is said to have arrived, and to which the funeral
procession hastens. The son of the deceased leads
it, dancing like a madman, and looking with savage

ASHANTEE CHIEF.

delight on a number of victims, who are hurried
along, with knives passed through their cheeks. The
reason of these knives is to prevent the victims from
devoting any person to destruction by an oath or

curse, at the time of their immolation. They arrive before the king, sitting in his usual form of state.

Discharges of musketry are now made for the space of an hour. The chiefs after firing their pieces run about like maniacs, attended by their sycophants, who wave their flags, and call out the "strong names" of their masters. The common soldiers retain their places. The women outside the circle of men, vociferate the funeral dirge at the utmost pitch of their voices. The head fetishwoman of the family rushes through the ranks, screaming as if in violent agony. When the noise has abated, rum and palm wine are drunk in abundance; and the females of the family come forth and dance. Then a present of sheep and rum is exchanged between the king and the son of the deceased.

Now the death-drum sounds its knell. Thirteen victims have been placed near the left side of the king. Each of the cabooceers casts a savage look on them. Then an executioner lops off the right hand of one of them, who is thrown down, and his head is severed from his body. The rest are mangled in the same way. The body of the deceased lady is carried to "the bush," where a large grave is made; here many other victims, principally females, are butchered. The heads of these victims are placed in the grave, and some retainers of the family are called in a hurry to assist in lowering the corpse; — when, just as it touches the pavement of heads, one of the freemen is stunned with a blow from behind; a deep cut is made in his neck; he is rolled in upon the lady's body, and the grave is instantly filled up. The "custom" often lasts for a week or ten days; and if it be a relative of the king's who has died, sacrifices are made every day. The carcases of the victims are thrown out for the vultures, dogs, and wild beasts to devour.

The funeral customs for the king or a member of his family are conducted on a large scale. Three or four thousand victims have been put to death on such an occasion, during a war when many prisoners were "on hand." When the king dies, all his chief slaves, in number above a hundred, who are distinguished by the large circle of gold which they wear round their necks, are put to death. Ashantee is then like a field of blood; for all the customs made by subjects during the late reign must be repeated along with that for the king himself. For some days no one is safe in the streets, and few people, even of the highest rank, venture out of doors, for men run about with swords, cutting down any whom they may meet.

These horrid customs prevail in the independent states around Ashantee. Dahomey used to be quite as bad. When the king of that country died, his wives began to break and destroy everything they could lay hands on, and then to kill each other. On one occasion, two hundred and eighty thus perished before the successor could reach the palace and stop the carnage. All these, and six of the remaining living wives were interred with the deceased monarch. We are sorry to learn that the new king of Dahomey is reviving the " customs " on a larger scale.

Enough of this sickening subject; which yet could not be omitted in a description of the " Africans at Home." In all this region it is blood, blood, blood ! And the pride is in gold, gold, gold ; and in glittering gewgaws which gold purchases. The great wealth (in gold) of the country seems to increase its savagism. Before leaving, let us take a glance at the royal household, and one or two other curiosities.

The power of the king is absolute over the lives and property of his subjects, so that he can instantly punish any one who has broken a law or spoken disrespectfully of himself. Yet he himself is bound by the laws which are made; and which, like those of the ancient Medes and Persians, cannot be changed. The customs of their forefathers must be maintained inviolate ; and a late king lost his throne by attempting to alter some of them. The captains and cabooceers, also, are consulted on all matters of war and peace, or other relations with foreign states, in order to make the country appear combined, and therefore more formidable to foreigners.

The royal household is usually very large. The king is permitted to have 3333 wives. A few only of these women live in the palace at the same time ; the rest reside at the royal country house, or in a part of the town consisting of two streets reserved for their use. This locality is enclosed, and guards are placed at the gates, which no persons are permitted to enter. Their female friends, and even the royal

messengers converse with them at the barricades.
When they go abroad, which does not often occur,
they are attended by a number of boys, furnished
with whips of elephant's hide, which they use freely
upon all persons who do not instantly turn away and
cover their eyes. Whipping and fining are penalties
inflicted on those who look at the king's wives. On
great public occasions, however, several hundred of
these royal dames accompany their consort, arrayed
in a profusion of silks and gold. Of course, it sometimes happens, that his majesty does not know how
many wives and children he possesses.

The cabooceers, also, practise polygamy on a large
scale. Infants are sometimes contracted in marriage
to elderly men; and a provisional contract is made
before the child's birth, as in India. It is therefore
dangerous to play with female children, lest they
should really be wives, and a heavy fine should be
the penalty. The women do not live in the same
house with their husband, but in a cluster of huts
by themselves, or under the care of their mothers.
Nor do they ever eat in their husband's presence.

One of the king's sisters is appointed governess, a
ruler of all the women in the country; and settles, or
tries to settle, all grave disputes amongst this sex.
They are, however, under the most absolute control
of their domestic lords. If any one is caught listening to her husband's conversation, the loss of an ear
is the inevitable consequence; or, if she blab out any
of his secrets, her upper lip is the forfeiture.

Where some people have so many wives, it follows

that many must have none, which is specially the case with slaves. To provide for this emergency, a number of females are set apart for the common use; and wealthy women bequeath slaves to the state for this purpose, as an act of religious righteousness. Other irregularities may be expected to occur. In fact, no distinction between right and wrong is made respecting the relationship of the sexes to each other; it is treated as a mere matter of property.

This covered porch or piazza, in which a great man sits, smoking, drinking, and gossiping, is the front of his house. A door through it leads into the yard and court, in which are a number of sheds or huts built of "swish," that is, of sticks and mud. The front of the wall is sometimes ornamented with various devices in plaster work.

The king is on public occasions magnificently appareled in silk and gold. His person is loaded with all kinds of ornaments of this precious metal, mixed with charms; and his "stool" or throne is covered with plates of gold. Gold adorns the belts and muskets of his guards, and forms the breast-plates and sword-hilts of his messengers. His treasurer carries blow-pan, boxes, scales, and weights of solid gold; and his linguists carry bundles of gold canes. All the other officers carry the badges of their office, made of gold. The chief slaves and servants of the household wear stars, crescents, or neck-bands of gold; and the royal executioner carries a massive golden hatchet.

As the chiefs vie with each other in a display of

their wealth, after the manner of royalty, the amount
of gold in Ashantee must be immense. Some parts of
the soil are said to be impregnated with this metal;
and in one stream, many thousands of slaves are
employed in washing for it. There are also gold
mines, in which large lumps are sometimes found
imbedded in loam and granite. The bracelets on
the arms of some of the cabooceers would weigh
several pounds each.

Consider this grand display of wealth by one of
the great cabooceers! He thinks himself free from
all faults which might cause a palaver and loss of
property; and he is too vain to keep the knowledge
of his riches within his own breast. He exhibits
them, once in his life, in a noisy procession through
the streets, in which his numerous slaves carry and
display his goods and chattels. Amongst these
valuables are gold chains for the neck, arms, and
legs; various ornaments for the ankles, consisting
of keys, bells, chains, and padlocks; similar ornaments for his wives, children, and captains; a superb
war-cap of eagle's feathers; fetishes and charms;
caps and silk dresses; purses, bags, &c.; other
articles made of monkey-skin; fans of tiger-skin,
with ivory handles, and adorned with silk; gold
swords; figures of birds, beasts, and fishes, in gold;
bows covered with silk and skin, and ivory arrows;
drums and other instruments of music, covered
with tiger-skin; many weapons of war; and a
variety of other articles. The ornaments of gold are
declared to weigh more than sixteen hundred ounces.

The population of Coomassie may be estimated at one hundred thousand; that of all the chief towns in the district is also large. Hence the great number of captives that are taken in their international wars; and as the kingdom of Ashantee is the strongest and most consolidated, it seldom wants a full stock of slaves. The soil is in general very rich, producing many valuable fruits and vegetables; together with cotton, indigo, bamboos, and oil nuts.

We have already mentioned the fetish, which is

THE FETISH MAN, AND THE GOVERNOR OF WYDAH.

the common worship of the negroes of Guinea. It is a species of demonology. Spirits of various kinds are supposed to reside in natural objects which have been properly consecrated,—spirits of both sexes, and requiring food for their support. Each town has at least one rude temple or fetish house erected in a grove. Many kinds of objects, animate, inanimate, and fanciful, are consecrated for the abode of these imagined spirits. Images abound. In some places the crocodile is worshipped, or dangerous serpents, or wild beasts. Certain rivers, lakes, and ponds are held peculiarly sacred. The fetish men and women work upon the credulity and superstitious fears of the people, and make them serve their own purposes of gain and power.

Under the same influence of fear, some negroes worship the devil, whom they suppose to be a great evil spirit ever intent upon mischief. So that when a person rises from his seat, his attendants are wont immediately to lie down on their side, and cover the spot where their master sat, lest the devil should slip into his place. But on the Gold Coast, instead of being honoured, he is annually expelled from the country with great ceremony. The people collect on a certain evening, furnished with muskets, sticks, and other noisy weapons; and shouting, hallooing, and making all the din that is possible, they beat about the houses. Then they rush out of town with flambeaux, and fire muskets, and shout as after a retreating enemy, till they imagine Satan to be driven far away from them.

We need not describe the forms of their puerile idolatry, or the tricks of the priests, who live by the offerings of a deluded people. These impostors even pretend to divine, by acting in concert with one another, and becoming possessed of the circumstances and private histories of individuals, which they disclose as if received by inspiration. They also announce what days are lucky and unlucky. Of the former there are not above one hundred and sixty in a year. On the unlucky days, men must not do any public business, engage in battle, or even march forward their troops.

Similar forms of superstition and immorality prevail throughout Ashantee, Dahomey, Fantee, and the smaller adjoining kingdoms. Their civil and social condition is also nearly the same. Slavery, bloodshed, polygamy, and fetish, with a childish pride in gold and gaudy apparel, prevail in these benighted regions. A little light is beginning to spread amongst the natives, especially on the coast, through the influence of Protestant missions from England, and the establishment of Liberia.

Native converts are penetrating into the country, and proclaiming the glad tidings of the Gospel: schools are established, and an example of peaceful civilisation is afforded. But the opposing obstacles from fetish priests, " customs," slavery, and polygamy are great and powerful; and the mass through which the holy leaven has to spread is great. Yet, if Mahometanism has effected changes in many nations of the Negro family, it may be expected that Christianity and a healthy commerce will be no less mighty, in pulling down the strongholds of a base superstition and bloody savagism.

CHAP. IX.

Eastward from Say. — Gando. — Royal Covetousness. — Sockotu. —
Sultan Bello. — Civet Cats. — An impudent Executioner. — Wurno.
—Sultan Aliyu. — The Pistols. — Providing for a Guest. — Journey
in the Desert. — Agades. — Its Palace. — Sultan. — Royal Procession.
—Men and Women. — Markets. — Court of Justice. — More of the
Desert. — A narrow Escape. — Effects of Thirst. — Route by Bilma.
— Skeletons. — Fate of Couriers. — Mutual Fears. — Blood Feuds. —
Salt Lakes. — Surgical Operation. — Sons of the Desert. — Plun-
dering.

WE must now return to Say, where we left the Niger,
and proceed on our travels eastward; in order to
visit one of the most populous and powerful regions
of Africa. This country has the general appellation
of the Howssa States, and contains several small and
tributary kingdoms or provinces, as Gando, Sockotu,
Katsena.

Canoes of all sizes are ready to transport you and
your effects across the river at Say. But if your luggage is very bulky, you must have one of the larger
sort. Such a boat is about forty feet in length, and
four to five feet in width in the middle; formed
of two hollowed trunks of trees sewn together in the
centre. It will carry three camels. The stream is

THE NIGER AT SAY.

here contracted by a rocky bank, and is only about
700 yards broad, but has a noble appearance.

The main route from this place eastward is pretty
much frequented; and the road is varied, being by
turns rocky, woody, and swampy. The people are
poor, and the villages and towns of no particular
interest. But here is a salt-hamlet, of which there
are several in this locality! It adjoins a large mound
of rubbish about 200 yards square, and from 20 to
50 in height, formed of the mould of the valley from
which the saline particles have been extracted. The
earth of the salt vale is put into large funnels made
of straw and reeds; so that when water is poured
upon the earth, it is strained through the funnels.
Being received into vessels placed underneath, it is
boiled, and the sediment is formed into small loaves
of salt. The product is of a greyish yellow colour,
and of tolerable quality, especially for culinary
purposes. The natives also extract salt from the
ashes of burnt grass, which has grown in a brackish
soil. Other kinds of salt are brought from the desert; but the produce of the pits is of very different
qualities.

This country, like that on the other side of Say, is
inhabited by Foolbe and Songhay, and is in a very
distracted condition. Travellers must keep a constant watch, to prevent being surprised by some band
of marauders. The principal towns contain seven or
eight thousand inhabitants, and are all walled and
fortified. A singular incident here befel one of Dr.
Barth's camels. It went raving mad, leaped about

in the most ludicrous manner, kicked in every direction, and at length fell to the ground.

The next place of importance is Gando, the capital of the Kebbi district, and residence of a powerful Pullo prince. He is a nephew of the reformer Othman, and like all his relatives, is a stern and bigoted Mussulman. He spends his life in a secluded, monkish manner, and would not allow Dr. Barth to see his holy face. The traveller was obliged to leave his presents in the palace, without speaking to its august occupant. But the sanctity of the sultan did not prevent his being quite alive to his temporal interests, and trying to extort the utmost from a stranger. At first, he signified his approval of the presents sent to him; but having heard that his guest had given a pair of silver mounted pistols to the emir of Sockotu, he refused to let him depart until he had received a similar gift. This was very mortifying, as the pistols were reserved for a person of more importance in furthering the traveller's interest; but the holy man would not be content with less. The town, which is situated in a narrow valley and surrounded with walls, is only noted for its onions and cotton cloth.

Sockotu, or rather Sackatu, is the capital of the province of Zanfara, and one of the chief and most populous towns in Central Africa. It is known to Europeans as the place where the gallant Clapperton died, worn out with sufferings and disappointments. It does indeed seem to require the patience of Job to travel through these regions with anything like

a happy equanimity: for all the kings and chiefs,
great and small, try to detain the foreigner as long
as possible, in order to get more *presents* from him,
and through jealousy, lest he should bestow his gifts
on a neighbour or a rival. Sockotu is surrounded
with a good wall, between twenty and thirty feet
high, and has twelve gates, which are regularly
closed at sunset. It has two large mosques, besides
other places for prayer; and is laid out in well
arranged streets. The dwellings of the aristocracy
consist of enclosures containing several houses built
in Moorish style. The inhabitants are chiefly Felattas,
possessing numerous slaves; and it is, therefore, a
Mahometan city, though the people are not so in-
tolerant as in Timbuctu and Jenné. The situation
of the town is healthy, being on a long ridge; but
an adjacent marsh and stagnant pools cause it to be
very agueish.

A stranger is first introduced to the vizier or
gadado. The vizier, during Clapperton's sojourn in
the town, was an elderly man, very polite, speaking
Arabic exceedingly well. The sultan seemed to
live in greater simplicity than some of the chiefs of
inferior places. Captain Clapperton passed through
several guard houses, and was then introduced to
Sultan Bello, seated on a small carpet, between two
pillars which supported the roof. The walls and
pillars were painted blue and white, in the Moorish
taste; and on the back wall was the sketch of an
ornamented fire-screen.

Sultan Bello's brother sold to Clapperton some of

the remains of Major Denham's baggage, which had
been lost in a military foray which he had joined.
"He told me that he possessed a great number of
slaves; and I saw many females about his person,
most of them very beautiful." The prince kept civet
cats, of which he had two hundred. These animals
were very ferocious, and were confined in separate
wooden cages. They were about four feet long,
from the nose to the tip of the tail; and resembled
a small hyena, except in the greater length of body
and tail. They were fed with pounded Guinea corn
and dried fish made into balls. The civet was

CIVET CAT.

scraped off every second morning, with a shell like
that of a muscle; during which operation the animal
was thrust into a corner, and its head held down
with a stick.

"I was sitting in the shade before my door, with
Sidi Sheik, the sultan's fighi, when an ill-looking
wretch, with a fiend-like grin on his countenance,
came and placed himself directly before me. I
asked Sidi Sheik who he was? He answered with
great composure, 'The executioner.' I instantly
ordered my servants to turn him out. 'Be patient,'

said Sidi Sheik, laying his hand on mine, 'he visits the first people in Sockotu, and they never allow him to go away without giving him a few goora nuts, or money to buy them.' In compliance with this hint, I requested forty cowries to be given to the fellow, with strict orders never again to cross my threshold."

This villain had applied to the governor for the office of executioner, which his own brother then held, boasting of his superior adroitness in the family vocation. The governor said, "We will try:—go fetch your brother's head." The wretch immediately went to his brother's house, and finding him quietly sitting in the doorway, struck off his head at one blow with a sword, giving him no notice or warning whatever of his mission. He then carried the bleeding trophy to the governor, and claimed the promised office, which was given to him. He has had plenty of work to do. The capital punishments inflicted in Sudan are beheading, impaling, and crucifixion; the first being inflicted on Mahometans, the two latter on Pagans. Wretches linger on the cross for a period of three days, before death terminates their sufferings.

During Clapperton's stay in Sockotu, provisions were regularly sent him from the sultan's table on pewter dishes, with the London stamp: and one day, meat was served to him in a white wash-hand basin of English manufacture.

A little north of Sockotu is Wurno, the capital of the great sovereign who reigns over the Howssa States, holding the provinces which we have described in a kind of subjection as tributaries. His empire extends to Songhay on the west, and Bornu on the east. He is a liberal man, not haunted with the ghost of Mahometan bigotry or asceticism. At the same time he wants energy of character, and is only a nominal warrior. His dominions are, therefore, held with a feeble hand, and the border country is in a state of much insecurity and distraction. This is specially the case on the western side, where the stern followers of Othman wield a firm sway, and are anxious to extend the reforms (so called) of a stern Islamism. Aliyu, on the other hand, is content with the present state of things, and has no zeal for proselytism; as is evident from his allowing a pagan people to skirt his eastern frontier. We shall glance at these Bedee when we come to them in our journey.

Aliyu, on hearing of Dr. Barth's arrival, sent him a supply of provisions, consisting of an ox, four fat sheep, and two large sacks of rice, each containing about two hundredweight; intimating his desire to see him immediately. He was found sitting on a raised platform under a tree in front of his dwelling. He received the traveller with great cordiality, shaking hands with him, and begging him to sit down in front of him. He said that he had heard of all his movements, had received his letter sent through the Sultan of Agades, and entered heartily into the views of his mission: so he was ready to form a commercial treaty with the Queen of England, and engage to protect British merchants and travellers. He affirmed that it would be his greatest pleasure to help in drawing the nations together in bonds of amity, which would conduce to the good of all: and professed great regret that Captain Clapperton, called Abd Allah ("servant of God") had died in his dominions, fearing lest this untoward event might arouse the suspicion of Europeans.

At the next interview, when Dr. Barth went to the palace with his presents, he found Aliyu in a room built of reeds, sitting on a wooden divan. The sultan is a stout man, of middle size, with a round, fat, good-humoured face; inheriting the features of his mother, who was a Howssa slave, rather than those of his father. He was quite frank, and had thrown off his paternal reserve, not even using the face-covering worn by Pullo princes in the presence of strangers. His dress consisted of little more than a grey tobe or smock-shirt. He was greatly pleased with his presents, chiefly consisting of brocaded garments of various colours, a carpet, razors, looking-glasses, sugar and spices: but was enraptured with the last offering, a pair of silver mounted pistols, the like of which he had never seen. With childish joy he frequently exclaimed, "I thank you, I thank you: God bless you, God bless you."

As the sultan was on the eve of departing on a short expedition, and the etiquette of the country did not allow a distinguished stranger to leave in his absence, Dr. Barth was obliged to wait in the capital till his return. But Aliyu sent him 100,000 kurds, equivalent to about 10*l.*, to defray his household expenses in the interim. He also furnished

him with all the papers that he desired.   What a
pity that other sovereigns do not resemble this negro
prince in his pacific and enlightened policy!   Verily
all the wisdom of the world does not dwell in Europe
and America.

One would like to see a real " city of the desert,"
if it were not for the dangers and difficulties of the
journey.   In twenty days' hard travelling from Wurno,
you could reach the ancient and royal city of Agades,
once the capital of a Desert empire, now in a half
deserted and ruinous condition.   The danger from
robbers in this district is not great, if you travel in
company with one of the large salt caravans, which
are under the protection of powerful chieftains;
though these are sometimes attacked by a hostile tribe.
But small companies of men are never secure in these
wild regions.   The present inhabitants chiefly consist
of the Tagama, Kelgeres and Kelowi : but the Tawarek and other Arab tribes infest the neighbourhood.

Here and there, if you keep the proper route, you
will meet with a well, a village, or even a small
town.   Sometimes you must travel several days without finding any water, which you must carry with you
in bags of skin.   Then you must stop a day or two
to recruit yourself and camels.   Strong and cold
winds blow over the rocky mountains, so that you
would be glad of a blazing fire at night.   The brushwood which grows in the valleys is a fine covering
for ostriches, antelopes, and lions.   The last-mentioned animal is an active thief, though apparently
not very ferocious.   It has scarcely any mane, and

differs in this respect from the lion of central Africa, whose mane is large and beautiful. These wild beasts hunt in companies of four and five, and will not hesitate to steal a camel.

The people of the desert dwell in small villages of huts, built of mats attached to stalks of corn or to young trees, and roofed with branches covered with hides. They subsist chiefly by cattle breeding, hunting, stealing, and convoying caravans. Their manners are very free, and the morals of both sexes are described as extremely loose.

The naturalist could find some objects of interest in the desert. There is a plant, called in Howssa "kumkummia," a species of euphorbia, which grows to the height of nearly two feet. It is very poisonous, and is used to anoint the tips of arrows. Then there is the "aido," a grass covered with large and strong prickles, very distressing to naked feet. One part of the country is nearly covered with the *Asclepias gigantea*, on the leaves of which the cattle feed. It has a milky juice (used by pagans to foment their "giya"), which spots clothes, and even injures the hair of horses. Acacias, dwarf laurels, and other stunted plants grow in the more fertile places.

Now suppose that we could be transported across this desert region, which we gladly leave to its present occupants, and that we could be set down in Agades itself. This once far famed city deserves a little notice. It used to be surrounded with a wall, but this has disappeared from one side, and what remains is in a dilapidated state. The southern part

P

of the town is almost entirely deserted, and many
ruined houses are found in every street. In the zenith
of its prosperity, Agades had a circuit of about
three miles and a half, and probably contained a
population of fifty thousand souls. Its greatest de-
cline took place at the close of last century, when
the conquests of the Tawareks destroyed its principal
markets; and a tide of emigration set in for Howssa.
Dr. Barth estimates the present number of inhabited
houses to be six or seven hundred, and the inhabitants to be about seven thousand. A large portion of
the male population are always from home, on mercantile expeditions of their own or in convoying
caravans, so that the armed force of the place at any
one time seldom musters more than six hundred.

More than fifty houses are raised to two stories, or
rather have a garret planted on their flat roofs. The
better sort have a vestibule, with inner apartments,
and a spacious court-yard, in which is an enormous
bedstead. Turtle-doves, goats, and young ostriches
may be found running about here, and plenty of
children. In the back court are several apartments
for the women. The great bedstead is a piece of furniture peculiar to the Songhay tribes. In Agades, it
is like a small house, built of strong boards, and
furnished with a canopy of mats. The dwellings
require to be spacious, as they sometimes contain a
little clan of people.

Let us look at the palace. It forms a small quarter
of the town, consisting of more than twenty buildings,
included in a large court-yard. The sultan's own

house is of neat appearance, well polished, and
furnished with a wooden door. The vestibule is
divided by a balustrade, so as to form a kind of inner
room. Passing through another door, you are ushered
into the presence chamber of the king. It is a
spacious apartment, forty or fifty feet square, the
low roof being supported by two massive columns of
clay. On these pillars are placed large boards, which
sustain lighter ones; on which branches are laid,
which are again covered with mats; and over all is a
firm coating of clay. On either side of the hall, is

AUDIENCE HALL OF AGADES.

an opening to admit light; and at the farther end,
another door leads to the interior of the palace.

When Dr. Barth was introduced to the sultan, he
was seated between the right column and the wall,
clothed in a white "litham," having the lower part
of his face covered with a white shawl. He saluted
the traveller, and immediately entered into a conversation about England, of which he had never heard,
though he had used "English powder." He expressed great indignation on hearing that the travellers had been wronged by tribes under his jurisdiction,
who had deprived them of presents intended for the

sultan himself. He vowed vengeance for this offence, which he afterwards made a pretext for enriching himself with the spoils of these tribes; since one part of his revenue consists of fines levied on marauders. The rest of his income is derived from the presents or contributions received at his accession, and a small tax on foreign merchandise and salt.

This sultan had been deposed a few years previously, to make way for another; but a restoration was effected; and subsequently, another change was made; so that, though the people adhere to one family of kings, they seem to think that a change of persons "is lightsome." His re-installation was now at hand; and Dr. Barth witnessed the procession. The ceremony was as follows. Abd El Kader was conducted from his private apartment to the public hall. Then the chiefs of two tribes, Itisan and Kelgeres, asked him to sit down on a couch made of palm trees, covered with mats and a carpet. He did so, but kept his feet on the ground, till the chiefs of the Kelowi desired him to lift them up on the divan, and so recline fully in Eastern style. This was to show the joint investiture of their new sovereign by all these tribes. A procession was then formed to the chapel or tomb of a Mahometan saint outside the town, where the sultan said his prayers, and on his return the company dispersed.

In the procession, the new prince rode first on a fine horse of the Tawati, a most famous breed, wearing a fine robe of coloured cotton and silk, with a blue bernoose over it, and in his girdle a golden handled scimitar. Then came several officers of the household. Next rode the chiefs of the Itisan and Kelgeres, in full dress and armour, consisting of sword, dagger, long spear, and immense shield. The sultan of the Kelowi followed, with a long train of his people on swift camels. The men of the town closed the procession, some on horseback, but most on foot, armed, and dressed in their best finery. Several of the costumes were very picturesque; and the whole had a gorgeous and martial appearance.

Some of the men of Agades are tall, with broad face and coarse features; and they allow their hair to hang down upon their shoulders. These belong to a mixed tribe of Berbers and Songhay. The Itisan chiefs were tall and slender, of light colour, and fine countenance. Their dress was simple but elegant, consisting of trowsers and tobes of a pepper colour, made of a mixture of silk and cotton, with embroidery.

Many of the women are of good figure and fair complexion, with fine black hair. The richer class dress well, in garments of white or coloured silk and cotton, and are fond of silver and other ornaments. Dr. Barth formed a very low estimate of their morals, from the freedom with which they behaved when the sultan and most of the men had left the town; so that he was obliged to be very reserved, and even to seclude himself more than he wished. There are several markets in Agades. That for live stock contained a number of camels. The vegetable market is not so well supplied, the stock being small, except of cucumbers, and Molukhia (*Corchorus olitorius*). The butcher's market has a sufficient quantity of meat; and numbers of large vultures are sitting on the ruined walls, ready to seize upon any kind of offal that may be let fall.

In another market or bazaar, held in a kind of hall supported by stems of the doom-tree, women sell a variety of ornamental and other articles; such as necklaces and beads, sandals, small boxes of leather and tin, and saddles. The leathern boxes or purses are very neatly made, of different colours, and a variety of sizes. The sandals, also, are very neat, and are highly prized throughout the country. The artisans in leather work are almost entirely women, who live together in a quarter of the town, which used to be separated from the rest by a gate. Though the inhabitants are Moslems, and are far from bearing good will to infidels, Christians, or Jews; yet they do not deny themselves in their favourite amusements of dancing and music. These pastimes, with gossiping, occupy the leisure time of the evening, and are often protracted to a late hour of the night. A spectator of one of their moonlight balls represents the young men as dancing in pairs, placed opposite to each other, stamping with the foot, and whirling round in circles; the performance meeting with the applause of numerous admirers, who signify their approbation by loud clapping of hands. Besides the usual players on instruments, one musician attracted attention, by performing a solo on a sort of guitar, accompanying it with an extemporaneous song.

AGADES IN THE DESERT.

There is a crowd of persons assembled in the
vestibule of a house detached from others, and
furnished with a verandah! It is the residence of
the cadi or judge, who is listening to an interesting
lawsuit. A stolen camel has been traced to the
possession of a townsman, who proves that he bought
it of a man who swore it was his own property. The
complainant, who lost the camel, wishes to recover
its price from the defendant, who had bought and sold
it again under suspicious circumstances. After hearing the evidence adduced on both sides, the judge
decides in favour of the defendant.

Dr. Barth was, on the whole, pleased with this
city of the desert; though he had to submit to some
inconveniences from the bigotry of the Mussulmans,
whose religious zeal is especially excited at the time
of a religious festival. Though shorn of its former
splendour, Agades did not present any appearances
of misery and want. On the contrary, the inhabitants seemed to enjoy life with a considerable degree
of cheerfulness. Its healthy situation, partial civilisation, and germs of national vigour, afforded some
pleasing ideas of prosperity. The looseness of its
morals may be attributed to the numerous caravans
which are passing through it, especially in connection
with the salt trade of the desert.

The vast region which lies beteen Tripoli and the
heart of Africa, forming the eastern skirt of the Sahara,
has been crossed by several enterprising travellers.
But it is not, therefore, either easy or secure. There
are two principal caravan routes through it, the more

westerly one passing near Agades, and the easterly
passing through Bilma. By either of these, the
journey is fraught with many hardships and dangers.
High mountains of barren rocks and sand have to be
surmounted, and many intricate defiles to be passed,
vast plains must be crossed, of the dreariest description, with only here and there a spot of verdure;
whilst lawless tribes, hostile to each other and bent
on plunder, hover around, waiting for an opportunity
of becoming rich at another's expense. During most
of the route, water is scarce, and provisions are not
easily obtained. Cold winds and storms alternate
with scorching heat and clouds of sand.

Woe to the unhappy traveller who deviates from
the proper track, and gets lost in the desert! His
fate may be gathered from the narrow escape of Dr.
Barth, who left his companions to visit a remarkable
mountain near which the caravan would pass. He
took with him a few dry biscuits and dates, which
he soon found to be a very bad kind of food without
water. As the sun reached the zenith, the traveller
got tired and exhausted, and found at last that he
was lost. In vain he fired his pistols to give a
signal to his friends, and ascended one mound after
another, to try and catch a glimpse of the caravan.
When the sun set, he intended to light a fire, but
could not muster strength to gather wood; and
therefore scrambled to an old tree, under which he
might lie down. After reposing for an hour or two,
he discovered a large fire in the valley, which he
hoped to be that of his companions. He fired again

and again, but received no response. He tried to
sleep, but could not; and lay tossing on the ground,
feverish and restless, longing for the dawn of
day. Collecting all his strength, he then loaded his
pistols with a heavy charge, and fired once, twice.
The sound seemed loud enough to wake the dead;
strongly did it echo and reverberate from the opposite hills, and roll round the valley. But all in
vain.

"The sun that I had half longed for, half looked
forward to with terror, at last rose. 'My condition,
as the heat went on increasing, became more dreadful; and I crawled around, changing every moment
my position, in order to enjoy the little shade afforded
by the leafless branches of the tree. About noon,
there was of course scarcely a spot of shade left —
only enough for my head, and I suffered greatly from
the pangs of thirst, although I sucked a little of my
blood, till I became senseless, and fell into a sort of
delirium, from which I only recovered when the sun
went down behind the mountains. I then regained
some consciousness, and crawled out of the shade of
the tree, throwing a melancholy glance over the plain;
when suddenly I heard the cry of a camel. It was
the most delightful music I ever heard in my life;
and raising myself a little from the ground, I saw a
mounted Tarki passing at some distance from me,
and looking eagerly around. He had found my
footsteps in the sandy ground, and losing them again
on the pebbles, was anxiously seeking traces of the
direction I had taken. I opened my parched mouth,

and crying, as loud as my faint strength allowed
'aman, aman,' (water, water,) I was rejoiced to get
for answer 'iwah, iwah,' and in a few minutes he
sat at my side, washing and sprinkling my head."
The man then gave him a draught, set him on his camel,
and carried him to his friends, who almost despaired
of his safety.   The traveller's throat was so dry, that
he could scarcely speak and could eat little for three
days; after which he began to recover strength.

Major Denham and Captain Clapperton, who took
the route from Tripoli to Bornu by Bilma, describe
some parts of their desert journey as having been very
toilsome and distressing.   The caravan lost many
camels through fatigue; and they often passed
numerous skeletons of unhappy persons, chiefly
slaves, who had died of exhaustion on their way to
Tripoli.   Near one well they counted more than a
hundred, some of which had the skin still attached
to the bones.   During a day's journey of twenty-
six miles, they passed 107 of these skeletons.   No
wonder!   The poor slaves are marched with chains
round their legs and necks, with a scanty supply of
provision, and with no warm clothing.   Their privations, therefore, must be great; for the traveller
says, "it was the eighth day since our camels had
tasted water,—and at night it blew a hurricane."
Again he writes, "During the last two days, we had
passed on an average from sixty to eighty or ninety
skeletons each day; but the numbers that lay about
the wells at El Hammar were countless; those of two
women whose perfect and regular teeth bespoke

them young, were particularly shocking. Their
arms still remained clasped round each other as they
had expired; although the flesh had long since
perished, by being exposed to the burning rays of
the sun, and the blackened bones only were left.
The nails of the fingers, and some of the sinews of
the hand, also remained; and part of the tongue of
one of them still appeared through the teeth. We
had now passed six days of desert without the slightest appearance of vegetation, and a little branch of
the *suag* (*Capparis sodada*) was brought me here
as a comfort and a curiosity. On the following day
we had alternately plains of sand and loose gravel,
and had a distant view of some hills to the west.
While I was dozing upon my horse about noon, overcome by the heat of the sun, which at that time of
the day always shone with great power; I was suddenly awakened by a crashing under his feet, which
startled me excessively." It was treading upon skulls.
We shall not envy the Arabs their desert home.

Sometimes couriers are sent from Bornu to Moor-
zuk; but only the Tibbu will undertake this arduous
service. Two are always sent; for the chances are
against both of them returning safe. They are
mounted on the finest maheries (or swift dromedaries); and carry with them a bag of parched corn,
one or two skins of water, a brass basin and a wooden
bowl, a little meat cut in strips and dried in the sun.
A bag is suspended under the tail of the maheri to
catch the dung which falls, that it may serve for fuel
at night. The journey occupies about forty days,

travelling at best speed. It is wonderful that such
couriers can be found.

The Arabs acknowledge that it is a most exciting
circumstance when two caravans are about to meet
each other in the desert; and they have songs to
commemorate such events. As soon as a dark object
appears in the distance, the stern question comes
home to every heart, Is it a friend or a foe? Are they
travellers like ourselves, or are they a body of plunderers? Both parties are subjects of the same
feelings, and both prepare for action. Guns are
loaded, the cattle are sent into the rear, and the
men form in front, as if to meet an enemy. Great
joy it is when the strangers are discovered to be
friendly, when they can exchange salutations and
news, and furnish each other by barter with any
commodity that either may stand in need of.

When different tribes of Arabs meet, there is
another danger besides that of bandits. There may
be a blood-feud between the parties, If an Arab's
friend, kinsman, or even one of his clan has been
murdered, he must avenge his death on the criminal
or on one of his friends. Retaliation follows: and
thus a blood-feud is perpetuated from father to son,
through successive generations.

"Two Mesuratas (Arabs of a town near Tripoli),
who had killed a Tibbu chief and his followers two
years before, were of our party; and although the
Tibbu had taken ample vengeance by murdering
twenty-five men for eight, five of whom they had assas-
sinated in the night since our passing the road, yet

they contended there was blood between them, and
we all feared a disturbance. This morning it broke
out, and was very near being serious: the Arabs'
guns were twice presented, and had any blood been

MESURATA CHIEF.

spilt on either side, we should have probably been
all prisoners to the Tibbu, or if victorious, have
sacked their whole town."

It seems that a relation of the deceased chief went
to the tent of one of the Mesuratas, and talking of
the · death of his kinsman, shook his spear at the
Arab, who seized his gun and shouted the alarm.
Both parties flew to arms, and a fight seemed imminent. Captain Denham and a Fezzan merchant,
however, went unarmed to the Tibbu (who were
evidently afraid of the Arabs), declared the cause of
the offence, and pointed out the offender, who they
said ought to be punished. The dispute was after-

wards referred to Hadj Mohammed Abedeen, to be
decided "according to the book." He first made
the parties swear that they would abide by his decision, and then, in presence of the chiefs of both
sides, opened the Koran, and read therefrom. It
was found written, that if any man lifts his hand
higher than his shoulder, in a menacing attitude,
though he should not be armed, the adversary is not
to wait the falling of the blow, but may strike even
to death. This law was in favour of the Arab, who
could and did prove, that the Tibbu chief had
raised his hand above his head, armed with a spear,
to attack him, when he shot him dead. This decision
settled the matter; though the crowing of the Arabs
for gaining their cause was so great as almost to
cause a new quarrel, by aggravating the Tibbu.

Near Bilma, are several lakes, in which are great
quantities of pure crystallised salt, beautifully white,
and of excellent flavour. A coarser kind, also, meets
a ready sale throughout Sudan. The Tawareks help
themselves to salt from the wadeys of the Tibbu,
without taking the trouble to pay for it, as they
have a thorough contempt for buying any goods which
they can steal.

Would you like to see the wild Arabs performing
a surgical operation on a sick man? Here is a
specimen. A merchant of Tripoli, travelling in the
caravan, has been suffering on the road from an enlarged spleen. He is advised to undergo the operation of burning with a red-hot iron; which the Arabs
think an unfailing remedy for most internal disorders.

He consents. They lay him down on his back in the sand, where five or six men hold him steady. The rude surgeons commence their work by burning him in three places under the ribs of the left side; each wound being of the size of a sixpence. Whilst the iron is again heating, a number of thumbs are pressed into his side, to know if he feels pain : and their rough pressure is so great, that the sick man declares he feels pain all over. The operators then make four more brands near the former ones; then turning him over, they make three larger ones near his back bone. Finally, an old Arab, who has been feeling his throat, declares that he requires a large burn near the collar bone. The patient submits to this savage treatment with admirable patience, and getting up, drinks a large draught of water, and remounts his camel for the journey. We should think that this mangling must either end or mend the sufferer.

Wild and lawless are these children of the desert. The escort of a caravan think themselves privileged to lay hold of any thing or any body which comes in their way, and to help themselves to whatever they need. When any of the camels die of fatigue, they try to replace them without money. When they are hungry or wish for a little flesh, woe to the shepherd who crosses their track, or in fear has fled at their approach. "What, not stay to sell their sheep, the rogues! We'll take them now without payment" (as if they would ever have paid for them, except in blows!) So a dozen of the escort start off in the direction of the sheep-marks, and scouring the valleys, at length discover the hapless fugitives. There are about twenty persons, including men, women, and children, having ten camels to convey their tents and goods, with about two hundred head of cattle. Their retreat is intercepted by some of the freebooters, whilst the others dash forward, and in a moment the capture is made. "The most rapid plunder that I could have conceived quickly commenced. The camels were instantly brought to the ground, and every part of their load rifled. The poor women and girls lifted up their hands to me, stripped as they were to the skin; but I could do nothing for them beyond saving their lives." The chief soon came up, and seemed ashamed of the paltry booty, and was moved by the tears of the sufferers. "I seized the favourable moment, and advised that the Arabs should give everything back, and have a few sheep and an ox for a feast. This was finally agreed to: the women's wrappers were thrown down, and the robbers went off with ten sheep and a fat bullock.

The chief of the escort sent forward a messenger with a camel and man, to the sheik of the next place, announcing his approach. Before reaching the town, they found the messenger stripped naked, and tied to a tree, and almost famished, having been twenty-four hours without food. He had been attacked by eighteen men, who had stripped him and taken away his camel and attendant, saying, that the latter should have his throat cut if he were not ransomed: "they cared nothing about the chief nor the sheik either." This bandit-tribe consists of about a thousand, who subsist chiefly by plunder. They live far in the desert, where no large body of men can follow them, for want of water; as there are no wells for four days in the line of their retreat.

Thus these wandering tribes live with every man's hand against his neigbour, plundering wherever they can, and expecting no better treatment from a stronger party who may fall in with themselves. It is merely a question of who happens to be the most powerful. They are perfect adepts in thieving, as well as in plundering; and in this art, the women are not inferior to the men.

CHAP. X.

PURSUING our journey eastward from Wurno (from which we deviated in order to visit Agades), we traverse a varied country of hill and dale, rocky deserts, fertile valleys, and large forests, intersected with rivers.   Here are many valuable trees yielding food and medicine, extensive cotton grounds, and rich fields of onions and corn; so that the markets of the towns are well stocked with provisions.   One of these was observed to be attended by nearly ten thousand persons, and was largely supplied with cotton, millet, slaughtered oxen, fresh butter, and onions; exhibiting a degree of civilisation and comfort which one would scarcely expect to find in a third-rate African town, imbedded in a deep forest.

Negroes are pretty sharp and cunning; but they

are no match for Arabs in the accomplishment of
deception. The biter is often bit: of which the
following incident is an example. The Governor of
Katsena coveted an Arab youth in the service of Dr.
Barth, and enticed him away by splendid promises.
This lad had travelled much, having accompanied
Ibrahim Pasha's expedition to Syria, and another
expedition to Kurdofan; and had thus learned many
things useful to a traveller. So that the doctor, who
had hired him for the whole journey to Timbuctoo
and back, was a little disconcerted by the loss of his
services. The governor did not reflect that a man
who tricks one master is quite ready to trick another,
when occasion offers. He mounted the young Arab
on a good horse, and dressed him in a fine bernoose,
that he might wait upon him when he was accompanying the doctor out of town in a gay manner.
At evening the youngster took an opportunity of
slipping away, with horse, dress, and accoutrements;
and set off for his own country with the spoils;
leaving the emir to digest the loss and affront as he
best could. It doubtless proved a standing joke
against him; as the Africans do not easily forget a
ludicrous blunder perpetrated by another; especially
when connected with the idea of being "served
right."

The country now changes and becomes clear of
wood, except here and there a few large shady trees,
resorted to by women of the country selling re-
freshments. The villages are numerous, and the
road is thronged with people of all conditions. This is

a sign of our approaching Kano, the great emporium
of Howssa. "But I had no sooner passed the gates,
than I felt grievously disappointed. For, from the
flourishing description of it given by the Arabs, I
expected to see a city of surprising grandeur. I
found, on the contrary, the houses nearly a quarter of
a mile from the walls, and in many parts scattered
into detached groups, between large stagnant pools
of water. I might have spared all the pains I had
taken with my toilet (having dressed in an elegant
naval uniform, with all its equipments); for not an
individual turned his head round to gaze at me; but
all intent on their own business, allowed me to pass
by without notice or remark."

As the town is none of the cleanest, it is happily
provided by nature with one of her own scavengers. This circumstance introduces us to the vulture, a large, ugly, filthy bird which frequents most
towns in tropical climates, especially those of the
east. We have met with it in previous parts of our
journey: but now it becomes very common, and is
often found in large numbers. However ungainly
this vulture may be in its appearance and habits,
it is a great blessing to the natives, who respect its
useful services, and are careful not to destroy any of
the species. As the white ant clears the country of
rotting timber; so the vulture devours every kind of
animal refuse which it can find in the towns. It
sits perched on walls near the market and other
frequented places; and no sooner does its keen eye
see any kind of garbage fall on the ground, than it

instantly pounces upon it, and claims it for its own.
It devours all dead animals that may lie about the
fields where wild beasts do not venture to come,
and the bodies of slaves, which are never buried. In
some places, as in Ashantee, it saves the country from
a pestilence by ridding it of the corpses of the victims
of a bloody superstition.

Kano contains from thirty to forty thousand inhabitants, more than half of whom are slaves; besides
a great many visitors from every quarter of the
compass. It is about fifteen miles in circumference,
and is surrounded with a high clay wall and double
ditch. Its fifteen gates are of wood, covered with
sheet iron, and furnished with guard-houses. Only
a fourth of the enclosed ground is occupied with
houses; the rest consists of fields and gardens. The
governor's residence is like a walled village, including
a large space with a mosque and several towers.
The market is very large and well regulated, having
separate quarters and booths set apart for the sale of
different articles; which embrace all kinds of live
stock, vegetables, and other provisions, fruits, and
many descriptions of merchandise. Amongst the latter are mentioned sword blades, knives, and scissors;
writing paper, armlets and bracelets of brass and
silver, pewter rings, and other trinkets; beads of
amber, coral, and glass; silks; turban shawls, tobes,
and other dresses; coarse woollen cloths and calicoes;
Moorish and other gaudy dresses; Egyptian linen,
checked or striped with gold; crude antimony, tin,
iron, &c. &c. Captain Clapperton bought here an

English green cotton umbrella, for three Spanish dollars.

A custom prevails in this market of the seller returning to the buyer a discount of two per cent. on the purchase money, "by way of blessing:" that is, in plain language a "luck-penny." The sheik of the market regulates the prices of all the wares, for which he is entitled to a small commission on every sale, amounting to something more than a half per cent. Bands of musicians are stationed at some of the booths, to attract customers.

The butchers of the market are said to practise all manner of tricks with their meat; and even to stick sheep's wool on a leg of goat's flesh, to make it pass for mutton. Near the shambles are cook-shops in the open air; consisting of a fire, before which a large number of small bits of fat and lean meat are roasting on wooden skewers. These tit-bits are scarcely larger than a penny-piece; and when cooked, are placed on a mat, from which the guests are helped.

The slave-market is held in two long sheds, one for males, the other for females; where they are seated in rows, and gaudily decked out for sale. They are inspected by buyers with as much scrutiny as any cattle in England; the tongue, teeth, eyes, and limbs being carefully examined. When purchased, the trappings with which they were adorned are sent back to ornament others: and if any defect be found in them, they can be returned within three days.

"At seven in the morning, I waited on the

governor. He informed me that the sultan had sent
a messenger express, with orders to have me conducted to his capital, and to supply me with everything necessary for my journey. He now begged
me to state what I stood in need of. I assured him
that the King of England, my master, had liberally
provided for all my wants; but that I felt profoundly
grateful for the kind offers of the sultan, and had
only to crave from him the favour of being attended
by one of his people as a guide. He instantly called
a fair-complexioned Felatta, and asked me if I liked
him. I accepted him with thanks, and took leave.

I afterwards went by invitation to visit the Governor
of Hadyja, who was here on his return from Sockatu,
and lived in the house of the wan-bey. I found this
Governor of Hadyja a black man, about fifty years of
age, sitting among his own people at the upper end of
the room, which is usually a little raised, and is
reserved in this country for the master of the house
and visitors of high rank. He was well acquainted
with my travelling name; for the moment I entered,
he said, laughing, " How do you do, Abdallah? Will
you come and see me at Hadyja on your return?"

I answered, " God willing," with due Moslem
solemnity.

" You are a Christian, Abdallah?"

" Yes."

" And what are you come to see?"

" The country."

" What do you think of it?"

" It is a fine country, but very sickly."

At this he smiled, and again asked,

"Would you Christians allow us to come and see your country?"

"Certainly."

"Would you force us to become Christians?"

"By no means: we never meddle with a man's religion."

"What! And do you ever pray?"

"Sometimes: our religion commands us to pray always: but we pray in secret, and not in public, except on Sundays."

One of his people abruptly asked what a Christian was?

"Why a Kafir" (infidel), rejoined the governor. "Where is your Jew servant? You ought to let me see him."

"Excuse me; he is averse to it; and I never allow my servants to be molested for religious opinions."

"Well, Abdallah, thou art a man of understanding, and must come and see me at Hadyja."

I then retired, and the Arabs afterwards told me that he was a perfect savage, and sometimes put a merchant to death for the sake of his goods. But this account, if true, is less to be wondered at, from the notorious villany of some of them.

The women of this country are not satisfied with their natural beauty, but they have recourse to art to heighten their charms. For this purpose they dye their hair blue, as well as their hands, feet, legs, and eyebrows. The paint is made by decomposing an old indigo-dyed garment. They then mix a little of it with water in a shell and operate on themselves, holding a feather in one hand, and a looking-glass in the other. Both men and women colour their lips and teeth with the flowers of the tobacco plant and another tree. The juice of these flowers gives them a blood-red appearance, which is highly esteemed.

You have admired the politeness of a Frenchman: but the Negroes of Kano are not far behind him in urbanity of manners. See, one of them is addressing a friend whom he has met! He lays one hand on his breast, and making a low bow enquires, "How do you do? I hope you are well. How have you passed the heat of the day?"

A bride pretends to great bashfulness; which is a mere sham. When she is being conducted to the house of her husband, attended by friends and slaves carrying her dower, she whines all the way, saying, "Oh, my head! my head! Oh! dear me! my head!" Yet the husband has generally known his wife some time before this formal marriage takes place. Besides, both parties have their hands and feet dyed, during three days before the marriage ceremony is performed; when the bride attends the bridegroom to apply his henna plaisters with her own hand. Yet she whimpers when she is publicly going to him! So truly does it happen everywhere; "The more politeness the less simplicity."

On the eastern side of a mount in this town there is a hole in the rock, said to be the foot-print of the camel on which Mahomet rode to heaven. On asking the Negro who pointed out this sacred spot, "if the Prophet's camel had only one leg," he replied "Oh! God did it." This ends all controversy on such points of faith.

Jugglery appears to be common here, as well as in India, and other countries of the east. The performers, who are probably Arabs from Barbary, carry about snakes in a bag, and make them dance to the sound of a little drum; and play other tricks

ARAB JUGGLER.

with them. These snakes are very venemous, and often exceed six feet in length. But the poisonous fangs are extracted; and the juggler is also furnished with a roll of cloth wound round his right arm, to protect him from harm, in case the animal should become too exasperated and try to bite.

Kano is celebrated for its dyed cloth. The whole of the processes are performed here. The cotton is grown, spun, wove, and dyed in indigo. This shows how abundantly Central Africa could furnish England with some of the articles that it much needs.

If a free commercial intercourse could be opened up
with these parts of the country, cotton, indigo and
rice might be obtained in any quantity that could
be desired.   They are raised by the Negroes with
little trouble, for their own use and native trade;
and therefore they could be grown for foreign
markets.   Some native shirts are really handsome.

THE "GUINEA-FOWL" SHIRT.

The foot-soldiers of this country are generally
armed with bows and arrows; the cavalry with
swords, shields and spears.   Captain Clapperton
mentions it as a singular fact that these men were
equipped with the identical swords which once

belonged to the knights of Malta. They had been
sent from Malta to Tripoli, and thence brought
across the desert to be sold to the Negroes of Central
Africa. Such are the changes of human things.

Going eastward toward Kooka we may either pass
through Gummel and other considerable towns, along
Dr. Barth's route; or we may go more to the south,
by Murmur and Katagoom with Captain Clapperton.
Let us adopt the latter; as it leads us to the last
earthly resting-place of the gallant traveller's companion, Dr. Oudney. A little on this side of Kano,
whilst the captain was resting under the shade of a
tree, being oppressed with ague, he was accosted
"with infinite archness and grace" by a pretty
Felatta girl, going to market with milk and butter,
neat and spruce in her attire as a Cheshire dairy-
maid. "She said I was of her own nation: and after
much amusing small talk, I pressed her, in jest, to
accompany me on my journey; while she parried
my solicitations with roguish glee, by referring me
to her father and mother. I don't know how it
happened, but her presence seemed to dispel the
effects of the ague." The traveller adds that the
making of such butter as ours is confined in Africa
to the Felattas; and that it is both clean and excellent.

The people of this country are very eager for
charms, and pester every learned stranger to write
for them some prayer which will preserve them from
evil. Captain Clapperton says, that in a town on
the other side of Kano, he was much troubled with

importunities for such safies. His washerwoman
positively insisted upon being paid with a charm,
which would have the effect of causing people to
buy earthenware from her; and no reasonings would
persuade her to the contrary, or make her believe
that it was beyond human power to grant such a
spell. When people are so superstitious, no wonder
that they are easily duped.

Three of the governor's wives visited the traveller,
and after examining his skin with much attention,
observed, with real looks of compassion, that it was
a thousand pities he was not black, for then he would
have been good-looking! He asked one of them, a
buxom lass of fifteen, if she would have him for a
husband, provided he could obtain the governor's
consent. She immediately began to whimper, and
on being urged to assign the reason, said, that she
did not know what she could do with his white legs.
The ladies were attended by an old woman and two
young slaves, and while with him were very merry.

These women only spoke the sentiment which is
entertained by most of the Negroes, and especially
the Negresses of interior Africa north of the Equator. They really do think a white skin to be a
defect. It does not suit their taste; it has a ca-
daverous appearance; they prefer the dark or
copper-coloured. And perhaps they are not far
wrong in having this preference, if we consider how
soon a European skin loses all its beauty in tropical
Africa, and becomes of a dead sallow hue, without
life or expression; while the dark skin shines and

glistens with the fat underneath. The flat nose is another thing.

We now arrive at Murmur, a small town, about a 'day's journey from Katagoom. Dr. Oudney, who was united in the expedition with Major Denham and Captain Clapperton, was in company with the latter at the time of his falling a victim to the African climate. He had been unwell and was still very weak, when he was attacked with ague in the Bedee country. He then felt that it was all over with him; "I once hoped to conduct the mission to a successful termination, but that hope has vanished:" and he gave directions about his papers after his decease. He rallied, however, so as to be able to see the Governor of Katagoom, and to prescribe for the sick of that town, who visited him in great numbers. Many men and women also came for remedies against impotency and apprehended calamities; supposing that the medicines of the white doctor could ward off every imaginable ill of life. "The women were particularly fanciful in these matters; and were frequently importunate to receive medicines that would preserve the affections of their gallants, ensure them husbands, or what was highly criminal, effect the death of some favoured rival."

After this, Dr. Oudney was seized with a diarrhœa, which greatly weakened him. His cough also continued (he was in a consumption) and he suffered from inflammation, for which he was cupped by a native in the manner we have before described. Unable to ride on horseback, he was carried on a

litter placed on a camel's back : till they reached
Murmur, where they were obliged to stop. Next
morning he drank a cup of coffee and desired to
proceed; "but before he could be lifted on the
camel, I observed the ghastliness of death on his
countenance, and had him immediately replaced in
the tent. I sat down by his side, and with unspeakable
grief witnessed his last breath, which was without a
struggle or a groan." He was buried under an old
mimosa tree, a little outside of the town.

Dr. Oudney died at the age of thirty-two, "a man of
unassuming deportment, pleasing manners, steadfast
perseverance, and undaunted enterprise : whilst his
mind was fraught at once with knowledge, virtue,
and religion." His surviving companion felt something like that which Mungo Park experienced when
he lost Mr. Anderson at Sansanding : "I shall only
observe, that no event which took place during the
journey, ever threw the smallest gloom over my
mind, till I laid Mr. Anderson in the grave. I then
felt myself, as if left a second time lonely and
friendless amidst the wilds of Africa." Honour to
the memory of these brave men! We must not
let them pass away without a notice.

Let us now enter Katagoom, which lies in
12°17'11" north latitude and 11° east longitude. The
town is of a square shape, with a gate in each side,
defended by platforms. It has a double wall, each
twenty feet high; and three ditches, each fifteen feet
deep and twenty feet wide. The best houses are of
the Turkish form already described, some of them

having two stories. The inhabitants are estimated at from seven to eight thousand. The governor's residence occupies a large enclosure in the centre of the city. Let us suppose ourselves to have been of Clapperton and Oudney's party when they were introduced to him; and the following would be our description of the interview.

He was sitting without any ceremony or armed men, on a low bank of earth covered with a rude canopy. Only three old men were in his company. He shook hands and desired us to sit by his side. The modesty of etiquette induced us not to accept this high honour; but to sit on the floor before him, along with his counsellors. He offered us some Goora nuts, and we presented the articles which we had prepared for his Highness. In this case our present consisted of a tea-tray, ten yards of red silk, an Indian palempore or bed coverlet, a piece of white linen cloth with gold stripes, a pound of cinnamon, and the same quantity of cloves. He was very much pleased with the articles, especially with the tray, when its use was explained to him. He asked if we wanted slaves or anything else; for all that he had or could procure was at our disposal. When answered in the negative, he again inquired, "What, then, do you want?" When informed that we only desired his friendship, with permission to collect the flowers and plants of his country, and to see its rivers, he exclaimed: "Wonderful! You do not want slaves; you do not want horses; you do not want money; but wish only to see the world! You must go to the Sultan Bello, who is a learned and pious man, and will be glad to see men who have seen so much. You shall have all, and see all that is in my province; and I am sure my master will grant everything you wish." He then came down from his seat, sat by our side, and shook hands with us :— which is here a sign of great respect from one grandee to another.

After this, the governor paid the travellers several friendly visits, and was visited by them in return. He desired to see and know the use of their astronomical and other instruments, and had them explained to his cadi or judge, and to the chief people. He showed them his palace, which was a very respectable building; and introduced them to his favourite wife, a jolly and good-looking Negress. He begged a small supply of English powder, which he saw in a box; and then attended the captain to see him fire at a target. "I fired twice, and happened to hit the mark both times, at a distance of sixty or seventy yards; when he called out, 'The Lord preserve me from devils.' Yet in token of his approbation, he threw over my shoulders with his own hands a very handsome tobe. The cadi had made the pilgrimage to Mecca, was an intelligent man, and acquainted with Arabic literature."

The Africans believe in omens, as well as other people. A servant, in rising to receive the Goora nuts presented by the governor's orders, overturned a pot of honey which was also a gift, without breaking it; though the honey was spilled. This

R

was considered a·most propitious circumstance by his Excellency, who ordered some poor people to be called in to lick up the honey. No sooner said than done. A number ran in, fell down on their knees, and amidst a good deal of wrangling soon made an end of the sweet.

Everything is large in Africa. A rat, or bandicoot, was caught in Katagoom, measuring two feet seven inches from the nose to the top of the tail. It was of a light grey colour, with black tail and round head, covered over with long hairs. Vermin of such a size must be very destructive; and we should rather they were caught by natives than by ourselves.

Before reaching Bornu, we must pass through the Bedee country; which lies between the two kingdoms of Howssa and Bornu. The Bedees speak the Bornuese dialect and acknowledge a certain sort of dependence on the Sultan; but they are really under their own government, if such it may be called. They have never received the tenets of Mahometanism; so that they are called infidels by their neighbours, and are treated as outlaws whom any one may kill or enslave. Their country is full of dense forests and morasses, which make it difficult for an enemy to penetrate; though it is being encroached upon from either side. It forms a kind of neutral territory, separating two powerful kingdoms from each other, and doubtless preventing many wars between people who cannot be amicable. The Bedees are much more rude and simple than their neighbours, who have received many arts of civilisation from the Moors. They are said to be very fond of dog-flesh, and they fatten these animals for the butcher.

The Mahometans accuse the Bedees of having no religion, which appears to be true in so far as outward forms are concerned. Yet they seem to live under the impression, or at least the sense, of a supreme power; for when they kill any beast for food, they hold it up to heaven, in acknowledgment of the bounty of an "unknown God." It is necessary to be very cautious in receiving what a Moslem says about other people's religion. They have no idea of any other godliness than that which consists in formal prostrations, fastings, and pilgrimages. They smile at the idea of a Christian praying in private, which they regard as a mere subterfuge or equivocation; and they call us Kafirs or infidels, as well as the Pagan Negroes. When they know of a Christian who carries about his "book" and reads it, and when they have watched him (which they do) and seen that he really does perform private devotions, they entertain a different opinion of him. We know this by experience. When we have shown them our "book" in the shape of an Arabic Bible, they have looked at it with veneration, and have heard us read out of it and explain some passages, often exclaiming "Wonderful!" Shereefs and learned Moslems (not Moors) have conversed with us about religion, and have gladly received a Psalter, or other portion of the Scriptures in Arabic. But when a

man makes no profession of religion, either because
he has none, or because he conceals it from motives
of policy, Africans of all kinds regard him as an
infidel. Boldness and consistency in one's faith is
honoured both by Pagans and Moslems.

It was at a dilapidated town, called Ngurutuwa, a
little north of the route which we are pursuing
towards the capital of Bornu, that Mr. Richardson
died. He was associated with Dr. Barth and Mr.
Overweg in their researches through these parts of
Africa, and was actively pursuing the objects of the
expedition of which he had the principal charge,
when he sank under the effects of the climate. He
was an energetic man, and had made the friendship
of some of the native princes. He separated from
his companion at Katsena, that they might pursue
different routes to Kooka (or Kukuwa); and, though
suffering from bodily indisposition, was pressing
forwards to the capital, where he hoped to rest and
recruit a little. He reached this obscure place one
evening, quite exhausted, and breathed his last, all
alone, early next morning. His grave was made by
his servants under a wide-spreading tree in the
vicinity, where it was visited by his companion a few
days afterwards.

Your hardihood would now be tried in passing
through dismal swamps, beside large lakes, and
through arid wastes, exposed to many vicissitudes of
the atmosphere, and to dangers from roving bandits.
Yet here is a beautiful tree, called the kooka. It is
very tall and erect, and is sometimes twenty-five

feet in circumference. The trunk and branches taper off to a point; the wood is porous and spongy; the bark is copper-coloured, soft, and covered with a gummy exudation. Its leaves are small, growing in clusters from twigs; its flowers are large and white, something like the garden lily. The fruit is larger than a cocoa-nut, having a hard shell, containing some powdery matter and seeds; its dark green changing to brown as it ripens. "The tree, whether bare of its leaves, in flower, or in full bearing, has a singularly grotesque naked appearance; and with its fruit dangling from the boughs like eastern purses, might, in the imagination of some eastern story-teller, well embellish an enchanted garden of the Genius of the Lamp." The dried leaves, being glutinous, are used by the natives in making sauces, and are eaten boiled with dried meat. They are also used to fatten cattle. The mealy part of the fruit is pleasant, and put in water makes a cooling acid beverage.

Another tree peculiar to this region is the goorjee, which resembles a stunted oak. It has a beautiful dark red flower, not unlike a tulip, which is used to give a red tinge to the mouth and teeth, and to season some kinds of food.

The Sultan of Bornu was described by Major Denham as a mere puppet, possessed of no authority, a kind of state prisoner. He resides at Birni, which we pass through on our way to the real capital where the sheik lives. Birni is a walled town, containing some ten thousand inhabitants, but with-

out any splendour. An interview with the sovereign
is thus described by Major Denham.

We were first conducted to the gate of the Sultan's
mud edifice, where a few of the court were assembled
to receive us; and one, a sort of chamberlain, habited
in eight or ten tobes or shirts of different colours,
the outside one of fine white tufted silk of the manufacture of Soodan. In his hand he carried an
immense staff, like a drum-major's baton, and on
his head he bore a turban exceeding in size anything
of the kind we had before seen. This was, however,
but a trifling one to those we were destined to behold
at the audience on the following morning. The
Sultan shortly after sent word that by sunrise the
next morning he would receive us. In the evening,
a most plentiful, if not delicate, repast was brought
to us, consisting of seventy dishes, each of which
would have dined half a dozen persons with moderate
appetites. The Sultan himself sent ten, his wives
thirty, and his mother thirty; and for fear the
English should not eat like the Bornuese, a slave or
two was loaded with live fowls for our dinner. The
meats consisted of mutton and poultry, and were
baked, boiled, and stewed.

Soon after daylight we were summoned to attend
the Sultan of Bornu. He received us in an open
space in front of the royal residence. We were kept
at a considerable distance while his people approached
to within about a hundred yards, and passed by him
on horseback; then, dismounting and prostrating
themselves before him, they took their places on the

ground in front, but with their backs to the royal
person, which is the custom of the country. He was
seated in a sort of cage of cane or wood, near the
door of his garden, on a seat which at the distance
appeared to be covered with silk or satin; and
looked through the railing upon the assembly before
him, who formed a sort of semicircle extending from
his seat to nearly where we were waiting. Nothing
could be more absurd and grotesque than some, nay
all, of the figures who formed this court.

Large bodies and large heads are indispensable
for persons who serve the court of Bornu; and those
who unfortunately possess not the former by nature,
or on whom lustiness will not be forced by cramming,
make up the deficiency of real protuberance by an
immense wadding, which, as they sit on the horse,
gives the belly the curious appearance of hanging
over the pummel of the saddle. The eight, ten, or
twelve shirts of different colours, that they wear one
over the other, help a little to increase this greatness
of person. The head is enveloped in folds of muslin
or linen of various colours, though mostly white, so
as to deform it as much as possible; and those
turbans which seemed to have been most studiously
arranged, had the effect of making the head appear
completely on one side. Besides this, their persons
are hung all over with charms, enclosed in little red
leather parcels strung together; the horse, also,
has amulets fastened round his neck, on parts of his
head, and about the saddle. A little to our left, and
nearly in front of the Sultan, was an extempore de-

claimer, shouting forth the praises of his master, and
his illustrious pedigree. Near him, was one who bore
a long wooden frumfrum, on which he ever and
anon blew a blast, loud and unmusical.

Such, it appears, was the state ceremony adopted
by the former negro kings, and which the vizier
wishes the Sultan to continue, in order to amuse him
and his courtiers, and to please the people, that the
power may continue in his own hand. An ugly
black eunuch called for the presents, which were
carried unopened to the royal presence. But the
visitors could only get a faint glimpse of the Sultan,
through the lattice-work of his pavilion or cage;
which sufficed, however, to show that his turban was
larger than that of any of his subjects, and that
his face from the nose downward was completely
covered.

Angornu, the ancient royal residence, is a much
larger place than Birni, and has a very large
market, sometimes attended by a hundred thousand
persons. Linen is described as being here so cheap
that most of the men have a shirt and pair of trowsers. Some beggars endeavoured to attract the pity
of charitable persons, by holding the remnants of
trowsers in one hand, and lifting up their shirt with
the other, crying out in a doleful voice, "But
breeches, there are none! But breeches, there are
none!" The only persons armed near the Sultan's
person, were some hundreds of Negroes in blue
tobes, who were outside the court circle. Each of
these carried an immense club with a large nob, a

bow and arrows slung over his back, and a short
dagger.   When a chief is riding, a footman runs
behind, carrying four spears.   There are many
strangers in Angornu, principally traders from different countries.

CHAP. XI.

Bornu. — Dashing Entrance into Kooka. — Interviews with the Sheik.
— Mode of Life. — Looseness of Manners. — Two guilty Girls. —
Market. — Shifts for Money. — A Lion for sale. — Houses. — Penal
Decisions. — Rockets and Musical Box. — Quack Doctors. — Strange
Presents. — Poor Barca Gana. — Mandara. — Its Troops. — Sultan in
State. — Men and Women. — Beauties. — Fight with a Panther. —
Battle with the Felattas. — Disastrous Flight. — The Shuwas. — The
Marghi. — New Mode of Duelling. — Substitutes for Dress. —
Kanuri people. — Pullo Country. — Meeting of the Rivers. —
Adamawa. — Yola and its People.

WHEN a large caravan enters Kooka (or Kukuwa) it
is received with much state and ceremony. The
Bornuese love on these occasions to make a display
of military power, not only for vanity's sake, but also
to intimidate the Arabs, who form the usual escort
of the caravan. The latter have a great contempt
for the prowess of Negroes, which often consists more
in vaunting than in actual valour. Here, then, are
several thousand Bornuese horsemen drawn up in
regular order, waiting for the approach of their
friendly visitors. As soon as they see them, a loud
shout is given, followed by a blast from their rude
horns; and they dash forward, as if making a charge
in battle, till they come within a few feet of the

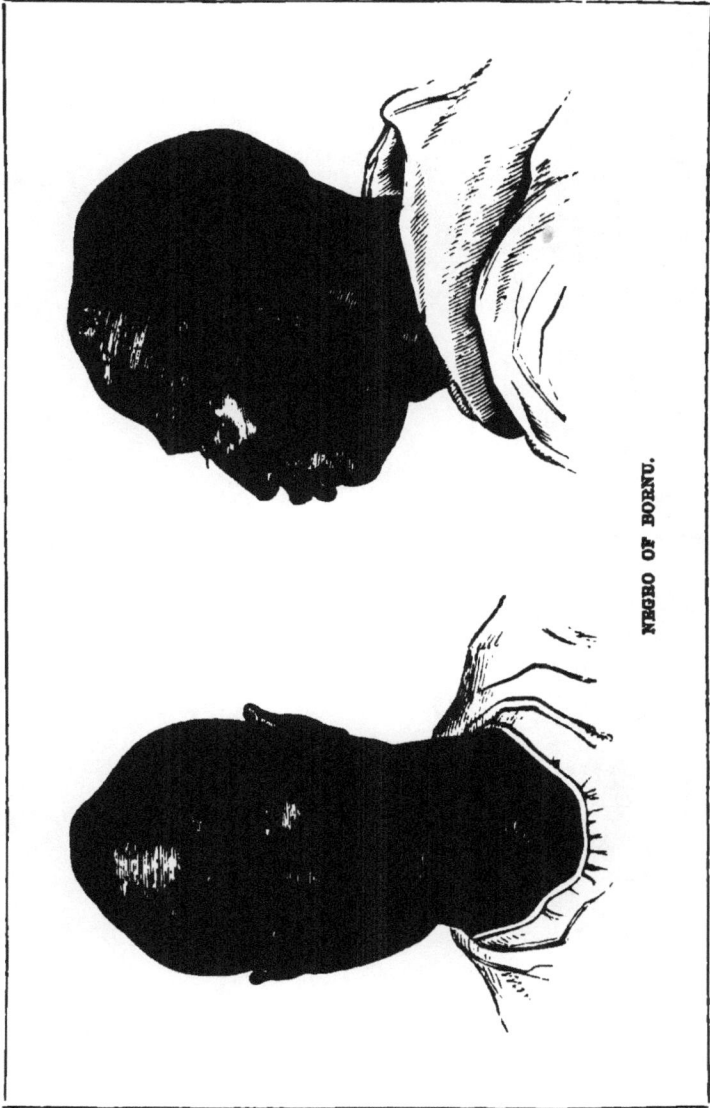

NEGRO OF BORNU.

strangers. Then wheeling round, with great expert-
ness, they form one large cavalcade, shaking their
spears over their heads, and crying out "Blessing!
blessing! sons of your country! welcome, sons of
your country!"

Conspicuous amongst these horsemen are the
sheik's body-guard, clothed in coats of mail composed of iron chain, and wearing a similar cap as a
kind of helmet. Their horses' heads also are protected against the thrust of a spear by plates of
metal, which cover all except the eyes. The chiefs
of the escort alone enter the gates, and pass along a
broad street, through a line of spearmen, to the
sheik's residence. His general now directs the
strangers to be admitted, and they pass, one by one,
up a staircase, where they are brought to a stand by
the crossed spears of Negro soldiers. Permission of
entrance is given, and the sheik is found sitting on
a carpet, in a dark room, dressed in a blue tobe and
a turban. Two Negroes are on each side of him
armed with pistols, and a brace of these weapons lie
on the carpet by his side. Fire-arms are also
suspended on the walls of the chamber.

When the Europeans had been thus introduced to
his highness, he inquired the object of their coming.
On receiving their reply, he bade them welcome.
He said that he would further their object, that he
had ordered huts to be built for their accommodation,
and that when they had recovered from the fatigue
of their journey, he would be happy to converse
with them.

Next day they proceeded to the palace with their presents, and had to go through a good deal of ceremony; which contrasted strongly with the plainness of the sheik's personal appearance. There were passages lined with sitting attendants, who forcibly prevented the strangers from advancing too quickly, by holding their legs and feet, from which they had abstracted the slippers. The visitors were seated on clean sand, laid on each side of an earthen bank covered with a carpet, on which the sheik reclined. He expressed his pleasure with some of the presents, and his satisfaction at knowing that he had been heard of in England; intimating to his counsellors that this was in consequence of their having defeated the Begharmis. The general who had conducted this successful expedition, happening to be present, inquired if the Sultan of England had heard of him also: and being answered in the affirmative, replied, " Ah! then your king must be a great man!" A sentiment which was re-echoed from all sides.

Major Denham observes, that besides occasional presents of bullocks, camel-loads of wheat and rice, leathern skins of butter, jars of honey, and honey in the comb, — five or six wooden bowls were sent to them, every morning and evening, containing rice with meat, and paste made of barley-flour, savoury but very greasy. Sweets made of curds and honey were also given; a camel-load of fish, bream and mullet, was thrown down before their huts, on the second morning after their arrival, and lest this should not suffice, another was sent in the evening.

Dr. Barth describes the Sheik Omar, who was ruler of Bornu when he visited it, as a benevolent and cheerful man, simply dressed, reclining on a carpeted divan at the back of an airy hall, the clay walls of which were neatly polished. He was frank in his manners and free in his conversation. The vizier at this time was Hadj Beshir, who was soon afterwards put to death, leaving seventy-three sons, besides daughters; for he kept a harem of more than three hundred female slaves.

We have perhaps more information about Kooka than about any other town of Interior Africa. This results from its central situation. All European travellers, proceeding from the north into the interior of the continent, must pass through Bornu, as it has the desert routes on the north side, and is flanked by Lake Chad on the east. It is, doubtless, the most important kingdom of Central Africa to foreigners who travel overland. It may also prove the easiest way into the interior by water, up the river Shary into the lake. Could a highway of peaceful communication be made up the navigable part of the Niger, and from it across to the Lake Chad, through this populous and partly civilised district of Africa, great results might be expected. These people already desire the luxuries and manufactures of more advanced nations, and try to imitate what they see in strangers superior to themselves. They pride themselves upon possessing and wearing articles of foreign material, and they have a considerable love of trading. Their princes

generally desire communication with more polished
countries.

In Kooka, there are three principal tribes of inhabitants, the Bornuese, the Shuwas, and the Kanem-

KANEMBOO SPEARMAN.

boes. The first are the proper natives of the country,
being Negroes, with large mouths, flat noses, and beautiful teeth. They are courteous, good-natured, and
timid. But the Shuwas are Arabs, having all the worst
qualities of that people, being treacherous, proud,
cunning. They are the chief breeders of cattle, and
speak a good Arabic dialect. The natives are very
simple in their manner of life; they grow a kind of
mullet, which forms the staple diet of the common
people. It is eaten raw, parched, or boiled as rice.
When made into flour, and mixed with fat and
honey, it is regarded as a luxury. Rice, onions,
and beans are also used. Bread is only eaten by the
rich.

The Bornuese are Moslems, and are rigid in performing the five daily prayers and ablutions. They seldom have more than two or three wives, and the poorer people are obliged to be satisfied with one. But the rich have harems of slaves. The women are not good-looking, and disfigure themselves still more by their tattooing, having twenty cuts on each side of the face, one cut on the forehead, six on each arm, and more on other parts of the body. They cover their head and face, and kneel when they address the male sex; they approach their husbands on their knees, and enter his bed at the foot.

The morals of the people are described by Major Denham as very loose, though the sheik was endeavouring to reform them. A husband can divorce his wife when he pleases, by returning her dower; and the lady can also demand her freedom under certain circumstances. In such a state of things, purity of morals is impossible, and the people were generally opposed to the reformations attempted by their ruler. In his zeal he seized two unfortunate girls and ordered them to be hanged. They were both under seventeen years of age, and the severity of the sentence raised the commiseration of all the people. Efforts were made to turn the sheik from his purpose, but he persevered in his resolve, until a Mahometan doctor declared that such a punishment would itself be a sin, since there was no authority for it in the Koran; that the law of the prophet prescribed a mark of disgrace, not death, for such offences; and that the purposed execution would be visited on the land by the vengeance of Heaven.

The sheik was finally obliged to relent, but ordered the girls to have their heads publicly shaved, which is a mark of infamy.

What is that man doing, looking for something over the door of his wife's apartment? He wishes to enter, but must take care that one of his wife's friends has not hid a shoe there; for if he should pass under her slipper, his head has been under her foot, and she will be master of the house. Thus the game of " who shall be uppermost" is constantly going on, notwithstanding the depressed condition of the female sex.

If you wish to make any common purchases in Kooka, you will find a small market every afternoon. But here is a large one, or kind of fair, held once a week! This is a grand affair, attended by twelve or fifteen thousand persons, and furnished with all kinds of commodities, arranged in order in separate places. What a variety of dress and figure is exhibited by this motley assembly of Negroes and Arabs, drawn from many different countries and tribes! It is a picturesque and interesting spectacle to see the people only. What a variety of merchandise for sale! Here is the place for buying materials for a tent or dwelling; mats of all kinds, poles and stakes, and frameworks. Next, there are oxen for slaughter or burden, ox and camel bags, camels themselves, and horses. These are ranged round the sides of the market. In the interior, you would find dealers in native and foreign merchandise. Of the former, are cloths, leather work, kola nuts, salt, natron, copper,

silver, slaves. Of European goods are calicoes, cam-
brics, coarse silks, woollens, cloths, beads, sugar,
paper, needles, sword-blades, muskets, razors, &c.
The Arabs sell dresses, shawls, spices, frankincense,
&c. So that everything which you could desire for
consumption or use in Africa may be bought at this
weekly bazaar.

Each merchant squats down where he pleases in
the open space of the market. Brokers and retail
dealers have stalls, which they erect in any place
that they fancy. The motley scene is enlivened with
the barber's whistle, the fun of the professional story-
teller, the amusements afforded by the serpent-tamer
and conjurer. Cakes, sweetmeats, nuts, boiled beans,
dry dates, sour milk and water, are offered as refresh-
ments to the exhausted market goers. There is a
difficulty in the way of completing your purchases,
which is a most harassing and tedious business.
What money must you give? Cowries or kurdi
have of late become the chief currency; but a
novice will not relish the trouble connected with
them. These little shells are not fastened together
in strings of a hundred each, as on the Gold Coast;
but they must be counted one by one. No person
will take even a takrufa, or rush sack containing
20,000 shells, without first seeing that he has received the entire number. Practice makes perfect,
and the natives become very expert in counting
cowries; but it is a herculean task for a foreigner to
count out 500,000 of them, which a merchant has
sometimes to do. A pound sterling is equal to about

s

12,000 cowries; consequently, fifty of them go to a
penny. As 100,000 are reckoned a load for a camel,
twelve camels would be required to carry 100*l.* in
cowries.

But people are not obliged to take cowries in
payment. Few farmers will do so. Here a new
difficulty arises. You wish to buy corn for your
horse, and you have only the substantial dollar in
your pocket. What are you to do? You must first
buy cowries; then sell the cowries for *shirts;* and
with a shirt you can buy corn, and with no other
medium of exchange. Throughout this district, and
away southward, a shirt is money. The country
people will seldom take anything else in return
for their goods; except that trifling articles may
sometimes be bought for beads or needles. A traveller was so hard pressed in passing through one of
these rural districts, that he was obliged to take
his servant's shirt from his back, to buy a little
corn, for the peasants would not take his dollars or
cowries.

Amongst other articles offered for sale was a
young lion. "He walked about with great uncon-
cern, confined merely by a small rope round his
neck held by his keeper, who had caught him when
he was not two months old, and having had him for
a period of three months, now wished to part with
him. He was about the size of a donkey-colt, with
very large limbs; and the people seemed to go very
close to him without much alarm; notwithstanding,
he struck with his foot the leg of one man who stood

in his way, and made the blood flow copiously.
They opened the ring which was formed round the
noble animal as I approached, and coming within
two or three yards of him, he fixed his eye upon me
in a way that excited sensations I cannot describe,
from which I was awakened by the fellow calling me
to come nearer, at the same time laying his hand on
the animal's back. A moment's recollection convinced me that there could be no more danger
nearer than where I was, and I stepped up boldly
beside the Negro; I believe I should have laid my
hand upon the lion next moment, but after looking
carelessly at me, he brushed past my legs, broke the
ring, and pulled his conductor away with him, over-
turning several who stood before him, and bounded
off to another part where there were fewer people,"—
as he did not like company.

The best houses in Kooka are good and spacious
edifices, consisting of several court-yards and apartments, with an inner court leading to parts of the
dwelling reserved for women. Each wife has a
square space for herself, in which is a handsome hut.
There is often an upper story, or rather some upper
chambers like turrets on the roof, appropriated to
the use of the owner of the mansion. The walls
are made of reddish clay, smooth and polished, and
ornamented in different ways. The domestic animals
have a court-yard near the entrance allotted to their
use. These dwellings exhibit a good deal of taste
and refinement in their construction, and show what
Negroes can and will do, when they have a model

set before them, and sufficient means to execute a copy.

Some judicial proceedings of the Sheik El Kanemy may tend to exhibit the manners and ways of this people. A freeman had caught the slave of another man along with his wife. The sheik commanded the guilty parties to be hanged together. The owner of the slave objected to this decision, alleging that the woman had been always trying to seduce his slave; and that therefore if he were hanged through the woman's fault, her husband ought to give him the value of a slave, as he was a poor man. The other dissented from this proposition. The sheik exclaimed, "Ah! how often is man driven to destruction by woman; yet of all his happiness she is the root or the branch!" He himself paid the poor man for the slave, and the sentence was executed according to the judgment pronounced.

Another circumstance caused no little stir amongst the women of Kooka. Some complaints were made that during the absence of the army on a grand expedition, the females had been seen too often in the streets, and with their faces uncovered. Of course "when the cat is away, the mice play." But some reporters had been left behind. Their husbands also, who had not heard their voices for some time, complained on their return, that the fair sex had acquired a habit of loud talking; and therefore inferred that during their absence they had been too free in the use of their tongue. In consequence, the women were summoned before the sheik, who

SHUWA AND MARGHAY LADS.

severely lectured them; giving strict admonitions to the single ladies about propriety of conduct, and ordering the matrons who had slaves not to go out of their house or receive visitors at home.

A quarrel took place one evening, when a Shuwa stabbed an Arab, who died of his wounds. The brother of him that was slain demanded the vengeance of blood. The Shuwa proved that he had thrice commanded the man to go from his door, " if he had any faith in the prophet," but that he refused, and continued to molest him, till his anger was aroused, and he stabbed him several times. The judge in this case had decided that after so solemn a warning the deceased ought to have gone away; that his refusing to do so was a sign he had no faith; and that his obstinacy was the cause of his own death. An appeal was made to the sheik, who acknowledged that the Book orders "an eye for an eye, a tooth for a tooth, and life for life;" but suggested the propriety of the pursuer's taking a fine instead of blood. But the vindictive Arab demanded justice, and the sheik said that his enemy was legally in his hands. On hearing which decision he took the Shuwa outside the walls, and beat out his brains with a club. This affair created much sensation in the town.

It may be imagined what effect an exhibition of rockets would have upon a people who had never seen fireworks. When one was sent over the town, it caused a panic and universal scream. A musical box called forth exclamations of wild astonishment.

The sheik himself cried out "Wonderful! wonderful!"
Then covering his face with his hands, he listened
with rapture to a plaintive air which it played. But
a man near him, having interrupted his happy trance
by a loud exclamation, he gave him a blow that
made all the company tremble. He swore that such
an instrument would be cheap at a thousand dollars.
The box was afterwards presented to him, and he
studied it till he understood the stops.

Quack doctors are found in this as well as in
other regions. A charm is written, and some herbs
are applied to the stomach or other part of the body,
so that imagination effects most of the cure. The
natives are surprised at the potency of European
medicines; having no idea that a little powder could
produce such influences on the human frame. Prac-
tical experience, however, of a good dose changes
their unbelief into admiration, and elicits the usual
cry of "wonderful! wonderful!"

On the annual festival held in commemoration of
Abraham's offering up Isaac, the rich people give
away garments to their followers. The sheik El
Kanemy gave away more than a thousand tobes, and
as many bullocks and sheep. He was a noble and
generous man, though subject to those bursts of
passion from which an autocrat is seldom free.
Major Denham mentions an occurrence that took
place whilst he was in Kooka, which illustrates the
disposition of that prince. His favourite general,
Barca Gana, who was also governor of six large
districts, fell into sad trouble. The sheik had inad-

vertently sent him a horse which had been intended
as a present for another person, and the general
was requested to return it. He was so offended
at this procedure that he instantly sent back all the
horses which the sheik had given him, saying, that
in future he would ride his own beasts or else walk.
His master forthwith sent for him, reproached him
for his ingratitude, had him stripped in his presence and a leathern girdle put round his loins,
and ordered him to be sold to the Tibbu merchants,
for he was still a slave.

The disgraced favourite fell on his knees, acknowledged his punishment to be just, and begged that
his wives and children might be provided for by the
royal bounty.   Next day, the chief eunuchs and
officers fell down before the sheik and asked for
Barca's pardon. The culprit came in at this moment
to take leave, when the sheik threw himself back on
his carpet, burst into tears, and allowed the wretch
to embrace his knees. Then, calling them all his
children, he pardoned the penitent. In the evening
there was a general rejoicing, and Barca Gana
dressed in new robes rode round the camp, followed
by the chief officers. He had had a narrow escape,
and would doubtless profit by the lesson which he
then learned. The vicissitudes of life under an
eastern despot are often very striking.

The people applauded this act of clemency in the
sheik, but they did not approve of all his doings,
which were sometimes very harsh and arbitrary. He
had no mercy in exacting the keeping of the Rhama-

dans with the strictest fasting. It is well known that
Mahometans fast during this month from sunrise to
sunset; but this abstinence is usually limited to
eating. The sheik applied it also to drinking, and
to every act of gratification; so that if a man was
caught suffering his thirst to get the better of him,
or visiting his wives, during the day, he was sentenced to receive four hundred stripes with the
horrible coorbash. Now the heat in Kooka was
excessive, and the people fainted for want of water.
Many went down to a well and had buckets of water
thrown over them, as the only means of allaying
their sufferings. No wonder they grumbled at the
stern edict.

One unfortunate man was caught asleep, and the
wife of another man stretched by his side. Being
at once presumed to be guilty of breaking the
Rhamadan, the man was sentenced to receive four
hundred lashes, and the woman two hundred. The
informer received her dress and ornaments, which
were instantly stripped off. Her head was shaved,
and she was suspended by a cloth round her middle,
when a powerful Negro inflicted the penalty. She
was carried home senseless. The man was taken up
in a similar way, and obliged to kiss his instrument
of torture. They strike on the back, but the end of
the thong has a knob which winds round to the
breast or stomach, and usually renders the brutal
punishment fatal. This poor creature emitted blood
from his throat and bowels after receiving half the
number of strokes, and died soon after they were

completed. One hundred stripes with a milder weapon were inflicted on a rogue who stole and sold ten camels; theft being reckoned by the sheik a less heinous crime than breaking the Rhamadan. So do others, besides the ancient Pharisees, " strain at a gnat and swallow a camel."

Another act of cruelty rendered the ruler of Kooka still more odious to his people. He was always severe against the failings of the female sex, and one day he sent out his emissaries to collect women of a bad reputation. Five of these unfortunates were sentenced to be hanged in the market-place, and four to be flogged. Of the latter, two expired under the lash. The former had their heads shaved, and were dragged round the market with a rope round their necks; they were then strangled, and their bodies thrown into a hole. This severe proceeding roused the anger of the whole population of the town against the sheik. More than a hundred families quitted the place to go and live in other towns where such rigour did not exist; saying, that it was impossible to exist in Kooka under such tyranny, and where malicious spies might easily procure their doom to an ignominious death. The rest of the women expressed their abhorrence in an unmistakeable way. For it is common to welcome the Aid, the principal Moslem festival, held in honour of Isaac's deliverance, in a very lively and gorgeous manner. But on this occasion the sheik received no presents, and his running footmen obtained no new dresses. The women who were

wont to array themselves in their best attire, and
standing at their doors scream out a welcome to him
as he passed, omitted doing so; and the joyous
festival went off in gloom and disgrace.

South of Kooka is the Mandara country, the sultan
of which entered into alliance with the Sheik of
Bornu, for their mutual defence against the Felattas,
who had encroached upon the pagan territories from
the west. Mandara itself was with difficulty rescued
from their grasp. The sultan became Mahometan,
and built a new capital, called Mora, in a strong
situation encompassed by hills. On the surrounding heights there are some wild tribes of pagans,
called Musgo, who form a kind of slave-preserve for
Bornu and Mandara. Whenever slaves are wanted,
an expedition is sent against them; and if they do not
buy a respite by a present of slaves and horses, they
know what will be the consequence to themselves.
In order to procure this present, they must make
war on other tribes in their vicinity; and thus a de-
populating warfare is constantly going on.

Here is a splendid cavalcade, consisting of many
hundreds of horsemen, well mounted, dressed in fine
tobes of different colours, blue, scarlet, and striped;
and in the midst of them, a small company clothed
in striped silk, their saddles and horses adorned with
skins of the leopard and tiger-cat! They are preceded by men with instruments of music resembling
trumpets and clarionets. They are the cavalry and
the body-guard of the Sultan of Mandara, who keeps
up an appearance of state that would not be expected

in this outlandish region. If you pay him a visit, etiquette requires that you ride up to the place of interview at full gallop; though in so doing, you would probably ride over some persons in the way. But you must stop for nothing. Dismounting at the palace gate, your slippers are pulled off by attending servants, and entering the court, you find his majesty seated on a divan covered with a handsome carpet and silk pillows, surrounded by his eunuchs and nobles dressed in silk and coloured cotton. The principal men are in front, having their backs turned to the sultan. A native grandee, going to be presented or to deliver a message to the prince, sits in front of the eunuchs, with his back to the throne and his eyes on the ground, and clapping his hands utters such expressions as these: "May you live for ever! God send you a happy old age! Blessing! blessing!"

The men and women of Mandara are better looking than the Bornuese, not having so much of the flattened features. The ladies are highly esteemed for beauty in Kooka, and slaves from this province fetch a high price. Their hands and feet are small, and they have a considerable protuberance behind; qualities much prized by those who keep harems. In their own mountainous region, they trouble themselves with little clothing, and often dispense with it altogether. The Mandarese chiefly live on vegetables; and their most esteemed dish is made of paste, mixed with hot fat, pepper, and onions.

The hills of this district produce iron, which is

manufactured in a rude way by native blacksmiths.
They also abound in wild beasts, especially those of
the panther and leopard species. These animals watch
for their prey with great cunning, often waiting a
long time for human beings, till some one has left
his company and can be attacked alone; on whom
they spring from behind. They seldom make an
assault where resistance may be anticipated, but are
ferocious enough when they are wounded. Listen
to this account of a fight with a large panther! It
had killed a Negro on the road, and was sucking his
blood, when a company of horsemen came up. A
Shuwa immediately sent his spear through the neck
of the beast, which rolling over broke the weapon
and bounded off with half of it in its body. Another
man thrust a second spear through its loins, on
which it turned with a strange howl to spring upon
the pursuer. At this moment an Arab shot it
through the head, and it fell dead. It measured
eight feet two inches from the nose to the end of
the tail, and was of a yellow colour, beautifully
spotted.

The company of Arabs, with whom Major Denham
and his friends had traversed the desert from Tripoli, had been very anxious for a razzia of some
kind, in order to obtain booty in slaves before returning home. They had begged the Sheik of
Bornu to allow them to make a forage in the direction of Mandara. He, nothing loth, agreed; but
really with a different object from theirs. He
thought he might use them advantageously to

MUSGU CHIEF AND SLAVES.

humble the Felattas, as the Arabs priding themselves on their guns despised Negroes armed only
with bows and spears. Accordingly, Barca Gana
was sent with three thousand horse, in company of
Boo Khaloom and eighty Arabs. Major Denham, by
much entreaty, obtained permission to accompany
this expedition.

When they reached Mandara they wished to attack
the Musgoese, from whom they would doubtless
have obtained a large booty. These people wear no
clothes except a leathern girdle. They are armed
with a spear, a shield of wicker work, and a small
weapon which they throw with considerable dexterity. But when attacked by a large body of troops,
they are obliged to fly behind the broad rivers,
where the enemy cannot follow them for want of
canoes. In these razzias the men are generally
butchered, the women and children carried off, and
the granaries plundered or burned. They pay
tribute and make peace-offerings in slaves.

The Sultan of Mandara did not wish to let the
Arabs enter the Musgo country, which he desired to
keep as a slave-preserve for himself. So he joined
some of his own troops with the army of Bornu, and
sent them against the Felattas, who would probably
make a stout resistance. The sheik and sultan
appear to have had the same object in view to
humble their old enemy, and to give their boasting
friends the Arabs some serious work to do. In the
latter part of the scheme they succeeded. Boo
Khaloom and his men rushed on a strongly en-

trenched town of Felattas, under a shower of poisoned
arrows, to take it by storm. A desperate fight
ensued, and the Arabs were kept at bay. Barca
Gana and about a hundred of his spearmen hastened
to their assistance, but the rest of the united forces
of Bornu and Mandara kept out of bow-shot, coolly
looking at the fight. The Felattas seeing this,
pressed their foes valiantly, and their horsemen
coming up charged them in turn. Only the most
desperate valour saved the little company of assailants
from utter destruction, for all their friends took to
flight, headed by the Sultan of Mandara. This prince
was ready to share the spoil if the town had been
captured, and quite as ready to run away in case of
failure. He had no desire to expose himself or his
men to the shot of a single arrow.

Barca Gana, who had brought down eight men with
his own spears, had three horses shot under him,
two of which died immediately, being wounded by
poisoned arrows. The retreat was a desperate affair,
as no help was afforded to the defeated band by
their own army, which had scampered off. Boo
Khaloom died of a wound which he had received in
his foot from a poisoned shaft. Forty-five of the
Arabs perished, and most of the rest were wounded,
so that more died afterwards. Their bodies became
instantly swollen and black, like that of their chief,
whose corpse was saved from being dishonoured by
the enemy. The wounded horses, also, as soon as
they drunk water at a stream which they crossed,
dropped and died; whilst blood gushed from their

mouth, nostrils, and ears. The baggage was left in the hands of the victors.

Major Denham, who had gallantly joined in the mêlée, had several narrow escapes for his life. He was assailed by the pursuers, whom he beat off, when his horse fell with him. He was then wounded and stripped naked, and the plunderers began to quarrel about his clothes, when he crept under the belly of a horse and darted off into a wood. Again pursued he made for a stream, and was letting himself down the precipitous bank by means of a tree, when a large serpent darting at him so petrified him with horror, that he let go the branch and fell into the water. This saved his life from both enemies, revived him, and gave him strength to swim across. Reaching the two defeated chiefs and six Arabs pursued by Felattas, he was taken up on horseback by the shiek's Negro, Maramy, amidst a shower of arrows. Soon the pursuit cooled, as the enemy were intent upon the baggage which was left with them, and Boo Khaloom ordered an Arab to throw a bornouse over the major's back, which was suffering dreadfully from the sun. This was shortly before the warrior dropped from his horse and expired. Crossing a stream, the major fell down exhausted on the other side and swooned. Maramy again helped him on his horse and conducted him to Mora. After riding forty-five miles on the bare back of a lean horse, in a state of nudity, the gallant officer was more dead than alive. He got a shirt from one man on promise of repaying him with a new one.

The deposed Sultan of Angornu, living at Mora in
a leathern tent, commiserated the Englishman, and
offered him his own trowsers, which he took off for
that purpose. When these were refused, the prince
in poverty shed tears because he had no others to
give. Then calling a slave, he stripped him of his
drawers, which he put on himself, and gave his own
to the stranger. They were now accepted, and
Mai Meegamy (be his name honoured!) became the
major's friend till he left the country.

The Sultan of Mandara, who had behaved so
shamefully in running away from the fight, refused
any help to his friends, even in his own capital,
and would not give the famishing Arabs a handful
of corn. He even kept their deceased chief's clothes
and horse-trappings. But he began to prepare for
defence, as he expected the Felattas would soon pay
him a visit; and his allies, as they left Mora, were
charitable enough to wish them all success against
such a cowardly knave and traitor. It was, however, quite just that an expedition whose very object
was the plunder of innocent Negroes, should signally
fail. The defeated party had to endure much suffering before reaching Kooka, as they had little to eat
on the road.

The sheik tried to console his guest and general
for their defeat, and helped to repair their personal
losses out of his own purse. He laid the whole blame
upon the Mandara people, and assured the Major,
that if he would accompany him in a projected expedition against Mungo, he would see how his people

could fight, when he was with them. The gallant
officer, nothing daunted by past reverses, expressed
his willingness to go, at which the sheik was much
pleased.

Another route southward from Kooka lies a little
to the west of that which we have just pursued, and
leads us to Adamawa, which appears to be the limits
of Mahometanism and civilisation in the interior of
Africa, north of the equator. It leads through the
fertile province of Ghamdergu, inhabited by Shuwas,
some of whom we have already met with; a small,
slender, light-coloured people, of considerable industry and activity. We have had a specimen of
this tribe in Barca Gana, who was taken as a slave
when young; and having gained the favour of the
Sheik of Bornu, was raised to the highest posts of
honour in the kingdom, though still a slave. But
Barca was of a strong herculean frame of body,
which, with undaunted courage, gave him great
superiority amongst a people who fight with spears.
The country here is low, flat, and marshy; and wild
hogs abound in the woods. The inhabitants are
poor, with little of the civilisation of life.

After the Shuwas you would find the Marghi, a
pagan tribe, and almost savage. The men wear beads
and iron rings on their wrists and ankles, and sometimes an iron chain round their waist. They have no
covering except the funo or apron about their loins.
It is a fertile country, abounding in corn, with numerous small towns and villages. These people have a
novel and singular way of settling disputes amongst

T

themselves. Instead of boxing or shooting each other, or fighting with sword or spear, like inhabitants of more civilized countries, they leave the trouble and danger of a conflict to their cocks, who are naturally provided with weapons for this purpose. The two litigants repair to a holy rock, each carrying a cock, to whom he entrusts his honour and interests. These feathered animals are then set against each other, and the owner of the winning bird gains the cause against his adversary. Both parties are satisfied with the issue of the encounter, supposing it to be decided by a supernatural power to which man must submit.

Proceeding southward, through a mountainous region infested with bandits, we should arrive amongst the Kanuri people. They generally go naked, except having a narrow strip of leather about their loins; but this is often deemed unnecessary. The men are tall, of fine form, and of various shades of colour, from the glossy black to a light copper hue.

COVERED GRANARY.

Travelling in these districts, you would require to practice a good deal of abstinence, and be satisfied with a little of very simple fare. Your principal food would be the fruit of the *toso* tree, or the Bassia Parkii, and an esculent root called *katakirre*. The latter is about the size of a potato, its pulp resembling a radish, but softer, more succulent, and more nutritious. It has a milky juice which forms a grateful restorative in this parched land. The plant grows with a single blade about ten inches in height, but the root is often a foot or eighteen inches beneath the surface. It is one of nature's merciful provisions for man in a thirsty region.

The Pullo country lies to the southward, consisting of a mountainous and rugged wilderness, until you reach a large plain intersected by important rivers. Here the Benuwy and the Faro meet. The latter is about six hundred feet in width, and two feet deep, flowing with a strong current. The Benuwy is half a mile broad, with a deep and powerful stream, which flows westward to join the Niger, and is called by Europeans the Chadda or Tsadda. This will probably be found a good channel for navigation, when the time for Africa's civilisation shall arrive.

Crossing this noble river and ascending the Bagella mountains, generally enveloped in clouds, we see the hamlets of the Batta people perched on the tops of hills. When the waters are out, this mountain appears like an island in a huge lake. The wild natives keep to their hilly eminences for defence against the encroaching power of the Foolbé or Felattas. In their manner of life they seem to resemble the Musgo (who dwell a little eastward) and other Negroes of mountainous districts. ·

Yola is the capital of Adamawa or Fumbina, much of which has been subjected by the Mahometans. The town is about three miles in circuit, and may contain 12,000 inhabitants. The houses

consist of clay huts built in courts of the same
material. Adamawa only exports slaves and ivory;
the former of which find their way to the Niger and
foreign climes. There are whole villages of slaves,
who cultivate corn for their owners. The soil is
fertile. The woods abound with the elephant and
rhinoceros. The wild bull and ayu, an animal somewhat like the seal, are also found in the district. In
return for their ivory and slaves, the inhabitants
import cloths, calicoes, beads, and salt. The neighbouring people are Battas. We believe that no
foreigner has entered Yola. Dr. Barth who penetrated thus far, through many difficulties and dangers,
was positively forbidden to enter the town. As the
natives have suffered so much from the encroach-
ments of the Foolbé, they are naturally jealous of
strangers, especially of those who professedly come to
see their country.

HAMLET OF KANEMBO CATTLE-BREEDERS.

CHAP. XII.

IT is now time to take a survey of the Lake Chad, which covers a surface of many thousands of square miles in the immediate vicinity of Kooka. This large expanse of water has been an object of great interest to foreigners, though it is not so to the people of the land. It is in fact of no use to any one, save to the wild people who inhabit the islands with which it is studded. At some future period, it may be an important part of African geography, and one of the most delightful spots of its central regions.

The Biddomas, who dwell in the isles of this lake, are one of the wildest and most savage tribes of men. They have large mouths, a sunken eye, and flat features: their look is morose and repugnant, and their

T 3

neck long. The men let their hair grow, and plait
and twist it into knots. In early years they collect
beads and other ornaments, which they wear round
their necks, but which are given to their wives on
marriage. They go about armed with a spear; but
when they visit the shores, are shy and reserved in
their manners. They seldom come to the mainland
except when they want to get or steal something; for
they are confirmed and adept robbers. They traverse
the lake in canoes which they manage with great ex-
pertness; and keep the entire navigation in their
own hands. Hence it is impossible to attack them
in their homes, to which they quickly convey all
stolen property.

The banks of the lake are generally swampy, the
soil consisting of black mud, in which rushes and
reeds grow luxuriantly. Wild fowl are abundant on
the margin, and the waters teem with excellent fish.
Do you ask what those people are about in the water,
women and children encircling the shore in a kind
of single file? Watch them, and you will see that
they are driving a quantity of the finny tribe before
them into the shallows, where the frightened fish are
easily caught by the hand, or even leap ashore, in
a vain attempt to escape from their pursuers. Now
a fire is made: and a stick being run through the
mouth into the belly of each fish, it is stuck into the
ground close to the clear flame. The roasting fish
can be turned by the tail, so that both sides are
cooked; and the repast which they afford is far from
despicable. They resemble mullets. A great quantity

are caught with nets in the Yeo, which flows into the lake a little north of Kooka, and being dried, are sold in all towns of the vicinity.

Continuing to pass northward, along the western side of the lake, we traverse a district full of wild beasts, and reach the town of Burwha. This is a frontier town of five or six thousand inhabitants, which has a high wall and dry ditch, and is otherwise defended in order to keep off the Tuarick Arabs who infest the deserts. In proceeding farther, we enter a forest of acacias and underwood, a favourite haunt of elephants and other monsters; and in which is Woodi, the little capital of this district, governed by a sheik. Stay! there is a snake of no ordinary size! It is like a coluber, of horrid appearance, not less than eighteen feet long. If you kill it you will find in its belly several pounds of fat, which the natives esteem highly as a specific for the diseases of cattle.

At the north-western corner of the lake is Lari, a small town standing on an eminence. Its dwelling huts are built of rushes, round and conical; with a mat hung up at the only aperture, which serves for door, window, and chimney. A screen of mats is used to divide the little house, when part is allotted to the women.

In this vicinity, are a number of petty villages, inhabited by the Kanembo, consisting of a cluster of huts erected under the shade of a tree. The men wear only the funo, and a singular head-piece, being a cap with a red bandage and a crown of

bristling reeds.   They are adorned with a necklace
of white beads, and with several greegrees or charms.

KANEMBO CHIEF AND MAN.

They carry a spear, shield, and javelins; and when
mustered by their chiefs, form an essential part of

the army of Bornu. A great many of the Kanembo live in Kooka, constituting one element of its population; but their rude manners do not appear to be much altered by living in the capital.

It was in a pretty hamlet of the above description, called Maduwarrie, that Mr. Overweg breathed his last. This zealous traveller is probably the only European who ever visited the islands of the lake: and he would have had some curious information to give about its wild inhabitants, if he had survived. His health had suffered from the humid climate in which he was pursuing his discoveries; and one day, whilst shooting in the marshes, he was seized with cold, followed by a fever, under which he rapidly sunk. He left no regular journal or papers that were of any use; only a number of scraps, which he had intended to form into a diary; but which were unintelligible to any body but himself.

Should you wish to survey the northern side of the lake, you must have an escort of Arabs. The country is very wild, forming the southern border of the desert; and is inhabited by a few tribes of its roving inhabitants. They once held the extensive government of Kanem; but made themselves so obnoxious to the neighbours by their predatory habits, that a combination was formed against them, by which a great part of them were cut off. They now have only a few temporary settlements, ready to be abandoned at the first alarm of a foe.

The whole country is over-run with large and small bands of robbers. Your own escort would

prove as great plunderers as any from whom they
could protect you; so that you would find yourself
to be really associated with lawless bandits, and
would have to brave the consequences of their fighting with the natives. The distracted state of the
country cannot be surpassed. Every one's hand seems
to be against his neighbour; and the differing tribes
plunder one another whenever opportunity occurs,
living in a constant state of alarm. On this account
you could not reach the east of the lake by passing
along its northern border; which would otherwise
be the best route.

Therefore we must start again from Kooka. To
travel close by the lake would be almost impossible,
from the marshy character of its shores, the in-
numerable hosts of mosquitoes which frequent the
margin, and the wild beasts which we have already
mentioned. How little the elephants care for man,
may be gathered from a hunt perpetrated by Major
Denham and some of the sheik's people. Finding
three large elephants grazing near the water, the
hunting party prepared for action. The footmen
were ordered to remain behind, and four horsemen
approached the game. At first the creatures did not
seem to care for their hunters, or the wild cries which
they uttered; but afterwards they gave a loud roar
that shook the forest, and moved slowly off, the
largest keeping in the rear. He was intercepted, and
a spear was thrown, which struck him under the
tail. He only gave a roar, and lifting his proboscis
discharged a volley of sand that nearly blinded the

horsemen. He turned towards the place where the footmen were stationed, who all scampered off as fast as possible; and the major's servant was so frightened that he did not recover the shock that day. The noble beast went onward at a clumsy rolling walk, which kept the horses at a short gallop. The last of two balls which struck him gave him a moment's uneasiness; a spear flew off from his tough hide; and the hunters wisely left him to himself.

Eight elephants now appeared, doubtless summoned by those which had been annoyed, and came towards the hunting party, who thought it prudent to drive them away. But the creatures allowed the men to approach them closely before they would even turn their backs; not caring for the spears that were thrown at them, and only frightened at flashes from the guns. Throwing out a great quantity of sand, they majestically retreated. A number of birds, somewhat like thrushes, were perched on their backs, said to be very useful to the elephant in picking off vermin from those parts of his body which he cannot reach. It is a wonder that the huntsmen were not all killed; since, though the elephant is comparatively harmless, he often becomes infuriated when attacked, and blinding his pursuer with sand, seizes and crushes him to death.

Passing through Angornu, which we have already described, we coast the lake to Angala, a town situated near its most southerly point, where it is formed into a kind of gulf. Angala is the capital of an ancient government subject to Bornu: and El

Kanemy had married the daughter of its sultan.
She was now divorced from him, and lived near her
father, who had built a house for her occupancy, and
furnished her with a large establishment.

"She was a very handsome, beautifully formed
Negress, of about thirty-five, and had imbibed much
of that softness of manner, which is so extremely
prepossessing in the sheik. Seated on an earthen
throne, covered with a Turkey carpet, and surrounded
by twenty of her favourite slaves, all dressed alike,
in fine white shirts, which reached to their feet; their
necks, ears, and noses thickly ornamented with coral;
she held her audience with very considerable grace.
Four eunuchs guarded the entrance; and a Negro
dwarf, who measured three feet all but an inch, the
keeper of her keys, sat before her with the insignia
of office on his shoulder, and richly dressed in Soudan
tobes. This little person afforded us a subject of
conversation, and much laughter.

"Miram inquired whether we had such little
fellows in my country; and when I answered in the
affirmative, she said, '*Ah gieb!* what are they good
for? do they ever have children?' I answered, 'Yes!
that we had instances of their being fathers to tall
and proper men?' 'Oh! wonderful!' she replied;
'I thought so: they must be better than this dog of
mine; for I have given him eight of my youngest
and handsomest slaves, but it is all to no purpose.'
The wretch, and an ugly wretch he was, shook his
large head, and slobbered copiously from his exten-

sive mouth, at this flattering proof of his mistress's partiality." '

Shortly after this, on their return from Loggun, a gallant young Englishman died at Angala. He was ensign in a regiment stationed at Malta; and had readily volunteered to join Major Denham at Kooka, when it was found expedient to send help to the mission. He made an extraordinary journey across the desert, and proceeded with his companion along the south of the lake. But his constitution began to give way, and he became so seriously ill that the major hastened with him to Angala, where they had been hospitably received, and where every attention was paid to the dying officer. He rallied for two days; then a cold shivering came upon him; nature was exhausted, and he expired without a groan, aged twenty-two. As the sun was sinking, his body was interred in a deep grave, under a clump of blooming mimosas, north-west of the town, and a large pile of thorns and of the prickly tulloh were placed over, to protect it from being disturbed by hyænas.

Mr. Toole's death was perhaps hastened by the rapid manner in which they had to travel from Loggun, which was threatened by the Baghirmis, and by the want of proper provisions on the way. The Sheik of Bornu came with an army, hastily gathered, to repel these invaders; and the hostile forces met near Angala. The enemy, who were in great strength, came forward boldly and offered

battle; which the sheik declined, as he could not
get into so favourable a position for fighting as he
desired.   The alarm at Angala and Angornu was
great; as the departure of a kafila for Soudan had
deprived the sheik of thirty Arabs, his best warriors.

The Baghirmis seeing his hesitancy to fight, and
attributing it to fear, now ventured to attack him in
the plain near which he had encamped.   He disposed
his few Arabs and forty Musgo musketeers on his
flanks; and hoisting his green flag in the centre,
moved forward in the midst of his Kanembo spearmen.   Two guns were in front, which had been
mounted by Mr. Hillman, a carpenter connected with
the British mission.   The Baghirmis came forward in
a solid mass, five thousand strong, with two hundred
chiefs at their head, and made directly for the centre
where the standard of the prophet was unfurled.   The
artillery drove them back.   Then they fell on Barca
Gana's flank with so much impetuosity, that all but
himself and a chosen band gave way.   Here Maramy, Denham's friend and preserver in the fight
with the Felattas, fell by the thrust of a spear,
whilst he was drawing his own from the body of a
chief whom he had killed.   The Bornuese horse and
Arabs now closed upon the Baghirmis, who fled.
Only one of their two hundred chiefs is said to have
escaped.   Seven sons of the sultan were among the
slain, and seventeen hundred men of less note.   Numbers were killed by the villagers in their flight; and
many were drowned in a stream which they attempted
to cross, pressed by Kanembo spears.

All the people praised "the guns, the guns, which made the dogs skip." The sheik, afraid that too much might be made of the guns, said, that truly the guns were wonderful, but that he lifted up his hands in prayer, and from that moment the victory was decided. The booty gained by the conquerors was considerable; four hundred and eighty horses, two hundred women, two eunuchs, and the baggage of the princes. Fifty of the women, belonging to the sultan's sons, were choice females of great beauty, and were given up to the sheik. Besides these, a crowd of slaves were taken, and sold in the Kooka market for two or three bullocks a-piece.

Going eastward, we reach Showy on the Shary. This is a fine river, about half a mile wide at this place, and flows gently into the Chad, at the rate of two or three miles an hour. In the centre of the stream, opposite the town, is a beautiful island. A sail down the river presents some exquisite scenery, from the variety and richness of the foliage which lines the banks. The trees are hung all over with creeping plants of various colours; which, by the long windings of the stream, are displayed to great advantage. About a dozen miles from the lake is another island, uninhabited, but abounding in game of various kinds, and with centipedes, scorpions, and porcupines. Crocodiles, hippopotami, and buffaloes swarm about the river. Near its mouth are other small islands covered with reeds and bamboos; and the banks here are very marshy, swarming with mosquitoes and other noxious insects. The nearest

island of the Biddomas to this part of the lake is
said to be a three days' voyage for a canoe.

Giraffes abound in this district.   On being chased,
they move away awkwardly, from being so low behind, seeming to drag the hinder legs after them:
they are not swift.

GIRAFFE.

The chief inhabitants of this country are a tribe of
Shuwas, more simple and unsophisticated than those
of the west.   The men have fine large features with
much expression of countenance, and a long bushy
beard.   They do not live in towns, but in tents of
dressed hides and huts of rushes, subsisting chiefly
on the milk of their camels and cows.   Their camps
are circular, with two entrances, by which to drive
in and out their cattle.   They despise the Negro

nations around them, though they are necessarily
subject, in the way of tribute, to the king in whose
territory they reside.

Major Denham expresses himself as greatly pleased
with the simple manners of these Shuwa Arabs.
They salute a stranger by clapping their hands
gently, and then extending the palms towards him,
exclaiming, "Are you well and happy?" One of
their chiefs, a patriarchal man, looked at the European for some time with great earnestness, and at
last said, "What brought you here? They say your
country is a moon from Tripoli?"

"To see by whom the country is inhabited, and
whether it has lakes and rivers and mountains like
our own."

"And have you been three years from your home?
Are not your eyes dimmed with straining to the north,
where all your thoughts must ever be? Oh, you are
men, men, indeed! Why if my eyes do not see the
wife and children of my heart for ten days, when they
should be closed with sleep they are flowing with
tears."

He asked if it was true that the dollar came out of
the earth? And upon having the matter explained to
him, said, "You are not Jews?"

"No."

"Christians, then?"

"Even so."

"I have read of you: you are better than Jews.
Are Jews white, like you?"

"No; rather more like yourself; very dark."

U

"Really. Why, are they not quite white? They are a bad people."

On taking leave, he took my hand and said, "I see you are a sultan. I never saw any body like you. The sight of you is as pleasing to my eyes as your words are to my ear. My heart says you are my friend. May you die at your own tents, and in the arms of your wives and family."

"Amen."

There is something romantic in the language and manners of these Shuwas, who seem to be imbued with the poetic spirit of the east. A girl sits down by your tent, covering her face, but leaving her bosom bare; "A happy day to you! your friend has brought you milk. You gave her something so handsome yesterday, she has not forgotten it. Oh! how her eyes ache to see all you have got in that wooden house! (pointing to a trunk.) We have no fears now: we know you are good: and our eyes which before could not look on you, now search after you always. They bade us beware of you, at first, for you were bad, very bad: but we know better now. How it pains us that you are so white!"

Aisha, the daughter of a chief comes to revisit the stranger, two days after the fight, and with weeping eyes says, "A happy day to my friend! What can he think of Aisha's not having seen him for two days? But what could she do? Eight of her father's house fell beneath the spears of Amanook! She was obliged to stay and mourn over them; but she mourned more in her heart that she saw not her

friend! Still they deserved her tears, for they were
brave and beloved. But then the whole camp would
have wept for them, and the stranger was alone, and
had nobody to bring him milk:— no, no, she was
wrong. Last night she would have come, and had
passed the barrier: she feared nothing but giving pain
to him she thought of, — but she knew not herself.
The hyænas howled; they came near her: her heart
was small, and she turned back!"

Being pressed to enter the tent, the girl gets
frightened, and exclaims, "Wait here! sit down
here on the sand! Aisha is now frightened at her
friend! What does he ask her to do? Would he
see her beaten with leather thongs till she bleeds?
Would he have her brother's dagger red with her
blood — the blood of her heart, which now beats so
strong, and bids it go to him it beats for, while her
head tells her to fear? Aisha's heart is weaker than
her head: her eyes have seen her stranger friend,
and have seen none like him!"

If this be not making love, what is? A present
being offered, with an admonition to return to the
camp; she replies, "I go; for it is now day. What,
take pretty things from her friend now, when she
knows his eyes have no pleasure in her! No — No!
She now leaves him: but when night comes, and all
her house will be singing over the dead, then Aisha
will have no fears — she will leave the tent: but her
stranger must come with his gun, and protect her from
the hyænas." Poor daughter of the desert! We fear

she had lost her heart for a stranger, in a way that might form the subject of an interesting romance.

We have said that the colour and religion of a Christian are great scarecrows for the people of Africa. •And this not only with the Negroes. The Shuwa girl pitied the white man's skin. Three wives of Shuwa chiefs are passing by the door of the stranger's dwelling in the city; and after some consultation, they venture to approach him. The eldest begins:

"What do you here? You do not buy or sell? Is it true that you have no female slaves? No one to shampoo you after a south wind?"

"Quite true: for I am a stranger, and far from home and alone."

"You are a kafir, (infidel,) Khaled: and it is you Christians, with the blue eyes like the hyæna, that eat the blacks, whenever you can get them far enough away from their own country."

"God deliver me from his evil glance," said a girl, "is that true? Why they have been here now for some time, and don't seem very savage! Would it not be better to give him a wife or two; teach him to pray, like a Mussulman, and never let him return among his own filthy race?"

"God forbid," says the old woman, who begins to reason with her youthful and more merciful companion; and then cries out, "What infatuation is this? Why, I tell you again and again, he is an uncircumcised kafir! neither washes, nor prays! eats pork! and will go to hell!"

"Oh, oh! the Lord preserve us from the infernal devil!" And screaming aloud, they all run off.

The people of Showy are indolent and mirthful. The men do little but lounge about during the day. At night they fish in the river; and spend the other hours of darkness in dancing to the sound of a drum. The women sit near, with covered faces, and scream their approbation. But what is this merry party, amusing themselves near the river with a long skipping rope? They are black figures, unincumbered with any drapery but what nature has given them: fine figures too; and they perform the jumping and skipping very well. Gentle reader! they are young ladies of good size; who appear to be quite unsophisticated about the decorum of dress, and to see no necessity for covering their form from the eye even of a stranger. Let them romp away! And may they never know the shame of evil! When they marry they must wear veils.

Passing up the Shary, through difficult morasses and forests, and across tributary streams, we shall find our way to Loggun, the capital of a small kingdom. Its western gate leads to the principal street, which is very wide and has dwellings on each side, built with much regularity. The people come out to see us; and presently an officer from the palace advances, bending very low, and joining his hands. The slaves who attend him bow still lower. He has come from the sultan to give us a welcome, and now precedes us to the huts appointed for our resting place. As we pass along the street, every party that

we see advance and salute us in a similar manner.
The accommodation afforded us is good.

You are going to visit the sultan. Take your present with you. Ten huge Negroes, of high rank, bare
headed, and carrying large clubs, come and precede
you to the palace. Passing through some dark rooms,
you reach a large square court, where many persons
are assembled, all seated on the ground. In the
middle is a vacant space; and you are desired to sit
down there. Two slaves fan the air through a lattice
work, behind which the sultan is concealed. On a
given signal, the screen is removed, and you see a
living creature on a carpet, wrapped in silk tobes,
and having the head so enveloped in shawls that
only his eyes are visible. That bundle of clothes is
the sultan of Loggun. Before this bundle all the
court fall prostrate, and pour sand on their heads;
whilst eight funfrums and horns give an inharmonious
salute.

His majesty whispers a welcome. For it is not good
manners to speak loud in Loggun. You can scarcely
hear the gentlemen's voices, when they address you.
" Do you wish to buy some handsome female slaves?"
asks his majesty, who seems to have a mercantile turn
of mind; "for if you do, you need go no farther: I
have some hundreds, and will sell them to you as
cheap as any one."

If you go into the houses of the Loggunese, you will
find many of them busy at the loom. The women
are more industrious than the men, and their cotton
cloth is of superior quality, especially on account of a

fine glaze which they know how to impart to their indigo-dyed manufacture.   They are handsomer, have
a better carriage than the Bornuese, and are more
intelligent.   This last qualification is employed for
evil purposes as well as good.   " To give them their
due, they are the cleverest, and the most immoral race
I had met with in the black country."   This expression paints a strong character in a few words: but
seems to be not far from the truth.   Take the following little scene as a sample.

" The ladies of the principal persons in the country
visited me, accompanied by one or more female

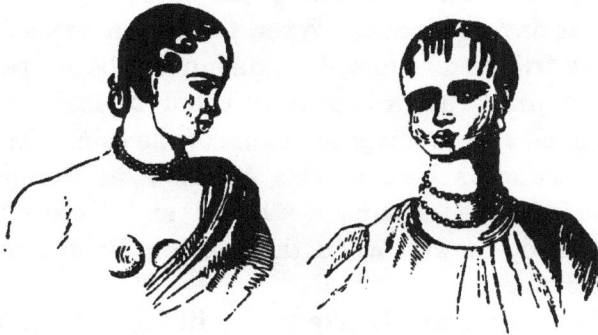

LADIES OF LOGGUN.

slaves.   They examined everything, even to the
pockets of my trowsers.   And more inquisitive
ladies I never saw in any country.   They begged for
everything; and nearly all attempted to steal something: when found out, they only laughed heartily,
clapped their hands together, and exclaimed, ' Why,
how sharp he is !   Only think, why he caught us ! ' "

The modesty of these ladies was on a par with their
honesty.

But here is something that is new in Negroland, a
piece of money or current coin! It is not, indeed, of
gold or of silver, or of the usual round shape. It is
composed of thin plates of iron, in the form of a
horse-shoe; which are made up into parcels of ten
or twelve, according to the weight; and thirty of
these parcels are equal to a dollar. Still, this coin
is subject to fluctuations in value, in order to suit
the sultan's convenience. Every week, at the commencement of the Wednesday market, a public pro-
clamation is made, declaring the value of the coin
for that day and week. When the sultan expects to
receive tribute or duty, he announces the currency
" below par : " and when he is about to make purchases, he always raises the value of the coin. There
are speculators here in this stock, as in European
countries; and they have " bulls " and " bears " in
Negroland, as well as in the London Exchange or
Paris Bourse.

We should scarcely like to live in Loggun. There
are two principal annoyances, thieves and insects.
To the former we have already adverted in the case
of the ladies; and the gentlemen do not seem to fall
far behind. When one of the sultans wanted a present equal in value to what had been given to his
rival, and the stranger rather demurred to this imposition; he was informed that the sultan's slaves
were the most expert thieves in the world, and that
if their master gave the word "Forage," no walls

could keep them out   This was a hint which could
not be neglected.   But who were these rival sovereigns?   They were father and son, mutually hating
each other, and each placed at the head of a political
party.   Their love and piety may be gathered from this
circumstance, that they both applied secretly to the
foreigner for a " poison which would not lie: " and
the son sent three young female slaves as a bribe.
Expressing abhorrence of such proceedings, " I had
the satisfaction of hearing myself, and all my countrymen, pronounced fools a hundred times over."

The country of Loggun swarms with mosquitoes
and other noxious insects.   This might be expected
from its situation, amid the woody marshes of a river
in a tropical climate.   The wonder is that any town
should be built in such a situation.   For the residents themselves are so troubled with mosquitoes,
that they often require to fill their huts with dense
smoke from wood fires, to get a little respite during
the hours of sleep.   Young chickens are sometimes
destroyed before they are properly fledged, by the
stings of mosquitoes: and a chief asserted that he
had lost two children, who were literally stung to
death by these venomous insects.   Strangers can
scarcely endure to remain in the place at some seasons of the year.   The malaria proceeding from large
stagnant pools which abound in the district, is almost
as fatal in producing fevers, as the insects are sure to
cause restlessness.   The capital is rather better situated in this respect than some other towns; but it is
bad enough.

CHAP. XIII.

AFTER these excursions about the Lake Chad, we
must proceed eastward.   But before entering a new
kingdom, and in some respects a new country, let us
pause for a moment, to consider our position, and
the ground which we have traversed.

We have passed through a vast extent of inhabited country from the western coast of Africa,
all more or less civilized.   The semi-civilization of
Senegambia merges into a higher type of refinement
when we reach the Niger; and this continues along
a line of midland towns, lying within a narrow belt
of latitude, until we reach Kooka, and the Lake

Chad. This improvement in arts and manners (we cannot say morals, except as to freedom from drunkenness), is owing to the presence and influence of the Moors and Mahometanism. We have looked at the Moors and Arabs in their own desert homes, to the north of this belt; and we have found them harsh, wild, and cruel; inferior to the central Negroes who have embraced Islamism, and who traffic with Barbary. Glancing at the south of this belt of towns, we have seen the pagan tribes merge gradually into barbarism; a fact which was strongly marked in our voyage down the Niger, and in our excursions to Mandara and Adamava.

Lake Chad, again, is inhabited in its islands by the wildest savages. Its northern border is over-run by Arabs, who also belong to the little desert. On the southern border, as we leave Bornu, we return towards barbarism; with a partial exception in Loggun and one or two towns on the caravan-route to the East.

To the south of this latitude, is a vast territory little explored, consisting of more than twenty degrees of latitude, and as many of longitude. Wandering tribes of Arabs rove in the north parts of this region: and the pagan natives are in a state of utter savagism.

East of the Shary is an immense country, principally desert. Tibbu Arabs dwell in the northern half, until it becomes utterly uninhabitable. Pagan savages live in the fruitful parts of the south. But we can find a passage through it traversed by

caravans, to Darfur and Nubia, and thence to Egypt
or Arabia.

We now cross the Logon, a river not so wide but
more rapid than the Shary. Its water is beautifully
clear, and not a ripple disturbs its surface. Here is
the richness and silence of nature. A crocodile slides
into the stream as you approach: and a hippopotamus,
which has been feeding on the grass, plunges into
the water. Again, all is quiet: till you hear the
leaping of fish, or the screeching of a hawk overhead.
We have now passed the boundary which separated
us from east Negroland and are in the country of
Baghirmi. The first portion of this territory is fertile because near the river. Herds of cattle range
through the swampy meadows, or wade in the
water: the maraboo stands "like an old man, its
head between its shoulders:" the pelican, the white
ibis, and the azure-coloured *dedegame* are seeking
their prey; ducks of many species skim the surface
of the water: and countless birds of bright plumage,
of many kinds and sizes, sport in the air. A few
hamlets of men peep through the trees.

But Dr. Barth found that the heart of man was far
from being in unison with this rich and peaceful
panorama of nature. When he arrived on the east
side of the river, the Sultan of Baghirmi was absent
on a warlike expedition; and the mind of the
governor was so poisoned with suspicions through
the report of some Arab travellers who had preceded
the European, that the latter was forbidden to
advance into the country. He was bandied about

from village to village near the river, and at last
made a close prisoner, till permission was given to go
to the capital.

The country had, indeed, suffered much from
enemies. After many successful conflicts with the

LANCER OF BAGHIRMI.

encroaching Felattas, it had succumbed to its eastern
neighbour, the Sultan of Waday, who plundered it of
its wealth, carried off many of its people, and made
it tributary. In addition, it was now suffering from
drought, and the ravages of worms and insects. Two
or three sorts of worms abound in millions, and
consume much of the produce of the people's labour;
who get their revenge by feasting upon the invaders
themselves when they have become large and fat.
As to white and black ants, they are like one of the
plagues of Egypt: for it seems almost impossible to

preserve anything from their ravages. An assault by
an army of the large black ant is thus described.
" In a thick uninterrupted line about an inch broad,
they one morning came suddenly marching over the
wall of my court-yard; and entering the hall which
formed my residence by day and night, they made
straight for my storeroom: but unfortunately, my
couch being in their way, they attacked my own
person most fiercely, and soon obliged me to decamp.
We then fell upon them, killing those that were
straggling about and foraging, and burning the chief
body of the army as it came marching along the
path. But fresh legions came up, and it took us at
least two hours, before we could fairly break the
lines and put the remainder of the enemy to flight."

Yet these ants have their use. They cleanse the
huts of the negroes, by devouring refuse, and killing
all kinds of vermin, not excepting mice. The stores
of corn which they lay up for future use are sought out
and plundered by the poor people. Different species
of the ant tribe, black, red, and white, fight with and
devour one another; so that their intestine wars tend
to keep down their numbers.

We are now prepared to look at Massena, the
capital of Baghirmi. It has a ruinous appearance:
indeed the walls are in such a condition, that the
gates appear to be only of nominal use. The houses
are of clay, thatched with grass, and of frail construction: so that they do not seem to be proof against
a violent storm. You may go to market any day
during some hours of the morning and afternoon;

and you will find a pretty good supply of onions, beans, groundnuts, milk, and red pepper; with a few sheep and cattle. Beads from Europe are brought here in large quantities, and are retailed in the adjacent petty states.

Here is the palace, — a large rectangular court, having other courts within it, some of which are full of huts. As the sultan is said to have between three and four hundred wives, each of whom has her own nest, constructed after her own taste; the agglomeration of these dwellings would present a singular appearance to a traveller, if he could gain admission into the women's quarter of the royal residence. And we can imagine the fright which must ensue from the fall of some of these frail tenements during a storm;—an accident which sometimes happens, filling the royal precincts with an uproarious noise of female voices, as if an enemy were storming the town.

Here, as at Loggun, a stranger must address the king seated behind a screen, so that his august features are not visible. It seems a very unsatisfactory mode of presentation; but etiquette must be preserved in every place. After receiving your presents, the sultan would probably offer in return a handsome female slave; as this is the most valuable commodity in these regions. If she be refused, he would send you a number of shirts, which you could dispose of in the market. The tribute which the sultan pays to the King of Waday, every third year, consists of a hundred male slaves, thirty handsome female slaves, a hundred horses, and a thousand

shirts: with ten female slaves, four horses, and forty
shirts to the inspector of the province. In order to
pay this demand, and also to satisfy the Sheik of
Bornu, he levies a similar impost on a number of
pagan tribes whom he has subjugated. Thus, slaves
form the larger currency, and shirts the small currency
of the kingdom! All foreign supplies come through
Waday or Bornu; the desert to the north being too
difficult for caravans to cross.

Baghirmi is nominally Mahometan. Between two
and three hundred years ago Abdallah introduced
Islamism, and extended the bounds of the kingdom.
Yet, though mosques are reared and the forms of
Mahometan worship are kept up, the hearts and
manners of the natives have not yet been converted.
The language is similar to that of Kooka. The
marriage tie is held in a very loose way; divorces are
easily made; and some of the people contract matches
merely for a limited period.

The sultan is returning in triumph after a campaign
against some pagan tribes! His procession exhibits
the characteristics of barbaric pomp and pride. The
lieutenant-governor rides first, surrounded by a troop
of horsemen. Next comes the *barma,* behind whom
a long spear of peculiar figure is borne, connected
with some religious superstition. The commander-
in-chief follows; and immediately behind him, the
sultan, on a grey charger, dressed in a war-cloth.
He is covered with a yellow bernoose, and is shaded
by two umbrellas, one green and the other yellow,
held over him by slaves. Six slaves having their

RETURN OF THE SULTAN OF MASSEÑA.

right arms clad with iron, fan his majesty with
ostrich feathers fastened on poles. Five chiefs and
other princes ride beside him. Some are clothed in
bernooses, some in black shirts, and some in blue;
their hands are generally uncovered. After this
motley group is the war-camel, on which a drummer
is mounted, beating two kettle drums, fastened one
on each side of the animal. Near him are three
mounted musicians.

The next part of the procession includes a long
line of the sultan's favourite concubines on horseback
dressed in black, each having a slave on either side.
The baggage camels follow; and the infantry bring
up the rear. When the monarch enters the town,
after some days spent in the camp, the principal
captives are led in triumph in the procession, and
are then subject to the insults of the harem: after
which they are made eunuchs or put to death.

As Baghirmi is chiefly a flat country intersected by
streams, it is rich in natural productions. The soil
is partly lime, partly sand. The people chiefly live
on Negro millet (*pennisetum*): but also grow sor-
ghum and beans (*sesamum*) with some ground nuts,
water-melons, and onions. They eat grasses, as the
Poa Abyssinia, and the leaves of certain trees which
are nutritious. Rice is here a wild plant. The
natives rear a little cotton and indigo for their own
use: and they have fine trees, the tamarind, palm,
monkey-bread, and sycamore. The whole population has been reckoned at a million and a half, of
whom many are slaves. They have few fire-arms or

bows, but chiefly use the spear and a kind of hand-bill.

We should have no disposition to pass through the wilds of Africa east of Baghirmi. Native traders and pilgrims perform that long journey in caravans; and according to their account, are subject to many hardships on the road. Still, it is nothing like

SYCAMORE TREE.

crossing either the Great or Little Desert of the north. For here are fertile spots and oases at no great distance from one another, where water and shelter may be had, and provisions may be obtained from wandering Arabs.

The first country is Waday, of which the capital used to be Wara: but a late sultan changed it for security to Abeshr, situated in a desert place, in the tribe of the Kelingen. It is a wild, straggling kingdom, nominally extending from 15° to 23° of east longitude. The country is mostly level, interspersed with barren mountains; and the northern portions are very desert. A caravan proceeds at the rate of about ten miles a day; and its journey to Darfur has been thus described by pilgrims. From Wara, you travel over rocky hills and a wide wilderness for seven days, when you will reach Doomta, a frontier town of Darfur. Your next march of eight days lies through Waday Bareh, a thickly peopled valley, to Kebkabiyeh a good town of the Jellaba, with clay houses and a market. About eight days more would bring you to the capital of Darfur, the route to which is partly through a wilderness inhabited by the Jellaba.

Where the people of this region are not Arabs, they are Negroes of the complete Negro type, living in the simplest and rudest forms of life: yet not so much savage, as uncivilized. It is chiefly from the neighbouring districts, that those slaves are procured whom the traveller on the Nile has seen brought down the river in cargoes to Egypt for sale. They are short in stature, dumpy, flat-nosed, thick-lipped, woolly-headed, black as a coal, almost naked, with little thought and little care.

Cobbé is generally called the capital of Darfur, though the king usually resides a little way off. But

native and foreign merchants have their residence in
this town, and with their numerous slaves form
the bulk of its inhabitants. The whole population
is about six thousand. They have a mosque, and
profess to be Mussulmen. But come! take a peep
within one of these mud walls, which inclose some
mud huts; and you may see men and women sitting
over their cups of booza, a fermented liquor made
from dhoora like that drunk by Negroes of the west.
Nor do the men limit themselves to the number of
wives prescribed by the Koran; but indulge in
polygamy to the extent of their means.

If you had goods to dispose of in Cobbé, you
would require all your wit, and even more, to save
yourself from being fleeced. There being no circu-
lating medium, trade is conducted by barter, in which
a practised native will always get the advantage of a
stranger. Nor would your property be safe at any
time out of your sight. Indeed, the character of the
people is wholly bad, being roguish and licentious
in the extreme.

Suppose we were admitted, with Mr. Browne, to
an audience of the sultan. We find him seated on
what must be called a throne, a bank spread with
small Turkey carpets, and covered with a canopy of
foreign light stuffs. Behind him, is a file of guards
armed with spear and shield, each having a black
ostrich feather in his cap. Some chief men sit on
either side of the throne, at a little distance: whilst
a crowd of spectators and petitioners fill the space in
front. A trumpeter of the king's praises stands on
his left hand, ever and anon reminding the people,

lest they should forget, that he is a person not to be despised: "See the buffalo, the offspring of a buffalo! a bull of bulls! the elephant of superior strength! the powerful sultan Abd-el-rach-man-el-rashid!" So that physical strength, not wisdom or goodness, is the great boast of a Darfurian monarch!

His majesty is a merchant on his own account, speculating in goods brought by the caravans. These are sometimes large, numbering two thousand camels; for Cobbé is on the line of route between the interior of Africa and all eastern places, as Sennaar and Abyssinia, Nubia and Egypt, and Mecca by Suakem and Jidda. It has therefore its full share of traffic, on which it principally depends.

The king is also a nominal husbandman; for when the annual rains introduce the sowing season, he goes out into the field with his attendants, and with his royal hand makes the first holes in the ground. Millet is chiefly grown; which being made into flour and boiled is eaten with milk, or with the juice of a bitter herb. Melons, gourds, Cayenne pepper, tobacco, and a little wheat are also raised. The tamarind, palm, and sycamore trees grow in favourable situations. All the wild beasts which we have met with in the interior infest the thinly peopled plains of Darfur, and prowl about the villages, to make a prey of the cattle, of which the people have abundance. Gold and copper are found in this region.

It is a toilsome journey of more than four hundred miles, through a barren district, from Cobbé to Sennaar on the banks of the Nile; but when this is

achieved, the great span of Africa has been nearly
traversed. The town of Sennaar depends on trade,
and is therefore better built and more refined than
other places in the neighbourhood. The houses are
made of clay mixed with straw. The best have two
stories and a flat roof, and the floors are carpeted.
The climate is unhealthy, though the soil is fertile.
The horses and cattle are very fine. A nominal
Mahometanism prevails.

One of the most singular institutions of this country
in former times was the frail tenure of royal power.
The king appeared to be a mere puppet set up to
amuse the people, but entirely controlled by the
officers of the court. A council of these dignitaries
could decree that it was no longer for the public
good that the reigning sovereign should continue to
exist; on which, he was put to death by an officer
who lived with him, as master of his household, and
a relation of his family. This officer did not consider
his bloody function to be at all derogatory to his
dignity, nor even to interfere with his friendship for
the royal personage. When the time had come for
the monarch to die, it was better that his throat should
be decently cut by a friend in his own palace, than
that he should be murdered by a mob or an as-
sassin. So also with all the princes except the eldest
who ascended the throne. The public advantage
demanded their death; and it was well for it to take
place in a decent and orderly manner. Princesses
were of no estimation in Sennaar, and were not
regarded with more respect than private women: so

that when their father was killed, they were very
badly off, if not previously married.

A long shirt of blue cloth is the usual clothing of
the people both men and women; the men sometimes
gird it round their waist with a sash. They always
go barefooted in the house.

If you professed to be a medical man you might,
like Mr Bruce, have obtained an interview with the
royal ladies. He was first introduced into a large
apartment full of black women without apparel, excepting a narrow piece of cotton round their waists.
One of these ladies in waiting led him into another
chamber better lighted than the former. Here, on a
bench covered with cloth were seated some of the
king's wives, clothed in the blue shirt above mentioned. But they also wore jewels of gold, large
rings passed through the under lip, the ears, and the
nose; with chains round the neck, the wrists, and
ankles. Their features were quite distorted by these
cumbrous ornaments, which pulled the lip and ears
out of shape and place. The most loved of these
queens was in bulk like an elephant. There was not
a vestige of real civilization in the regal pomp of
Sennaar. It is well done away with.

A great change has come over the government of
Nubia and its adjacencies, since Mehemet Ali took
possession of it, and made it a pashalic. The pasha
is in rank next to the viceroy of Egypt himself, and
has his seat of government in Khartum on the Blue
River, a little before it joins the White River.
Sennaar now receives an Egyptian garrison of four

or five hundred disciplined troops: so that the wondrous accounts of Burckhardt and others about it are antiquarian. Yet it is a pity that those accounts should be wholly forgotten; as they show some curiosities of human nature, when left to its own vagaries.

SOUAKIN CHIEF, EASTERN NUBIA.

At a great bend of the Nile, a little below Shendy, which used to be a great slave-mart, we fall in with a fine race of men called Berbers. This name is

sometimes given to any Nubian: but it properly
belongs to a small district consisting of a few villages
inhabited by Arabs of the tribe of Meyrefal. A tall,
slender, handsome set of people, are these Berbers;
of dark colour; showing nothing of the Negro shape
or countenance, except a little thickness of the upper
lip. Their hair is bushy, not woolly; and they have
a beard under the chin. They blacken their eyes, to
make them of-a-piece with the rest of their appearance. Young girls wear only a leathern girdle,
a custom which prevails in extensive districts of
Africa; the other natives have shirts or tunics.

These Berbers are a gay, frolicsome, and treacherous people; combining the fun of the Negro
with the cunning of the Arab. They have been spoken
of as full of all wickedness: but are probably not
worse than other denizens of these regions, though
their Arab astuteness renders them more clever in
sin. A Berber makes a good travelling servant, if
you pay him well, and trust him as far as you see
him: and you would not place more confidence than
this in the usual run of Africans. In the enclosure
of their dwelling-place, most Berbers have two
apartments for the family, a third for a storehouse,
another for strangers, and a fifth for public women.
The latter are accommodated for a season in different families, and so change about for the public
convenience. The inner court of the house is a place
for cattle and fodder. The furniture is like that
found in the dwellings of Negroes or Arabs. It
consists of a few necessary utensils, and a wooden

frame covered with reeds or strips of ox-leather, over which a carpet is thrown, to serve as a sofa by day and a bed by night.

The wily Berbers are said to trick strangers by means of the public women lodging in their houses. These females serve for decoys. When a luckless wight has been seduced by one of them, the master of the house pretends that a relative of his own has been dishonoured, makes a great fuss about the matter, and finally lets the stranger off on payment of supposed damages. This decoying is more easily effected by means of their drinking parties, in which they furnish large quantities of booza, until most of the guests are intoxicated.

The route through the Nubian desert to Eygpt is not so bad as most of those we have described. Stations and wells are more frequent in these parts : so that, with proper precautions, the journey may be made without much difficulty or suffering. But Arab guides sometimes wilfully deceive travellers, and lead them out of the right way, that they may make a gain of them, or plunder their effects in case of their perishing from want. The Simoom prevails here, like the whirlwinds of sand we have already mentioned. When overtaken by this blast, the Arabs kneel down and wrap their faces in their cloak : whilst their camels turn round and hold down their heads. The great fear is not of being poisoned, as Europeans commonly think, but of being stifled by the sand.

But melancholy accidents sometimes happen in

this desert; as may be seen from the following account furnished by an Arabian merchant who was travelling in a caravan. Their guide left the proper track in order to avoid a notorious robber who infested the district, and in doing so lost his way. The calamitous result was given in words to the following effect.

When we had performed five days' journey in the mountains, our stock of water was exhausted; and we did not yet know where we were in the wide desert. We determined therefore to go towards the setting sun, hoping thus to reach some part of the Nile. No relief appeared; and during a márch of two days without water, one merchant and fifteen slaves sunk down exhausted and died. Another feeling that he could not hold out much longer, and hoping that his camels might find the road to water better than men could, had himself tied on one of his beasts, and let them take their own way; but we never heard more of them, and they doubtless perished. After another day's journey, we came in sight of a mountain which some of us knew, but neither we nor our camels could travel farther. We laid ourselves under a rock to obtain a little shelter from the sun, and sent two of our strongest servants and camels to go and search for water. Our existence depended upon their success.

The two men pushed forwards, but before they reached the mountain where they hoped to find a well, one of them succumbed and fell from his camel. Unable to speak, he waved his hand for his companion to leave him to his fate, and to hasten onward. The other knew the country well, having frequently passed that way; but his eyesight failed from thirst, and he lost the road. Exhausted, he sat down under a tree, and tied the beast to one of its branches. The camel smelled water at a distance, broke its halter, and set off for the spring, which proved to be half an hour's journey from the spot where the man lay. Knowing the instinct of the animal, and assured that it was hastening to water, he got up and tried to follow its steps, but soon fell down and swooned. A Bedouin from the neighbourhood passing by, and seeing him in this condition, threw some water on his face and revived him. When he was restored, they hastened to the well, filled their skins, and returned to the place where we were lying. They found us still alive, though we had given ourselves up to death. Water quickly revived us, and after a short time we were able to pursue our journey, and we reached our destination in safety. We gave the Bedouin a slave for his trouble in saving our lives.

Instead of turning to the south from Sennaar, in order to have a peep at Nubia, we might have proceeded eastward with a caravan to Abyssinia. As this is the only independent country of native Africans who have retained a profession of Christianity, it may be well to see if their religion has done them any good, and made them superior to Mussulmen and Pagans. We fear, alas! that they are no better than their neighbours. Their religion is a mere formalism, of which they are very tena-

cious; it has no vitality whatever. Into the par-
ticulars of their creed we shall not enter, nor even
describe their ecclesiasticism. It much resemble the
Greek church in its forms, and in its utter want of religious principle. The laws of God seem to be entirely
disregarded, and the morality enjoined by Scrip-
ture to be quite ignored. There are three principal
sects of nominal Christians bitterly opposed to each
other, and the country has been torn by civil and
religious broils, which have threatened to exter-
minate the population.

Even since Mr. Bruce visited Abyssinia, where he
was detained for some years, it seems to have lost
much of its power and its barbaric splendour. Yet
it has not improved in simplicity. In Gondar, the
capital, haughty kings used to imitate many of the
customs of the ancient Persians, and they possessed
a large degree of authority which has passed away
with its attending pomp. Fifty years of civil wars
and constant broils with its neighbours, have greatly
reduced the kingdom, and changed the customs of
royalty.

Eighty years ago! What may not happen in
eighty years? Even in the fifty years which elapsed
between the visit of Bruce and that of Dr. (now
Bishop) Gobat, matters were greatly altered, and they
are now still more changed. The grandfather was
quite a different personage from the grandson. It is
curious, and it may be instructive, to observe the
contrast. A right royal despot was Mr. Bruce's
friend and detainer. We shall take a peep into

that traveller's book, and give a few cursory notes
of what was then passing in Gondar.   The crown was
a kind of helmet, in the form of a mitre, covering
the forehead, cheeks, and neck of the monarch.   Its
exterior was of gold and silver, of beautiful filligree
work.   The king put it on himself, after anointing
his own head with olive oil.   He covered his face in
giving audiences and on other public occasions, so
that nothing but his eyes were seen.   Mystery in-
spires feelings of homage!   He never walked but on
going into church, when his guards possessed the
entrances and kept out all people, save two officers
on whom he leaned.   He rode on his mule into his
palace, up stairs, and over his Persian carpets, to the
very foot of his divan.   He had six noblemen of the
bedchamber, and many other officers of state.   It was
death to sit on the king's seat.   He ate wheaten
bread grown in a certain province called the royal
province.

Persons presented to the king prostrated themselves before him.   They fell on their knees, then
on the palms of their hands, then stooped till their
forehead touched the ground, and they lay there till
told to rise.   This ceremony was mitigated in the
case of strangers, who were allowed to salute the
Abyssinian monarch in the same way as they do their
own sovereign.   To strangers of note, the king
allotted a village or two, which furnished them with
supplies of food.   He sent for any woman he pleased
to have, and made her his wife or concubine without
ceremony.   But the chief wife alone was queen.

When he elected a lady to this honour, the judge
pronounced in his presence and on his behalf, that
the king has chosen his handmaid Itaghe; then the
crown was placed on her head.   As there were many
royal princes, and only one could succeed to the
throne, the rest were sent to a mountain, where they
were maintained at the public expense.   The crown
was hereditary, but elective in the royal line; so that
the eldest son of the late monarch did not necessarily succeed his father.   This was in order to save
the country from an infant king.

The morals of the palace were imitated by the
people.   They had no marriage form, and no matrimonial bond, but that of consent, for as long a time
as the parties pleased.   The men used not to market
or carry bread or water, yet they washed all clothes,
even those of the women.   The women were covered
from the chin to the ground, it being a disgrace to
have even their hands or feet seen in public.   Will
you keep this in memory, and then receive, if you
can, this strange account of a bacchanalian revelry,
which Mr. Bruce describes as a real occurrence!

The guests are assembled in a quiet hall.   A living
bullock is bound and laid down outside the door.
A slight incision is made in its neck to save the
letter of the law, that its blood must fall on the
ground.   The skin is stripped from its buttock, and
thin pieces of flesh are cut out, without touching any
of the great arteries.   These are carried into the
chamber where the guests are seated at a table, one
gentleman between two ladies.   A number of thin

cakes are provided for every guest. Then each of
the ladies takes a delicate slice of quivering flesh,
and wrapping it up in a cake, thrusts it like a
cartridge into the mouth of the gentleman next to
her, on either side; so that each man is served in
turn by two ladies. When he is crammed, he per-
forms the same good office for his fair companions.
Then they drink together, and give themselves up to
all licentiousness such as cannot be here mentioned.

Oh! Mr. Bruce; was not this a caricature of their
revelries! bad indeed, but not *so bad?* We know
that in hot countries when a killed animal is cold
and has lost the blood, it becomes awfully tough ; and
it is a fact that Abyssinians eat raw meat, especially
beef steaks; yet we are scarcely prepared to receive
all this account, as easily as you represent the
Abyssinians swallowing cartridges of quivering flesh.
We suppose you did not see all this done with your
own eyes; and would you believe anything that a
native said?

A crowd of persons beset the royal residence early
in the morning, crying for justice from the king, to
whom they appeal. Such appeals are likely to be
often made in a place of such corruption as Gondar.
Whether or not his majesty satisfies them all, when
he is at leisure to attend to them, we cannot tell.
When there were no real applicants for justice,
fictitious ones used to be hired, and they really cried
out as if they were groaning under oppression and
wrong. The reason given for this strange custom
was a fear lest the king should be melancholy, from

feeling himself alone. Justice appears to have been summary enough, and cruel enough too. A capital sentence was immediately executed; whether it was hanging, crucifying, flaying, or having the eyes torn out and being driven into the fields to be devoured by wild beasts. Let the dogs eat the bodies of criminals!

Gondar itself is situated on a hill, and contains perhaps 10,000 inhabitants, for its population is greatly reduced. Its houses are round, built of stone and clay, and thatched in form of a cone. The palace is a large square edifice, the ruins of one built by the Portuguese. A few of the rooms are still tenantable, and huts are erected beside them; the whole surrounded by a stone wall thirty feet high. The streets of the town are very narrow, crooked, filthy, and often steep, as the city lies upon a rising ground.

The country is full of churches. The kings have built many: and others have been erected by rich people, in the way of atonement for their sins. They are generally situated on the top of a hill, and near a stream, to furnish water for the usual ablutions. They are planted round with a kind of cedar and the tall cusso tree, which give them a pretty appearance. They are circular in form, thatched, and surrounded with a colonade supported by wooden pillars. They are divided in the interior, to imitate the old Jewish sanctuary. You may enter barefooted, that is, if you are *pure;* (which is not the case with many men:) otherwise you must pray among the cedars. But

Y

when you go in, take care that your shoes be not stolen by the priests or monks, if they be worth stealing. The walls are hung with pictures or daubs of saints. There are no images or carved work; as this would be a breach of the second commandment of the Decalogue, which is not supposed to be broken by a worship of pictures.

The abuna or patriarch is in some respects a man of authority, at least in religious matters. If any men come to him desiring to be made monks, he gives the word of command, and they become monks without any other ceremony. In the same summary way he makes priests and deacons. Besides these ecclesiastics, there is a chief of the monks, chief priests, and scribes or copyists. The monks live in their own houses built round the church which they serve. The whole lot of ecclesiastics are, with a few exceptions, very ignorant and very stupid. Their great delight is to wrangle about useless or contro-verted points of religion. Poor Bruce was almost losing the royal favour because he would not decide that Nebuchadnezzar was a saint. The ground for this supposed saintship was the expression that he was God's " servant." These wrangles produce incessant quarrels and excommunications, often fol-lowed by bloody broils. The people are circumcised on the eighth day.

The importance of the sovereign, and along with it the lordliness of the male sex, seem to have been on the wane during the last century in Abyssinia. Dr. Gobat represents the grandson of the monarch who pleaded for the saintship of Nebuchadnezzar, (and whom he seems to have striven to imitate,) as an old man, living in a plain way, in a little circular house built amid the ruins of the ancient palace. Three large rooms and some small ones which remained of this noble structure were full of dust and filth. His majesty contented himself with one chamber, divided into two parts by a white curtain. But this king was a monk, who had exchanged the cowl for the crown; which was a great pity. The ignorant king asked the traveller if he had ever seen

ABYSSINIAN CHIEF.

anything like his palace? and was surprised to hear that in some parts of the world, men could still build beautiful houses of stone!

Dr. Gobat only gave the king a copy of the New Testament; which his majesty returned, saying, that he had plenty of books and would rather have received a piece of cloth, silk or linen; that all other white travellers had given him something as a present: that being a monk he prayed for these generous souls, and would do the same for him, if — Truly! Both parties were wrong. For what need has a monk of silks and worldly luxuries, when he professes to be

dead to the world? Unless, indeed, he wished to
sell the present in order to pay his soldiers. For
these poor wretches were driven to such extremity
by want of food and clothes, that one night they
pillaged the town on their own account; when Dr.
Gobat took a military way of defending his own
property. On the other hand, if it be customary for
a stranger to make a present to the king, from whom
he expects protection and help without paying taxes,
he ought to comply with such a custom, and not
damage a future visitor to the country. Though the
king be a monk, and the stranger be a missionary,
yet let the usage be kept up, if it tend to keep the
way open for other travellers. These may not care
for royal prayers, but they do care for royal protection and furtherance.

Well! we must suppose that in going now to
Abyssinia, we should find it divested of some of the
gilding given in Mr. Bruce's interesting and intelligent account. Perhaps, also, we should not expect to
see the eating of raw flesh from the rump of a living
animal: and it would be long before a nice time of
peace and quiet afforded an opportunity for one of
the old bacchanalian revels. But we should not wait
long to witness some of the dark features of Abyssinian character. Their ignorance, folly, vice, and
quarrelling, do not seem to have been mended by
more than half a century of religious prostrations
and sectarian janglings.

Dr. Gobat tells us of a little commotion that was
excited in the town by an act of the royal monk,

whose coffers needed replenishing. — A thief was the day before yesterday condemned to have his right hand and two feet cut off, that so he might not be able to steal any more.   This was taking a sure way of curing his thievish propensities.   As might be expected, the rogue died in the market-place where the punishment was inflicted.   Moreover, the hyenas were not deterred from copying his example, by a fear of sharing the same fate; for they stole away his dead body during the night.   This ought not to have been: since the king had not given permission for such a burial of the corpse.   Whose fault was it, that the felon's body was missing in the morning?   Why, we might foolishly think that it was the hyenas' fault, and that the king should punish them if he could catch them.   No such thing: this is not monkish logic.   It was the fault of the people who lived near the market-place, who ought to have guarded the corpse till their sovereign allowed it to be removed. So yesterday a number of the chief merchants were summoned to the palace, reproved for their neglect, and fined in the sum of two hundred and fifty dollars. They declined to pay, and were forthwith put in prison.   This morning, they have made a virtue of necessity, and the money is forthcoming, to help the king's exchequer.   The gentlemen are released, and their wives come to thank the sovereign for his leniency in letting them off so cheaply!

Opinions were divided on the subject of whether his majesty had done right or wrong in this matter. But there was some old statute, or there was said to

be one, about the propriety of guarding the bodies
of criminals exposed *in terrorem*: and as Abyssinians are so skilful in splitting hairs as to be able
to make a "saint" out of a "servant," many contro-
versialists were on the side of the royal monk, and
thought that he had law on his side. He certainly
had "possession," which is generally said to constitute "nine points out of ten." His lordly grandfather would not have adopted such a *ruse* to gain
the tenth point; but would have got the money at
once by the royal law of "might." And in doing so,
he would not have forgotten the property of a white
stranger, who had made him no "present."

At Debaree, south of Gondar, Dr. Gobat saw in the
market a man standing chained to a lad, begging
for money and crying out, "For my life, for my life!"
It seems he had murdered another man from motives
of revenge, and was sentenced to death. But this
punishment was commuted into a fine of two
hundred dollars, which he was unable to pay; and he
was trying to "raise the wind" by begging in the
public market. Surely the merchants of Gondar were
unfairly dealt with, if they had to pay two hundred
and fifty dollars for not watching a mutilated corpse,
whilst a deliberate murderer is only fined two hundred.
Justice does not appear to hold her balances rightly
in Abyssinia, even when under the guardianship of
a monk.

That the wisdom and morals of the Abyssinians
are not improved, may be gathered from the following
incident. One day on returning home, the visitor

found an elegant lady, who threw herself at his feet, saying, "I have heard that you know all things: I entreat you to assist me. I have the means of giving you everything that you may require. I have a son who has married a woman by whom he has had children. Now, another woman has given him medicine to make him love her; and since that, he is always running after her, and will never hear a word either of his lawful wife or of his children. I entreat you to give me a medicine to make him return to his wife and children."

Yet these people, who knew no distinction between physics and ethics, would wrangle from morning till night about the inscrutable nature of the Godhead, about saints, angels, and other mysteries of religion.

At the same time, the whole country was in a state of anarchy and war: and it seemed almost a pity that the Abyssinian Nebuchadnezzar had not left a successor of like spirit with himself. The better class of natives send their children to convents to learn to read and repeat psalms. But there are no books worth reading: and few can write. Some male slaves are kept to do drudge-work: and Dr. Gobat says that men do now go to market to buy provisions, but not cloth. When he was in the province of Tigré, its king was defeated and taken by the Gallas, who beheaded him next day: and the people were several times obliged to flee from their dwellings from an approaching foe. A swarm of locusts also passed over, darkening the sun, and committing the usual ravages.

Within the last few years, a complete change has

come over the politics of Abyssinia and its neighbourhood. A young man named Kassai, of obscure
origin, whose father had been employed by the
governor in the western province of Kuara, has now
obtained the sovereignty. He was a valiant soldier
in the army, and having been recommended by his
general to Ras Ali, the latter seeing his ability gave
him his daughter in marriage, with an official appoint-
ment under the dowager queen. Kassai quarrelled
with his mistress, defeated her army, and seized her
province of Dembea. Though at first repulsed by
Ras Ali, he made another attempt, surprised his
camp, defeated him in a decisive battle, and became
master of Amhara. He subsequently reduced Tigré,
and had himself crowned "King of the kings of
Ethiopia," under the name of Theodorus. Shoa,
which had become independent of Abyssinia, was also
reduced to submission. But new troubles soon arose,
principally in Tigré; and at the close of 1858 tranquillity was not restored. Theodorus was described
in 1855 as a handsome man, of middle stature, dark
brown complexion, and keen glance of the eye.
When Dr. Krapf then visited him at his camp, he
found that the old cry for "justice" was still kept
up; the petitioners coming to the king as early as
two o'clock in the morning. He attended to their
complaints till eight. This prince was courteous and
affable to Europeans, whom he desired to settle in his
country, in order to advance the useful arts amongst
the people: and it was the earnest wish of many
that he might be able to retain the government.

HEADS OF AFRICANS IN THE LAKE DISTRICT.

Mganga, or Medicine-man.   The Porter.   The Guide.

Minuya Kidogo.   Mother and Child.

CHAP. XIV.

WOULD you wish to visit the source of the Nile? We mean the Blue River, for the origin of the White Nile, which is the more important stream, has not yet been discovered. It is hoped that this long-pending question will soon be settled, as the " whereabouts " of the source has been pretty well ascertained. Still, travellers disagree as to the precise spot, and as to whether it issues as a separate spring from the mountain, or proceeds from the lake Nyanza. We may refer to this again.

But if you would see the source of the Blue River,

you cannot do better than follow the steps of Mr.
Bruce. His accounts of the country are now found
to have been correct; and no one has given a
more true and graphic description of the people,
in everything except as to their eating flesh from
living oxen. A princess who knew this eminent
traveller was alive when Dr. Gobat visited Gondar;
and she told him that the former sultan, her own
brother, had offered to Mr. Bruce " who was greatly
respected," the present of either a good market, or
the source of the Nile. If so, we suppose the
traveller chose the latter, but was satisfied with one
view of his singular possession. Yet we must remember that much of Abyssinian narrative is apocryphal.

Starting northward from Gondar, we find the
large lake of Tsana, forty-nine miles in length by
thirty-five in breadth in its extreme parts. It has
a few islands in its bosom, the natives said " forty-
five," Mr. Bruce thought about eleven; and he
instructs us to believe *them* in *nothing!*

On the northern side of Lake Tsana we find the
town of Maitsha. It is singularly constructed. For
example: one man builds a hut at the corner of a
field which he occupies, and his relations build other
dwellings behind his in adjoining fields; and so there
comes to be a large clump of huts, back to back, under
one large common roof. The whole is surrounded
with a thick abattis or thorny hedge, for the sake
of mutual protection. Miatsha consists of these
clumps of dwellings. Oats here grow wild, and reach

in height above the head of a rider: but this corn is not used by the natives; and they could not relish Scotch oatmeal cakes, made according to the receipt of Mr. Bruce.

Keeping near the Nile, which is full of windings, we should come amongst the Agows, a wild people, who have a great veneration for the river, and will not allow it to be desecrated. Messrs. Bruce and Co. must not ride across it, nor wash off the dirt from their clothes in the sacred water. The Agows would rather carry their baggage over the stream. Here is the first cataract, sixteen feet high, and about sixty yards across. On the tops of the neighbouring hills or mountains, you would perceive beautiful plains of verdure and villages of grass. Hail sometimes falls on these mountain tops; but no snow, — a phenomenon for which the natives have no word in their language. Above an almost impenetrable wood is St. Michael. Then on a gentle rise is St. Michael Geesh, where the Nile is not four yards broad. A little farther on, you see the church placed on an eminence, and down the hill beyond it, a verdant nook.

" I ran down the hill, towards the little island of green sods, which was about two hundred yards distant. The whole side of the hill was thick grown over with flowers, the large bulbous roots of which appearing above the surface of the ground, and their skins coming off on treading upon them, occasioned me two very severe falls before I reached the brink of the marsh. I, after this, came to an island

of green turf, which was in the form of an altar,
apparently the work of art: and I stood in rapture
over the principal fountain which rises in the middle
of it." This is the source of the Blue River. But
the White River, which is regarded as the more
important branch of the Nile, rises farther north
and west. The Blue source is in 11° N. lat., and
nearly 37° E. long.

When Bruce urged his guide to drink several
toasts with water from the fountain, the latter replied, " You must excuse me if I refuse to drink any
more water. They say these savages pray over that
hole every morning to the devil; and I am afraid I
feel his horns in my belly already from the great
draught of that hellish water which I drank first."
It was very cold. Yet he drank a bumper to the
health of the Empress of Russia.

From Gondar we might take an excursion south-
east to visit Shoa, if not afraid of meeting the fate of
Dr. Krapf. He tried to come in the opposite direction, but found the route very difficult and dangerous;
and was finally plundered of everything and made
prisoner by a petty chief. He seems to have had a
narrow escape with his life. It is to be hoped that
the " King of the kings of Ethiopia" will keep a
tighter rein over his vassals and governors, than was
done by his weak predecessors in royalty. If so,
travelling in Abyssinia may become safe, — a new
and excellent thing for the country. The region is
altogether mountainous, and the people are very insubordinate. If Theodorus can do for Abyssinia what

Mehemet Ali did for Egypt and Nubia, he will be a blessing to future generations.

We shall suppose that we have accomplished this journey, and have reached Ankobar, the capital of Shoa, situated in 9° 34′ 33″ N. lat., and 39° 35′ E. long., and 8198 feet above the sea level. Shoa is now again united to Abyssinia, and placed under a governor instead of an independent king. It may be called the Ethiopian highlands. It has a rich soil, a beautiful climate, and contains iron, coal, and sulphur. The people are Christian, after the Abyssinian or Coptic fashion, — which means very little that is good. They disregard holiness and righteousness of life. They fast nearly nine months out of the twelve, — which must be a great saving to the pocket, — but their morals are very loose. The late king had five hundred wives, which is a pretty good number for a Christian king; and most of the people who could afford it kept concubines and slaves. Of course they do not appeal to the Gospel for allowance in either of these practices, or in lying, thieving, or drunkenness. They seem entirely to ignore the precepts of the Bible, and only to retain it as a book for disputation. Dr. Krapf tried to settle in Ankobar, and was successful for a time; but was afterwards forbidden to enter the country.

They have a singular order of " detectives " in Shoa, which does not say much for the march of intellect amongst them. When the Lebashi is informed of a theft having been perpetrated, he gives his servant a dose of black meal and milk, after

which he makes him smoke a quantity of tobacco.
This has the effect, or supposed effect, of putting the
lad into a frenzy : when his master leads him through
the streets by a string tied round his body, crawling
" on all fours," and smelling about like a crazed
person or a dog. By and by he enters some house,
lies down on a bed, and sleeps for a time. Then the
Lebashi arouses him by blows, and makes him
arrest the owner of the house, who is regarded as
the thief without any other evidence, and is obliged
to pay for the stolen article according to its sworn
value. No wonder every one wishes to be friendly
with the thief-taker, and to use all prudent means
of securing his favour, before he takes his walks
abroad. The King of Shoa believed, or pretended to
believe, in the magic powers of this deceiver !

All the neighbouring tribes are Gallas, under
different names and having different forms of religion. There are a few Christians amongst them,
especially in Gurague, situated in about 8° N. lat.
Others are Mahometans. Most are pagans, worship-
ping the moon, some of the stars, and the Wanzay
tree under which their kings are crowned. The
Gallas, or as they call themselves Ormas, are a fine
race, with well-formed but savage countenance,
chiefly of a dark brown colour; though some are of a
fair complexion. Hence the young women are much
sought after by slave-dealers for the Arabian market.
They besmear their body and garments with butter,
which sends forth an unpleasant odour. In some
tribes the women ride beside or behind their hus-

bands; as it is considered degrading to go on foot. The Southern Gallas lead a pastoral and nomadic life. Their houses are built on the plan of the African round huts. The pagan tribes worship spirits, and have the usual magician-doctors and exorcists. Many of them will not eat fish or fowls, supposing the former to be of the serpent, the latter of the vulture species. We shall not weary the reader with any of their forms of foolish superstition or their silly tenets.

We should like to take a peep at the people inhabiting the corner or eastern promontory of Africa below Shoa, if we could by any means reach them. The distance from Ankobar is not very great, but we should not easily cross the deserts and mountains which intervene, through the tribes of Maidaites and afterwards the Somali. The wild nature of the country, the savage disposition of the people, the bigotry and jealousy of the Moslem chiefs, form an effectual barrier against our reaching them in this way.

Captain Burton did penetrate with considerable difficulty from the eastern coast of the Red Sea to Harar, which may be adduced as a specimen of other royal residences in this region. We shall imagine ourselves there.

The palace of the Sultan of Harar is a long shed, without windows, like a barn, made of rough stones and reddish clay. It is situated in a court-yard. Take off your shoes, and give up your arms, before approaching the royal presence ! For he is as great a man in his own estimation as the Czar of Russia is

in his. You will be introduced to him seated on a
raised bench called a throne, in a dark room, the
walls of which are whitewashed. Matchlocks and
polished fetters hang upon the sides of the chamber.
The sultan wears a crimson robe edged with fur, and
a narrow turban of white colour. His relatives are beside him, having their right arms bare. He salutes
you by snapping his thumb and finger, and asks the
usual question, " What do you want here ?" " Friendship and trade." A smile is the answer, — which
is a sign that your head is safe on your shoulders :
for you are in a lion's den. A motion of the hand is
made for you to retire :. and a dinner is sent you, in
the shape of a dish of shabty, consisting of cakes
soaked in sour milk, seasoned with red pepper and
salt. Eat and be thankful ! and get away as fast as
you can, lest the despot's humour should change !
He cares little for human life.

The town of Harar is about a mile long and half
a mile wide, surrounded with an irregular wall of
rough stones. The streets are narrow, encumbered
with heaps of rubbish ; for the dustman does not go
his rounds. The better houses are sheds of two
stories ; the rest are thatched huts. The place is
famous for mosques and tombs of Mahometan saints,
showing that it was once a large and powerful city.
The present population may be estimated at 8000
settled inhabitants : but the roving character of the
Bedouins makes it very fluctuating. Their religious
fanaticism is great, and their morals proportionately
loose. The Somali say that " Harar is a paradise

inhabited by asses." The people wear the usual tobe and sandals; to which some add drawers. If they abstain according to Moslem law from intoxicating liquors, they make up for its want by chewing tobacco, which is grown in the district. So also is excellent coffee.

You would reach Harar from Zaylah, a pretty good town on the coast, situated on a jutting bank of sand, with a half-savage population, consisting principally of Somali. It has had many masters, and is now said to belong to the Sheriff of Mocha, who farms it to a chief of the neighbourhood. Passing into the interior, the traveller must cross wild mountains, desert and fertile plains, forests and rivers. The frequent visits of roving marauders and wild beasts, who may be classed together, would require you to be continually on the watch during your journey. Encampments and villages would occasionally be met with.

We come to a village. It is a straggling concern, composed of a disorderly assemblage of mud huts. On entering one of these rude dwellings, through an aperture stopped by a moveable plank, we find an apartment divided into three spaces by low walls of wattled cane. One of these is for the men, another for the women, another for the cattle. The thatch is jetty with smoke, which is seldom allowed to escape; for smoke and dirt are enjoyed by the inhabitants, who deem them accessory to warmth. They are an indolent set of people; the men having

z

little to do besides tending their cattle; and the domestic arrangements of the women not being very recondite. They pound the grain of holcus and make it into cakes, which are eaten with sour milk, or with meat and broth.

Let us suppose an encamped tribe to be migrating. The master of the ceremonies shouts aloud, " Fetch your camels! Load your goods! we march!" The whole process of flitting is soon accomplished, and the heterogeneous assemblage moves forward. The stock may probably consist of two or three hundred cows, six or seven thousand camels, and twice as many sheep and goats. These are driven in divisions by two hundred spearmen, attended by boys and large pariah dogs. The sick and weak of the flock are carried on camels. Then comes the furniture of the tents, cooking apparatus, and extra apparel, packed on camels led by young women. The matrons follow, carrying their babies in shoulder lappets on their backs. The elder children are also used for baby carriers. The cavalcade proceeds at a slow pace, without much regard to order or quiet.

The Somali and their neighbours are armed with the spear and bow, and are much afraid of fire-arms, which they call an unfair and cowardly weapon, as bullets make no distinction between a brave man and a coward. Some of them used poisoned arrows, which we should think to be quite as cowardly. This poison is very deadly. It is obtained from an evergreen resembling a bay tree, round in form, growing to the height of twenty feet. Its root is something like liquorice, which is macerated, and the poison extracted by a particular process.

After these excursions to the south-eastern countries, we return to Gondar, that we may take a southerly route into the tropical heart of Africa. Not that we should like to travel in this direction, until we had more confidence in the people through whom we must pass. For, contrary to the supposition of ancient geographers, the equatorial regions are not burned up with the scorching sun so as to be uninhabitable. Nature has provided a black skin for the natives; and by this simple arrangement, men like ourselves, except in colour and mental ability, live and labour under the rays of a vertical sun.

Can we draw a bill of credit upon any of these natives? Shall we believe the accounts which they give of their own country? What confidence can we place in their testimony? Very little, certainly, if their interests were concerned in telling a lie; for they have no idea of truth being a virtue. But in ordinary conversation they may tell us pretty correctly what they have seen and heard; and if several of them, under different circumstances, give us similar information, we may place a general reliance on their description of men and manners. In this way only can we fill up a considerable void in our map of Africa, and connect the discoveries of late travellers. Krapf, Beke, Petherick, Burton, Speke, and Livingstone reached certain points of the interior; and there they received accounts from merchants and slaves, of countries beyond the range of their own personal adventure, which they have published for our edification. These accounts are generally meagre, but they afford an outline of parts of this "undiscovered" land. We therefore take them for what they are worth; trusting to the general statement, but not giving much credence to minute details, especially those in which the informants themselves were concerned. For all these people love to make a fine story about themselves, their adventures, and their heroism !

Let us travel for a few minutes in company with the tongue of Dilbo, a native of Sabba in Gnarea, who served Dr. Krapf in Ankobar, by order of the King of Shoa. This man, according to his own tale, had some experience of the countries south of Abyssinia. In his youth he had accompanied a band of slave-hunters to Kaffa, and thence to the neighbourhood of the Dokos (about whom we shall presently speak). In turn, an attack was made on Sabba, when he was captured and sold at Agabja for forty pieces of salt, and afterwards at Gonan for sixty pieces. His price was raised at Roggie to eighty pieces, and afterwards in Abeju to a hundred. At last a Mahometan gave silver for him in Aliwamba, to the amount of twelve dollars; and a widow in Ankobar transferred him to herself for fourteen. At her death he became the property of her brother, whose goods were confiscated by the King of Shoa, who lent the lad to Dr. Krapf. Such is part of the history of a slave! What was the remainder?

What a volume poor Dilbo might have written!
What a harvest of information he obtained, without
the trouble of sowing; and the crop was useless to
him, except to think about in his meditative hours!
Let us pick up a few gleanings, as we wish to
journey through these countries.

We could go, if we were native merchants, by a
caravan from Gondar to Gnarea; and if we were
willing to brave the difficulties and dangers of the
route for " filthy lucre's sake."   Most of the people
are Moslems, and their language is a dialect of
Galla.   Coffee grows wild, and is so abundant that
the tree is used for fuel.   The wilderness is full of
wild beasts, especially elephants.   The king is a
brave warrior and good ruler, who, sitting on a
wooden throne covered with a skin, administers
" justice " to all who come for it.   His capital, Saka,
contains 12,000 (?) people.   There are said to be
white elephants and white buffaloes in this vicinity,
which animals are held sacred.   Gnarea is a mountainous district.

Proceeding southward, we should reach the river
Gojob in twelve or fifteen days, and then come to
Kaffa, and its capital Suni, which is built on a hill.
The houses are of wood, thatched, and mean compared with those of Abyssinia.   Queen Balli was
sovereign when Dilbo visited Kaffa.   This bold
woman had seized the helm of government on the
death of her husband, and making her son general
of the army, took upon herself the management of
the home department.   She kept much retired; but

z 3

when she appeared in public, required due honour
to be paid to her rank; so that her dainty black feet
must walk on cloths spread before her.   The people
are partly Christian, of a very degenerate kind.   The
men have a place of public resort which no woman
can enter, where they spend the day together, only
seeing their wives at night.   A woman must not eat
or drink with her husband, under penalty of three
years' imprisonment.   Yet this does not seem to tally
with their obeying a female monarch, does it?   The
country has inward tranquillity, but wages perpetual
wars with its neighbours.

Could we travel safely through .these jarring
. elements of the human species, we should next arrive
amongst a singular species of men, the Dokos.   They
are a race of pigmies, only four feet high, of a dark
olive colour, living in a state of complete savagism.
They have no chiefs, law, clothing, or houses; pursue no art, not even that of agriculture; but live on
fruits, roots, mice, serpents, ants, and wild honey.
They have thick protruding lips, flat noses, and
small eyes; their hair, not woolly, is worn by the
women over their shoulders.   Their nails are allowed
to grow long, like the talons of vultures, in order to
dig up ants, and tear in pieces the flesh of serpents
which they devour raw.   The Dokos multiply rapidly,
but are hunted down by all their neighbours, to
whom they offer no resistance.   When captured,
they become docile and obedient slaves, who live on
a little, and are therefore prized by the people of
those countries.   This account of the Doko pigmies

has been corroborated by evidence from other quarters; and when Dr. Krapf was at Barava, a slave was shown to him of this description, said to have been brought from the liliputian race of the interior.

Somewhere on the left of the route which we have taken, is the kingdom of Senjero, where human sacrifices are offered to the supposed deities. In an olden time when the seasons were so jumbled together that the fruits would not ripen, the sorcerers ordered some children to be slain, and their blood poured on the throne and on the broken base of an iron pillar which stood at the entrance of the town, and which they commanded to be broken. The seasons then became regular; and in order to keep them right, certain families are obliged to deliver up their first-born sons, who are sacrificed at an appointed time. In imitation of these people, and from a crude superstitious fear, the slave-dealers on leaving Senjero throw a beautiful female slave into the Lake Umo.

It will thus appear that the natives get more savage as we approach the equator. From the pigmy Dokos we take a south-westerly course, in a stride of about 300 miles, to reach the tribes of independent Unyoro, who live in latitudes a little north of the equator. Our readers must really excuse this summary way of getting over a very wild and burning country, the inhabitants of which are rude in the extreme. This is, in fact, all that we know about them; and we have no desire for a near acquaintance, lest we should be murdered, sacri-

ficed, eaten, enslaved, or at least stripped of everything and left to starve in the wilderness. For the
same reason, we have taken a circuitous route, and
not one directly south from Darfur, which would
have been the shortest way into the regions which
we shall now visit.

Look at these slaves brought from the Unyoro!
They are of a dull black colour, with flattish heads,
prominent eyes, and projecting lower jaw, tattooed
in large botches encircling the forehead. They will
tell you about the land of their birth; that it
abounds in cattle and ivory, and is so hot that the
inhabitants care little about clothing. They think
that the Unyoro are a wide-spread people, composing
a number of independent tribes, perhaps under
different names, living about the northern parts of
the Lake Nganza or Victoria.

Passing through them, we enter the powerful
kingdom of Uganda, which lies under the equator,
and has subdued the dependent Unyoro who dwell on
its southern border. Let us listen for a moment to
an Arab merchant, whilst he tells us of his visit to
the capital of Uganda and its potent king. " Kibuja
is not less than a day's journey in length (!); the
buildings are of cane and rattan. The sultan's
palace is at least a mile long; and the circular huts,
neatly ranged in line, are surrounded by a strong
fence which has only four gates. Bells at the several
entrances announce the approach of strangers, and
guards in hundreds attend there at all hours. The
harem contains 3000 souls,—concubines, slaves, and

children. This palace has often been burned down
by lightning; on which occasions the warriors must
assemble and extinguish the fire by rolling over it.
The chief of Uganda has but two wants with which
he troubles his visitors, — one, a medicine against
death; the other, a charm to avert the thunderbolt;
and immense wealth would reward the man who
could supply either of these desiderata." (The late
king, the mighty Suna, was struck by the shaft of
the destroying angel in 1857, whilst riding in state
— that is, on his minister's shoulders — in the
midst of his army. Custom compels the new king
to live two years in retirement, during which time
his ministers have an opportunity of driving the
state coach.)

"The army of Uganda numbers 300,000 men (!),
each of whom brings an egg to the muster, and thus
something like a reckoning of the people is made. A
soldier carries one spear, two assegais, a large dagger,
and a shield; bows and swords being unknown.
They fight to the sound of drums, which are beaten
with sticks like those of the Franks; should this
performance cease, all fly the field. When the king
has no foreign enemies, or when his exchequer is
indecently low, he feigns a rebellion, attacks one of
his own provinces, massacres the chief men, and sells
off the peasantry. Executions are frequent, a score
being often slain at a time, to keep his subjects in
awe of him.

"Suna never appeared in public without a spear.
His dress was the national costume, a long piece of

fine bark cloth extending from the neck to the
ground. He was a terrible despot, boasting to the
Arabs that he was the god of earth, as their Allah
was Lord of Heaven. He claimed divine honours,
which his subjects readily paid; but was terribly
angry with the lightning. He shut up his sons,
numbering more than a hundred, in early youth, and
chained them in separate dungeons, where they must
continue till death, if not wanted for the throne.
He was awfully rigorous in justice (?); the only
punishments being death and fines. He was very
liberal to Arab merchants, whom he encouraged to
trade in his capital."

When Snay Ben Ameer arrived with a caravan,
the sultan ordered the erection of as many tents as
he might require, and sent him large presents of
bullocks and grain, plantains, and sugar-canes.
When after a repose of three or four days he was
summoned to the audience hall, he found 2000
guards outside armed only with staves. Suna was
seated on a cushion of bark cloth, dressed as usual;
two spears were near him; and his favourite dog, a
kind of greyhound, was by his side. The ministers
sat at a distance of fifty paces, between the king and
his guards; and the principal women were placed
out of sight, behind the visitor's back. The chamber
was lit with torches. A conversation took place
about Zanzibar and the politics of the whole country.
When tired of it, the despot rose up, and the meeting
dispersed. Snay received immediately whatever he
wanted; and it was intimated to the "king's stranger"

Ivory Porter.   PORTERS OF EAST AFRICA.   Woman.

Cloth Porter in Usugara.

that he might lay hands on whatever he pleased,
animate or inanimate. The Arab was wary of in-
dulging this prerogative. When he departed he
received a present of provisions for the road, and an
offer of two hundred guards to escort him. Suna
allowed no travellers to go north of Kibuja, lest the
distinction conferred by their visit should be shared
by inferior chiefs. He had a flotilla on the lake
Nyanza.

Crossing the river Kitanzure, which flows into this
lake, you would enter Karagwak, a hilly but fruitful
district, with a high range of mountains and rich
valleys. A tall, stout race of people inhabit these
highlands, where female beauty is (like amongst the
Moors) chiefly estimated by corpulence. Both sexes
are clad with the mbugu or short kilt, here made
of bark cloth. Their villages of shabby round huts
are scattered over the hills. Though the king has
a large store of fine cloth, presented to him by
strangers, yet he prefers the free and easy costume
of his subjects; from whom he distinguishes himself
by a pair of tight gaiters made of beads, reaching
from below the ancle to the knee. His palace consists of forty or fifty huts in a settlement by itself.
A pastoral people, the Wotoso, somewhat like the
Foolas of Senegambia, are scattered through this
country, the southern frontier of which is in about
2° 40′ S. lat. The next people are the Usui, who
bear a very bad name amongst travellers.

All this time, you have on the east of your route
the Lake Nyanza; whilst on the west are some

unknown tribes who merge into the Uzige and Urundi, on the northern parts of the lake Tanganyika. These newly-discovered lakes will require a passing notice.

Lake Nyanza or Victoria must be carefully distinguished from Lake Nyassi or Maravi, which lies a considerable distance to the south. (Much geographical confusion has arisen from supposing them to be the same.) The southern point of Lake Nyanza is in 2° 24' S. lat.; the middle of the expanse is about 33° E. long.; and it is 3750 feet above the sea level. Its water is very clear and sweet. There are some islands in its bosom, inhabited by a very savage and naked race of people. It has not been ascertained how far north it extends, but probably to the second or third degree of N. lat. Captain Burton judges, with much reason, that it occupies a hollow in the back parts of the "Mountains of the Moon," and that it is separated by a high ridge from the range which gives birth to the White Nile.

The ordinary caravan route would lead you from the south of Lake Nyanza, through Usukuma, to Kazeh the principal town of Unyanyembe. You might be surprised to find such a thriving place in the midst of a savage region. But it owes its prosperity to Arabs of the tribe of Omani, who have made it a central depot of merchandise for this part of Africa. Bringing their goods from the eastern coast opposite to Zanzibar, they send them from Unyanyembe to the tribes already noticed on the north, to the Lake Tanganyika on the west, and to a great many tribes on the south and south-west, including those around the Rukwa water or lake, which is situated between 6° and 7° S. lat., in the neighbourhood of a noted ivory mart.

There is nothing here which resembles a town. The Arabs live in oblong houses of clay called tembe, built after the fashion of those which we have seen in Central Africa. A verandah in front forms their usual lounging place, whence a strong door leads to a vestibule in which visitors can be received : then a passage conducts to a court-yard, where are separate chambers for the master and his goods, his harem and his slaves. This style of dwelling has been adopted by a few native chiefs and traders in the eastern districts. The Arab colonists of Unyanyembe do not exceed twenty or thirty; they seem to live very comfortably, and even splendidly. Their houses form little castles, substantial and capable of defence; their harems are well filled; their gardens are stocked with fruits and vegetables; they have flocks, herds, and slaves; and they receive regular supplies of wheat, fine rice, fruits, clothes, and whatever else they desire, by their caravans from the sea coast. But the climate is prejudicial to health.

A fine, enterprising, independent set of men are these Arabs; and the chief commerce of the lake districts is owing to their presence. About half a dozen of them are stationed at Kazeh, and others in adjoining places; the Negroes dwelling in clusters of hovels in their vicinity. They received the European travellers with great urbanity, and aided them in pursuing their

discoveries. Here your can recruit your stock of
African currency, which consists of beads, cloth, and
wire ; and along with ammunition you may procure
various comforts, including spices and drugs. The
Wanyamwezi of this region are the principal porters
of the merchandise of the caravans; as no adequate

A MNYAMWEZI.   A MHEHA.

beasts of burden have been reared to traverse a
country so diversified in its scenery and climate.

If you should be taken ill here, which is very likely
to happen in the rainy season, a doctor will be
strongly recommended. He tries the cautery, coat-
ings of powdered ginger, and similar counter-irritants.
Should his art fail, he insists that you are poisoned,
and that you ought to see a mganga or witch, celebrated for the cures which she has performed. The
old hag makes her appearance. She is covered with
wrinkles, "with a greasy skin, black as soot, set off

by a mass of tin-coloured pigtails; her arms adorned
with copper bangles, like manacles; and the impli-
ments of her craft, as usual, a girdle of small gourds,
dyed red-black with oil and use." She first demands
and receives her fee; and then proceeds to search
the mouth, and to inquire about poison. This question is perhaps a proof that deadly herbs are used
in the country. Taking a powder from one of her
gourds, and mixing it with water, she administers it
like snuff, so as to cause a violent sneezing. She
hails this sign with shouts of joy, then rubs the head
with another powder, and retires promising a cure.
But her propensities for intoxicating drink, which the
fee enables her to indulge, prevent her returning on
the morrow to see her patient.

Before visiting the other lake, which lies to the
west and reaches nearly to the centre of the continent, we had better glance at the people who live
between Kazeh and the eastern coast. It is a caravan route, with stations and villages at no great
distance from each other; so that there is little fear
of starvation from hunger or thirst, to the person
that is supplied with the money which "answereth
to all things." Nor will an armed party be in much
fear of robbers. Still, no one who reads the volumes
of Captain Burton's travels, will wish to take this
journey. The inconveniences and annoyances which
a traveller must endure are most oppressive, and
almost insufferable. It is difficult to say whether
the men or asses are most difficult to manage. The
latter are only half tamed, and are most unruly

animals, kicking, plunging, falling down, straying, and never going above two miles an hour, unless a stick is constantly applied by a person behind. By their misdemeanours you might sustain bruises on your body, loss of property, and be sometimes obliged to carry your own pack.

All the natives, escort, guides, carriers, slaves, and villagers, are as bad as bad can be; idle, cowardly, thievish, full of every kind of trick and deception. Your own hired people are insubordinate, quarrelsome, and ready to desert at a moment's notice. They stop when they please, hurry on when you wish them to go slow, and creep when you want them to hasten, always grumbling, and getting drunk whenever they can. The climate of this eastern region is oppressive, and subject to great alternations of heat and cold, fog and sunshine, fair weather and teeming rains. The *tzetse* appear here, and are not so respectful to men and asses as in the districts traversed by Dr. Livingstone; for they are very annoying to both species, though their bite is not fatal to them.

Proceeding eastward, you would first pass through a series of low jungles and desert plains inhabited principally by Wayamwesi. Black-mail is exacted by the chief of every place through which you pass; and it often requires a considerable time to settle the tax that must be paid. One of these petty "sultans" may be described as a sample of the rest: a tall, large-limbed, angular man, with a black and wrinkled skin; the grease and oil which drop from his pigtails imparting their unctuosity to the whole of his body. A cloth round his loins, and a tobe thrown over his shoulders, partially cover his gaunt limbs; whilst a portion of his legs and ankles are concealed with a deep ornament of brass and copper wire, and his sandals are decorated with discs of white shells.

· The Wagogo next attract your attention, in the table-land of Ugogo; a tribe of Negroes who seem to have mixed much with the Arab race, being greatly superior to their neighbours in physical appearance and attention to dress. Most of them have fine forms, and some of their females are handsome in a high degree. Similar remarks may be made on the Wahumba, who live to the north of the Wagogo.

Ascending the Usagara mountains, you come amongst the Wasagara, a set of short, black, beardless men; their only covering being a goat-skin apron slung over one shoulder. Their sultan is described as a little, grizzled old man, with wide mouth, a drunkard's eyes, a very thin beard, wearing long and straggling hair. His dress differed little from that of the sultan of Rubuga, but he wore a number of necklaces. Thus within a short distance, we find three contiguous tribes wholly differing in their physiological appearance!

Here the African sycamores abound. The branches of this splendid tree extend more than a hundred feet, and with their thick foliage form a most agreeable shade from a vertical sun. The fruit is a miserable fig, or rindy berry, eaten for want of other food. There are two species, one having a larger and thicker

A A

leaf than the other, and a loftier trunk or set of trunks.

The Rubero range of mountains, 5700 feet above the sea level, now crosses the traveller's route, and he must scramble as he best can through its difficult passes, intersected by numerous streams and deep gorges. In some parts of the "Tamarind" hills, Captain Burton and his party saw a great many skeletons lying about, the remains of porters and slaves who had perished from fatigue and the small-pox, which was committing frightful ravages amongst the natives. The climate of these islands is clear, balmy, and refreshing; so that in coming from the coast, you here first meet with the trees, beasts, and birds that prevail in the interior of Africa. For between these hills and the coast, the ground is low and covered with marshy jungles, over which rain or thick mist generally hangs.

The inhabitants of this steamy district are very degraded. The Wadoe, relics of a powerful tribe, are said to drink out of rough skulls. Their chiefs are buried with their bead ornaments in a sitting posture, and so that their forefinger may project above ground. Each is accompanied in his grave by a male and female slave, who are buried alive with their master's corpse, that they may wait upon him in the future state. The woman is seated on a little stool, supporting his head on her lap; the man is furnished with a bill-hook, to procure fuel for his lord in the other world! The Wakhutu are very mean in their physical appearance, in their worldly circum-

PARTY OF WAN'HUTU WOMEN.

stances, and in their moral character. They live in wretched huts, on dwarf cones of land which rise above the swamps. The vegetation of these marshes is so rank that grass grows upwards of twelve feet, and has stalks nearly as thick as a man's finger. These are famous lurking-places for runaway slaves and rogues; and the traveller has often to fight his way, as through a dense screen, receiving from time to time a severe blow from the recoil of the reeds, or a painful thrust from a broken stump inclined towards him. This is therefore a laborious, oppressive, and dangerous part of the journey.

The Wazaramo, next to the Arabs of the coast, have gained no advantage by their slight contact with a species of civilisation. They wear, as the peculiar badge or ornament of their tribe, a variegated collar of beads. They mat their hair into a number of forms with a pomatum of clay and oil; and their ordinary apparel is the loin cloth. They are impetuous, noisy, and impracticable; delighting only in revelry and drunkenness; having no religion but a few "customs" or superstitions of a fanciful nature.

A much shorter road to Lake Nyanza than that adopted by Captain Burton might be found from the coast: but the lawless character of the people prevents it being followed. Both Messrs. Rebmann and Krapf endeavoured to reach the interior from Mombaz; the former by way of Jaggar, the latter by way of Kikayu. But they were obliged to abandon their enterprise, after being plundered of their effects, and exposed to great hardships, and Dr. Krapf especially

to much danger. Their accounts of the impractica-
bility of the chiefs and people, and the bad conduct
of their own "porters," differ little from those which
we have already given.

Most people would find more comfort in reading
our description of the route from Kazeh to the coast,

AFRICAN STANDING POSITION.

which is far from being exaggerated, than in performing so laborious a pilgrimage. We can say little
better of a journey westward. However, it must be
pursued, at least in the pages of this volume. You
are therefore to suppose yourself back at Kazeh, due
south of Lake Nyanza, to traverse the district which

lies between you and Lake Tanganyika, by a westerly route.

The tribes through which you must now pass are similar to those already mentioned; only, there are small settlements of Arab merchants on the way, which greatly facilitates the transit of a caravan. The most important of these little colonies is at Msene, among the Wasumbah, who live in clusters of thatched huts, surrounded with stockades and moats for the purpose of defence. Their chief or sultan, savage in his appearance and dress, rules with a tight hand, and claims the most abject submission from his people, who never approach him but on their knees and with clapping of hands. The currency is in porcelain beads, the favourite colour of which is constantly changing by the freaks of fashion. This place is so exceedingly debauched in morals, that it is a kind of Circæan rendezvous for the most dissolute negroes of the district; and makes most caravans lose some of their porters, who are tempted to desert, that they may indulge for a season in boisterous revelry.

The whole of the region between and about the two lakes is called the "land of the moon," and is a garden of intertropical Africa; being pretty thickly set with small villages, and abounding in luxuriant vegetation. The ground is flat, but intersected with low conical or tabular hills. It is very productive of fevers and influenzas, which are as much dreaded here as in England; since the bodily constitution of the people is radically weak, and cannot bear up against

fierce distempers. These Wanyamwezi are of a dark
sepia colour, tall, and stoutly built, with crispy hair,
and thin short beards. Certain tattoo marks distinguish their different tribes or clans from each
other. Their usual dress is a kilt of cloth or soft
leather. Their favourite ornaments are beads, rings
of brass, and coils of copper or iron wire. Wives are
purchased, and polygamy is the order of the day
with those who can afford it. The sickness of a chief
often causes the death of many persons. It is as-
cribed to magic, and a mganga or sorcerer is summoned to find out the culprit. This he does by
inspecting the inside of a mystic fowl, which has
been killed and split into two parts. Blackness
or blemish about the wing is supposed to denote
treachery in children or kinsmen; in the backbone
it convicts mother and grandmother; in the tail it
accuses the wives, and in the thighs the concubines;
in the shanks or feet it condemns the common slaves.
When a class has thus been fixed upon as criminals,
its members are collected by the mganga, who
throws up another drugged hen, and singles out the
individual on whom it alights. Confession of guilt
is extorted by torture, and instant death is the
punishment. Men are speared, clubbed, beheaded,
or have their head crushed; women are impaled. If
the chief be long of recovering or dying, many victims are sacrificed; since the "custom" is continued
until some issue of his disease takes place. When
his disorder is the debility of intemperance and age,
many precede him into the other world; for in one

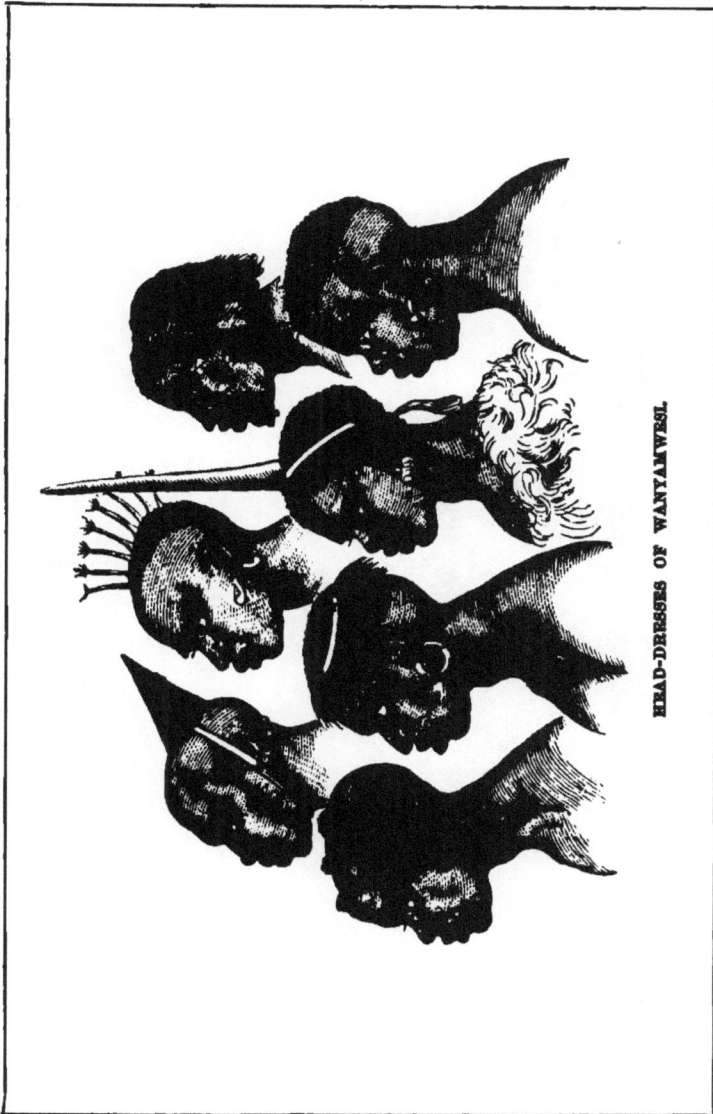

HEAD-DRESSES OF WANYAMWEZI.

house no less than eighteen persons, male and female, have been sacrificed to this horrid delusion.

Proceeding through jungle and swamps, you would reach Ujiji on the borders of the Lake Tanganyika, the great slave mart of these regions. The Wajiji and other neighbouring tribes do not materially differ from those which we have passed through. The lake is 1850 feet above the sea level, about 250 miles in length, and has an average breadth of twenty miles. Would you like to navigate this inland sea? Then you must sail in a rude canoe formed of a hollowed trunk, and propelled by paddles; creeping along dreary shores, which are skirted by miserable hamlets. Your savage crew howl, yell, and make an incessant noise with horns and tom-toms; an uncouth and ungovernable race of savages, who stop to smoke, eat, or wrangle, whenever they please. When going from Ujiji to the northern extremity of the lake, in order to avoid its inhospitable coasts, natives generally cross over opposite the island Ubwari, "a long, narrow lump of rock, twenty to twenty-five geographical miles long, by four or five of extreme breadth, with a high longitudinal spine, like a hog's back." Some parts are cultivated by its wild inhabitants, who are much feared by dwellers on the mainland. At the top of the lake is Uvira, a depot for young slaves, ivory, bark-cloth, grain, and iron ware, which are cheap here.

The Uzige live north of the lake, and to the west of them are the Wavira; south of whom are the Wubembe cannibals, and the Wagomu highlanders, who supply trees for the large canoes. The Waguhha possess the islands in the southern part of the lake; and through their country is the route to Uruvwa, at a distance of nine long stages, where the coast-trade terminates. Fifteen marches farther south would bring a traveller to Usenda, the capital of the chief Kazembe. Such are the accounts given by Arab traders of a region hitherto untrod by Europeans.

CHAP. XV.

As Lake Nyanza lies about the equator, and the
western side of Lake Tanganyika is nearly in the
longitudinal centre of Africa, the eastern half of its
central regions have been pretty well accounted for
by recent discoveries.   But what is contained in the
western half?   Here some vacancies in the map
remain to be filled up.   But a little insight into a
portion of this space has been given us (whilst this
volume has been in the press) by Monsieur Du
Chaillu, who penetrated from the western coast to a
distance of about 400 miles, between 2° north and
2° south latitude.   From his account we learn that

the coast range of mountains has other mountains
behind it; and, especially, that a little south of the
equator, a high range runs inward for several hundred
miles, extending beyond 14° east longitude.   This
hilly region is intersected by rivers, the courses of
which are not fully described.   Most of this country
consists of vast forests, inhabited by hostile tribes, who
wage incessant war with each other, and with wild
beasts and venomous reptiles which seem to claim
possession of the soil.   The people are very rude
and demoralised, given to witchcraft and similar
superstitions.

Some of the innermost tribes visited by Du Chaillu,
and others lying beyond his field of enterprise, are
addicted to cannibalism, feasting on the bodies of
enemies though not of friends.   Hence it appears
that the Africans living about the equator are unusually degraded; and this is probably the case
through the whole breadth of the continent.

Certain localities of this district are infested with
gorillas. This singular animal, of the monkey family,
approaches nearer to the human species in its form
and habits than the chimpanzee, ourang-outang, or
any other creature with which we are acquainted;
but it strikingly differs in the formation of the brain.
A full-grown gorilla is at least six feet high, very
muscular and strong, far surpassing the strength of
a man; so that it can break a tree of three or four
inches diameter with the greatest ease.   Its bones
are large and thick, its arms long, its chest ample, its
legs strong.   It is covered with hair, which is longer

in the female than in the male; and *has no tail*. It lives in caves, and feeds on vegetable produce, not

GORILLA.

eating flesh of any description. Its innate savage-ness is visible in its ferocious looks, especially in its

large and deep eye-balls; and it cannot be tamed.
The gorillas destroy all other animals in the vicinity
of their habitat, refusing to have friendly intercourse
with any other creature. Woe to the luckless
hunter who misses his aim, or fails to disable a
gorilla which he is pursuing; for it would instantly
pounce upon him, wrench his musket from his
hands, and beat out his brains with his own weapon.
Yet this creature is so devoid of everything like
"common sense," that although it enjoys warming
itself by a fire left by the negroes, it never thinks of
adding fuel to keep it burning.

As the localities in which it resides are very
limited, the species will probably become extinct, as
soon as man there becomes more civilised.

If we were to visit the innermost of the Fan and
other cannibals, such as the Osheba and Mashobo
(which we have no desire of doing); a stride of 400
or 500 miles would bring us somewhere in the
country of Matiamvo; which we might have reached
by a similar stride from the south of Lake Tanganyika. This distance, or even a shorter one from
Uruvwa (if the Arabs' account be correct), separates
the tribes described by Captain Burton from those
described by Dr. Livingstone, as the last-mentioned
traveller passed through a country adjoining that of
Matiamvo, and fell in with people who had been
there.

Matiamvo is the hereditary title of the king, who
is lord-paramount of the Balonda, and his capital
seems to bear the name of its ruler. His predecessor

in the sovereignty, who died early in 1854, was a
mad prince. · He would sometimes take a run
through the town with his sword, and decapitate all
whom he met, until he had made a heap of human
heads. If he took a fancy to anything which belonged to a stranger, he would order a whole village
to be sold in order to obtain his desire. When a
slave-trader visited him, he took possession of all his
goods; and after a week or two sent some men
to seize upon a village, murder the chief, and take
away the rest of the inhabitants for slaves, with
whom the trader was paid. Half-caste slave-dealers
used therefore to resort to his town, as a good place
for their unhallowed trade.

In the northern parts of Loanda the bloody custom
of Guinea prevails, in sacrificing a number of the
chief's servants at his death, in order to accompany
him into another world. Amongst the southern
tribes of the Balonda, this inhuman practice does
not exist. The Kanyika and Kanyoka live north of
the Balonda, but Matiamvo does not allow any
white person to visit them, as his chief supplies of
ivory are drawn from their country; so that he re-
tains a monopoly of this article. Ivory and slaves
are his principal exports; for which he receives
calico, gunpowder, salt, beads, and coarse earthenware. The present sovereign is more mild and just
in his government than his predecessor: still, his
power is absolute.

Let us look at the abode of Katema, a Balonda
chief, whose town lies in lat. 11° 35′ 49″ S., and

long. 22° 27′ E. It is a straggling village of huts,
rather than a town. Dr. Livingstone had a formal
presentation to Katema. He found him sitting on
a sort of throne, with about three hundred men
seated on the ground around; and thirty women,
who were said to be his wives, close behind him.
The main body of the people were squatting in a
semicircle, at a distance of fifty yards. Each party
had its own head man stationed at a little distance
in front; who, when beckoned by the chief, came
forward as his counsellors. Intemese then related
the stranger's history; and Katema placed sixteen
large baskets of meal before him, half a dozen fowls,
and a dozen eggs; expressing his regret that he had
slept hungry, as he did not wish any stranger to
suffer want in his town. He added: "Go home,
and cook and eat, and you will then be in a fit state
to speak to me, at an audience I will give you to-
morrow."

This very considerate conduct was exhibited by a
tall man, about forty years old, clad in a brown
coat with a golden band down the sleeves, and
wearing a helmet of beads and feathers. He carried
a large tail made of the caudal extremities of gnus,
having charms attached to it, which he waved in
front of himself, during the audience. He was in a
good humour and laughed much.

Next day he addressed his guests in the following
speech: "I am the great Moene (lord) Katema, the
fellow of Matiamvo. There is no one in this country
equal to Matiamvo and me. I have always lived

here, and my forefathers too. There is the house
in which my forefathers lived. You found no human
skulls near the place where you are encamped. I
never killed any of the traders; they all come to
me. I am the great Moene Katema of whom you
have heard."

KATEMA ON THE SHOULDERS OF HIS MINISTER.

Upon being asked what he would like to be
brought for him from Loanda, he prudently said
that anything from the white people would be accep-
table, and he would receive anything thankfully; but
the coat which he then wore was old, and he would

like another. He was pleased with the idea of
milking cows, which was a new thing to him. He
had a herd of about thirty fine animals; but they
were quite wild; and when one was wanted for
slaughter, it had to be shot like a buffalo. Katema
furnished guides.

Dr. Livingstone, on revisiting this chief after his
journey to the coast, gave him a cloak of red baize
ornamented with gold tinsel, a cotton robe, beads,
an iron spoon, and a small tin of gunpowder: when
he was greatly pleased with his present. On departing, he mounted on the shoulders of his spokes-
man, as the most dignified mode of retiring. The
latter was a slender man; whereas the chief was six
feet high, and stout in proportion: so that it was
only custom which enabled the bearer to sustain
his load.

Kawawa was another important chief in this district. His village, a little north-west of Katema,
consisted of forty or fifty straggling huts; but he
had a ferry over the Kasai, by means of which he
extorted a heavy tribute from all who could afford
to pay. The imposition which is thus practised
upon traders by all the tribes near the western coast,
is a great barrier to the exchange of merchandise:
but the natives are unable or unwilling to see the
evils of their short-sighted policy. The Chiboque
demand payment from every one who passes through
their country. This baneful custom has doubtless
arisen through the slave-trade; since the slave-
dealers are quite at the mercy of the chiefs of the

district, and are glad to pay any price for protection
or liberty of transit. Kawawa, who was otherwise
a kindly man, no sooner heard that Dr. Livingstone's
party had been fleeced of an ox by the Chiboque,
than he came forward with larger demands for himself. A fight seemed inevitable; as the chief demanded one of the party as a slave, besides a gun
and other things. These were peremptorily refused:
and the travellers prepared to force their way. Then
Kawawa allowed them to go as far as the river,
ordering the ferryman not to let them cross; and
the canoes were removed. But one of the party
perceived where a canoe was hidden amongst the
reeds: so that they borrowed it during the night,
and crossed in peace, leaving a few beads for the
ferryman. The Doctor expected that Kawawa would
some day lose his head by the order of Matiamvo, for
his extortionate conduct towards traders. Doubtless this would be the case as soon as the king heard
of his proceedings, which tended to impoverish the
country by keeping trade from the interior.

Here is a trick of the Chiboque! One of them
drops a knife near the ford of a river. Though the
travellers have been forewarned, yet a Negro cannot
resist the temptation of picking it up and putting
it in his basket. The owner of the knife has been
watching, and waits till all but the heads of the
party have crossed the stream. He then comes and
demands his property; and when it is given up,
requires a fine for the theft as it is called. There
is no remedy but to give him what he asks. For it is

customary that the finder of anything should show it to
his chief, and offer it to him; so that the latter may
restore it to the owner if sought for. When prac-
tising this deception, the Chiboque took care to keep
on their own side of the stream: and "it was
but rarely we could get a headman so witless as
to cross a river with us, and remain on the opposite bank in a convenient position to be seized
as a hostage, in case of my being caught."

On another occasion, when as large a present was
not given to the chief as he desired, he surrounded
the encampment with armed men, determined to
plunder it of everything. When expostulated with,
he said that one of the party had, in spitting near
the fire, allowed a small quantity of saliva to fall on
the leg of one of his men; and this "guilt" must be
washed away by the fine of a man, an ox, or a gun.
The person accused of this great offence acknowledged
that he had accidentally let a little saliva fall as
described, but that he had given the Chiboque a
piece of meat just before it happened, and had
wiped it off immediately. To save disputes, the
Doctor gave the injured man a shirt, with which
he was not satisfied. A few beads were added: but
as usual, the more that was given the higher their
demands rose.

The travelling party were really more than a match
for their assailants; and the chiefs of the latter had
incautiously come and seated themselves beside the
Doctor, by whose party they were surrounded: so that
in case of an affray, they would have become the first

victims. Finding that they could not succeed by
force, the natives tried a ruse. They said, "You
come among us in a new way, and say you are quite
friendly; how can we know it, unless you give us some
of your food, and you take some of ours? If you
give us an ox, we will give you whatever you may
wish, and then we shall be friends?" This was
agreed to. An ox was presented, and food demanded
in return. In the evening, the chief sent a very small

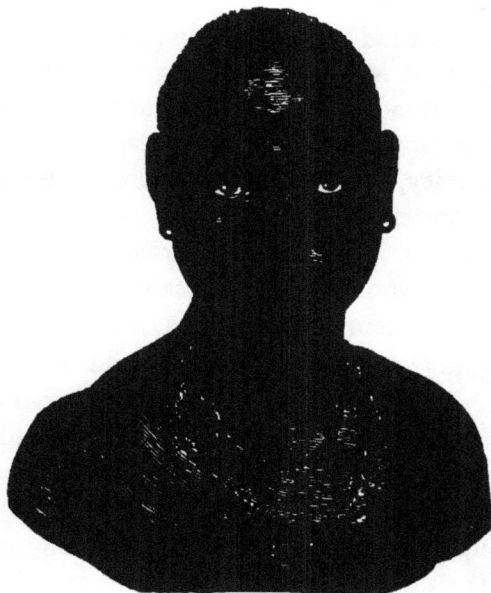

WOMAN OF CONGO.

basket of meal, and two or three pounds of the flesh
of the slaughtered ox! The travellers could not help
laughing at being so easily duped.

All the tribes bordering upon the Portuguese settlements on the coasts of Lower Guinea appear to be thus extortionate to strangers, so as greatly to hinder friendly and commercial intercourse with the interior. Otherwise, the inhabitants of Congo and its neighbourhood are far from being an uninteresting people, and are by no means devoid of intelligence. This is manifest from the conduct and character of those who are included within the bounds of the Portuguese government.

The Balonda men wear a girdle round their loins, to which a small apron of soft skin is attached both in front and behind. The women have nothing that can be called clothing. Yet the girls, indifferent to their own nudity, laughed at the Makololo men who had no back apron.

Strange to say, these naked barbarians are very punctilious in some of their manners: but this probably arises from superstitious fears. If their own fire goes out, they will not light it from a neighbour's. "They gave us food, but would not partake of it when we had cooked it; nor would they eat their food in our presence. When it was cooked, they retired into a wood and eat their porridge; then all stood up and clapped their hands, and praised Intemese (their chief) for it." An old man, who had been the companion of Matiamvo, was asked to sit down on the grass beside the traveller whom he was visiting. He refused with scorn, saying: "He had never sat on the ground during the late chief's reign, and he was not going to degrade himself now." Yet he accepted a seat on a half-burned log. He would not touch some cooked meat that was offered him, but would take it at home.

The Balonda seem afraid to remain in a spot which has been visited by death. They remove from the place; so that permanent villages are impossible. If they return to the locality, it is to pray to the deceased or present an offering. In the dark recesses of the forests, you might find human faces carved in the bark of trees, after the manner of the ancient Egyptian monuments; whilst offerings of small pieces of manioc-root or ears of maize are placed on the branches. Heaps of sticks are also made, after the manner of cairns, added to by every passenger.

Cabango, the most northerly village that has been visited in this region, lies in 9° 31′ S. lat. and 20° 31′ E. long. It consists of about two hundred huts, and ten or twelve square houses made of poles and grass, which belong to half-caste Portuguese traders. Information was here obtained that the town of Matiamvo lies about a hundred and thirty miles E.N.E. Some people from Mai described it as thirty-two days' journey, or about two hundred and twenty miles N.N.W. of Cabango; which would place it in about 5° 45′ S. lat. They mentioned another town, Luba, belonging to an independent chief, as eight days' farther, or in 4° 50′ S. lat. These visitors were as uncivilised as the Balonda, clothed in a kind of cloth made from the inner bark of a tree. Their chiefs do not admit strangers or fire-arms into their country.

The Balonda women are good-humoured, spending

their time in everlasting talk, funeral ceremonies,
and marriages. They spoil their looks by inserting
pieces of reed into the cartilage of the nose. A
funeral occupies four days of dancing, wailing, and
feasting. Guns are fired by day, and drums beaten

LONDA LADIES' MODE OF WEARING HAIR.

by night: and all the relatives, dressed in fantastic
caps, keep up the ceremonies with a spirit propor-
tionate to the amount of beer and beef provided.
When this provision is large, the remark is made,
"What a fine funeral it was!" A figure of feathers
and beads is paraded about on this occasion. There
is a general belief throughout this part of Africa, that
the souls of the departed mingle with the living, and
partake in some way of the food which is offered to
them. Sacrifices of goats and fowls are also made to
evil spirits, in order to appease them, when people are
sick. When a man kills another, a sacrifice is made
to lay his ghost.

The natives are not all quite black, but many incline to bronze, and others are much lighter. Heat alone does not produce a deep black, but heat with moisture. "Wherever we find people who have continued for ages in a hot, humid district, they are deep black; but to this apparent law there are exceptions, caused by the migrations of both tribes and individuals. The Makololo, for instance, among the tribes of the humid central basin, appear of a sickly sallow hue. The Batoka, who live in an elevated region, are, when seen in company with the Batoka of the rivers, so much lighter in colour, that they might be taken for another tribe; but their language, and the marked custom of knocking out the upper front teeth, leave no room for doubt that they are one people."

Amongst the inhabitants of Katema there is a love for singing-birds. They keep a kind of canary in cages because of the sweetness of their song. They have also tame pigeons. Singing-birds abound in some of the woods, and make a merry noise in the morning and evening. This forms a contrast with the northern tropic. Some sing as loudly as our thrushes, and the king-hunter (*Halcyon Senegalensis*) makes a clear whirring sound, like that of a whistle with a pea in it.

The Balonda are fond of agriculture: but immense districts of fine land are lying waste; and the very herbage is not eaten up by the wild cattle. They also catch fish, with which their rivers abound, in a variety of ways,—with nets, weirs, spears, snares, and the bruised leaves of a shrub which "poison" the finny tribe.

Before leaving these Balonda, let us pay a visit to Shinte, a noted chief, dwelling near the Leeba, a little south of the district which we have now described. Dr. Livingstone was accompanied to this town by a niece of the chief's, a tall Amazonian lady, named Manenko. This Amazon was a regular termagant, would have everything done her own way, and thought she could do anything. She was an accomplished scold and orator, and not only managed her own husband and people, but made the Doctor's party, and the Doctor himself, obey. Putting her hand on his shoulder, when he was resolved to go contrary to her will, she said, with a motherly look, "Now, my little man, just do as the rest have done." She marched forward with the party, accompanied by her husband and drummer. The former was merely a convenient companion; the latter thumped on his instrument till rain compelled him to desist. Manenko walked on, in the pouring rain, at a pace that few of the men could keep up with. When asked why she did not put on clothes (for she did not trouble herself with any garment) during the rain; she said that it was not proper for a chief to appear effeminate. The people all declared, "Manenko is a soldier."

This Amazon, according to the custom of the country, sent forward a message to her uncle that they were coming. She even went to a village to beg corn for her guest, ground it for him with her own hands, and brought it with an air which said, "I know how to manage, don't I?" Shinte despatched a messenger to bid the party welcome, accompanying his message with two large baskets of manioc and six dried fishes.

Shinte's town is embowered in bananas and other trees with large leaves. The streets are straight; the huts have square walls with round roofs, erected in courts surrounded with leafy fences. In some of the courts, tobacco is planted, or sugar cane, and bananas. Trees of the *Ficus Indica* afford a grateful shade to the inmates. Some of the people are very dark in colour, some are lighter; some have the Negro thick lips, elongated head, and flat nose; but others have well-shaped heads, and good-looking faces.

The chief received his guests, sitting under a banian tree, on a kind of throne covered with a leopard's skin. He was clothed in a kilt of scarlet baize edged with green, and a checked jacket. Strings of large beads were suspended round his neck, and his limbs were adorned with bracelets and armlets of copper and iron. On his head was a helmet of beads neatly woven together, and crowned with a great bunch of goose feathers. Close to him sat three lads with large sheaves of arrows over their shoulders. Behind him sat about a hundred women clothed in red baize; his chief wife being in front, wearing a curious red cap. The different sections of the tribe came forward, the headman of each making obeisance by rubbing his chest and arms with ashes. Then followed caperings, speech-making, clapping of hands by the ladies, music, &c. In the interludes of nine speeches, the ladies

sang plaintive ditties. Then Shinte rose, and so did
all the people. When a speech is approved of, this
is signified by clapping of hands, in which the chief
joins.

Manioc is here regarded as the staff of life. It is
easily cultivated. Beds are formed, in which pieces
of the manioc are planted, four feet apart. Beans or
ground-nuts may be sown between the rows: and
when these are reaped, the ground is cleared of weeds.
In about a year the roots are fit for food; the time
varying with the character of the soil. The plant is
esteemed good for three years. When a root is taken
up, a piece of the upper stalk is usually put into the
hole, and thus a fresh crop is provided for. It grows
to the height of six feet. The roots are three or four
inches in diameter, and from twelve to eighteen
inches in length. The leaves also are cooked as a
vegetable. It is cultivated in all the valleys by the
people of the villages, which generally consist of
twenty or thirty huts.

Blood relationships are formed by chiefs and people.
These are friendships of the most binding character,
literally cemented with blood. Two chiefs clasp each
other's hands, in which small incisions are made. A
little blood is taken from them and from similar cuts
on the stomach, and in the right cheek or forehead,
by means of a stalk of grass. The blood from each
person is put into a pot of beer, and drunk by his
neighbour. During the process, sentences are uttered
by their friends, who beat the ground with short

clubs. These blood-allies are bound not only to keep the peace themselves, but to warn the other party of any impending danger. The most valuable things which they possess are mutually exchanged as presents. Amongst the common people, the blood-tie is more easily formed: since a little blood squirting from an artery, whilst Dr. Livingstone performed an operation upon a woman's arm, constituted him her blood-relation. She considered herself bound to cook victuals for him any time that he might pass that way. Had he sooner known this custom, his lancet might perhaps have been of some service during his wanderings.

Sailing down the Leeba, we arrive at the place where it joins the Leeambye or Zambesi, nearly in 14° S. lat. The chief of the Barotse lives five days' journey east of this junction. The country here is overflowed during one part of the year; but it teems with animal life, and might as easily support millions of men as it now does thousands. Flocks of green pigeons are here met with; and many other interesting species of the feathered tribe. Here is the beautiful *trogon*, with bright scarlet breast and black back, uttering a peculiar note like that said to have been uttered by Memnon, which resembled the tuning of a lyre. In the quiet districts of the river, we find the *ibis religiosa*, large flocks of the white pelican, clouds of a black shell-eating bird, plovers, snipes, curlews and herons, *ardetta*, scissor-bills, spoonbills, the flamingo, the Numidian and other cranes, gulls,

the wading avoset, the *parra Africana*, &c. &c. Some
of these birds are singularly beautiful; others are very
curious in their structure and habits.

Fish are so numerous, that when the waters
retire all the people are engaged in catching, cutting
up, and drying the mullets that have been left on
the soil. The hippopotamus and other large animals
also abound; with immense numbers of insects.
Indeed, the valley teems with animal life.

Lower down, Lebonta is the frontier town of the
Makololo, built on a mound, like other villages in the
valley. Lebonta belongs to two wives of Sebituane.
Farther down, we come to the junction of the Chobé
with the Zambesi, in about $17\frac{1}{2}°$ of S. lat. and $25\frac{1}{2}°$
of E. long. A little way up the Chobé is Linyanti,
the capital of the Makololo. King Sekeletu was the
warm friend of Dr. Livingstone, furthered all the
objects of his undertaking to the utmost of his ability,
and generously supplied his wants.

Linyanti contains about 7000 people. It is built
in the midst of rivers and marshes, for the sake of
security; but this renders it unhealthy. The people
are of a light-brownish yellow colour, and have a
sickly hue compared with their olive-tinted neighbours. The Makololo ladies have the hue of the
half-caste: and in opposition to the judgment of the
Negroes of the north, they associate fairness of skin
with beauty. They drink large quantities of *booza*,
which is considered nutritious, and calculated to give
that plumpness of form which is highly esteemed.
They cut their woolly hair quite short, and anoint

themselves plentifully with butter, to make their skin
shine. Their dress is a simple kilt of soft hide,
reaching to the knees. They have also a skin-mantle
for full dress; and ornament themselves with armlets
and anklets of brass and ivory, so thick and heavy as
often to blister the skin. But these things are fashion-
able! Necklaces are also used. Beads of light green
and pink being the most esteemed, such colours are
of high price.

These women have much better ideas of beauty
and comeliness than their northern sisters in Bornu
and its vicinity. The latter like the flat nose, thick
lips, crisp hair, and black colour, which themselves
possess. But the Makololo ladies prefer not only a
light colour, but a proper symmetry of features.
"They came frequently and asked for the looking-
glass; and the remarks they made—while I was engaged in reading, and apparently not attending to
them—on first seeing themselves therein, were amus-
ingly ridiculous. 'Is that me?' 'What a big mouth
I have?' 'My ears are as big as pumpkin-leaves.' 'I
have no chin at all.' 'I would have been pretty, but
am spoiled by these high cheek-bones.' 'See, how
my head shoots up in the middle!'" They laughed
loud at their own criticisms and jokes upon themselves. A man, also, came alone "to have a quiet
gaze at his own features once when he thought I was
asleep. After twisting his mouth about in various
directions, he remarked to himself, 'People say I am
ugly, and how very ugly I am indeed!'" The natives
are sharp enough in perceiving the defects of others,

and giving nicknames accordingly: now they had an opportunity for the first time of seeing themselves.

Sekeletu was in 1853 a young man, about eighteen years old, of the dark yellow colour of which the Makololo are so proud, and about five feet seven inches in height. According to the custom of the tribe, he became possessor of his father's wives at his death; and he took two of them: the rest were given to influential chiefs. But the principal wife or queen passed to the late king's younger brother; according to a custom prevailing among the ancient Jews. However many wives the king may have, there is one who enjoys the title and position of queen; whose hut is called the great house; and whose children inherit the chieftainship. If she dies, another is chosen in her place.

On this occasion, the royal widows became so soon reconciled to their new lot, that the people made a song, to the intent that only the men felt the loss of their father Sebituane; for the women were so soon supplied with new husbands, that their hearts had not time to become sore with grief. A very pretty compliment to their highnesses!

When Dr. Livingstone travelled with Manenko and other chiefs, the inhabitants used to lend them the roofs of their huts, which are circular, and can be taken off at pleasure. The owners lifted them off, and brought them to the place where the travellers wished to lodge. Being propped up with stakes, they formed a sufficient shelter for the night. The numbers of large kind of game here are prodigious.

The lions are as big as donkeys; and their manes
make them look larger. Eighty-one buffaloes passed
slowly in file before the traveller's fire one evening,
within gunshot. Herds of splendid elands stood within
two hundred yards of the party, without exhibiting
any fear of them. In most districts of the Zambesi,
antelopes and smaller game are in profuse abundance;
so that no sportsman need want food.

We must leave the Makololo, with a description of
one of their dances. Their excitement is generally
shown and worked off in dancing and singing. In
the dance, the men stand nearly naked in a circle,
holding clubs or small battle-axes. Each roars at the
loudest pitch of his voice; whilst they simultaneously
lift one leg, stamp twice with it heavily, and lifting
the other, give one stamp with it. They also throw
their arms and head about in all directions. The
noise is tremendous, and the clouds of dust which rise
from their feet fill the air. "If the scene were witnessed in a lunatic asylum, it would be nothing out
of the way, and quite appropriate even, as a means of
letting off the excessive excitement of the brain: but
here grey-headed men joined in the performance with
as much zest as others whose youth might be an
excuse for making the perspiration stream off their
bodies with the exertion." The women stand by,
clapping their hands; but occasionally one advances
into the circle composed of a hundred men, makes a
few movements, and then retires. Poor things! they
do not like to be left altogether out of the fun. It is
too bad! On the Doctor's intimating that the dance

was hard work; Sekeletu's father-in-law admitted the fact, but said, "It is very nice, and Sekeletu will give us an ox for dancing for him."

The Batoka, who live to the east of the Makololo, do not differ much from them in manners. In a way contrary to the Balonda, the women are better dressed, whilst the men go about quite naked, without the smallest sense of shame. Their mode of salutation is to throw themselves on their back and roll on the ground, slapping the outside of their thighs, in token of a welcome. Even the big chief Monze rolled in this manner before his visitor, to the unspeakable disgust of the latter.

This tribe have the singular custom of knocking out their upper front teeth; the want of which gives them an uncouth appearance, and makes their laugh hideous. This folly has become a standing jest for the Makololo. The women of the Maravi, farther eastward, pierce the upper lip, and gradually enlarge the orifice until they can insert a shell. The lip then appears drawn out beyond the perpendicular of the nose, and gives them a moist ungainly aspect. There is no accounting for fashion! Sekwelu remarked, "These women want to make their mouths like those of ducks."

The Metabele, rivals of the Makololo, who live farther east, on the south of the Zambesi, do not differ greatly in their manners and customs from their western neighbours; and the same may be said of other tribes dwelling nearer to the Portuguese settlements. All these people, it may be remarked, are addicted to smoking a narcotic weed, which produces effects like the opium-eating of China; and which is capable of exciting them to a state of frenzy, when they partake of it largely, as they generally do before going into battle.

North of the Zambesi is a hilly and well-watered country, inhabited by the Basenga and Babisa or Movisa, who are much mixed up with Balonda and neighbouring tribes. Beyond them is Cazembe, which we have already mentioned as lying to the south of the lake district. Its capital, Lucenda, is described by Silvo Porto as a large town, with wide streets and spacious markets; having in the centre a royal palace containing a harem of 570 women. The government is most despotic, the laws are written in blood, and human sacrifices are frequent.

Silvo Porto's account of these people shows that they resemble the tribes described by Livingstone and Burton. They are barbarous, indolent, and vicious, though sometimes hospitable. They seem to know no distinctions of virtue and vice, and never to think of right and wrong, except in reference to present consequences from a breach of their own customs. Though their life is spent in so simple a way, " according to nature," without the prevalence of artificial wants and luxuries; and though their land teems with abundance, so as to supply all their need with a small degree of labour; they are far from enjoying happiness and ease.

Our readers must not suppose that a "state of nature" is a "state of bliss," according to the theory of some modern philosophers. One who went amongst the Africans for their good, whose patience and good nature have seldom been exceeded, who taught them many useful things, and who was ready to make all allowances for the ignorance and rudeness of barbarian life, sums up his account of them in these mournful words:—"Though all, including the chief, were as kind and attentive to me as possible; and there was no want of food (oxen being slaughtered daily, sometimes ten at a time, more than sufficient for the wants of all), yet to endure the dancing, roaring, and singing, the jesting, anecdotes, grumbling, quarrelling, and murdering, of these children of nature, seemed more like a severe penance than anything I had before met with in the course of my missionary duties. I took thence a more intense disgust at heathenism than I had before, and formed a greatly elevated opinion of the latent effects of missions in the south, among tribes which are reported to have been as savage as the Makololo."

Dr. Livingstone does not, in this category of their vices, mention slave-dealing, kidnapping, treachery, lying, drunkenness, plundering, want of natural affection, cruelty, and the other evils which proceed from polygamy and slavery. Captain Burton's account of the natives of the east is rather worse than Dr. Livingstone's; for his attendants evinced no respect, gratitude, or submission to his authority, such as the doctor experienced. According to the captain, these people live in rudeness and vice, without a single redeeming quality; striving only to gratify the

lowest propensities of their nature, in common with
the wild beasts of the desert.   Dr. Krapf's testimony
is of the same character.

We have said that Linyanti is situated in the
midst of rivers and marshes, for the sake of security.
It is indeed almost unapproachable from some quarters.   The banks of the streams are mostly marsh
land, covered with thick grass and reeds six or eight
feet high.   There is also a serrated grass which at
certain angles cuts like a razor, and clumps of pa-
pyrus, like miniature palms, an inch and a half in
diameter.   The climbing convolvolus, with stalks as
strong as whip-cord, binds all these reeds and grasses
into a thick mass.   The islands and dry places are
beset with brambles.

In penetrating to the south, the land is found to be

THE TSETSE.

flat and marshy, as far as the lake Ngami; after which
it soon becomes desert.   A great annoyance in these

districts is the tsetse, or *Glossina morsitans*, an insect which attacks cattle, horses, and dogs; but does not here afflict men or wild beasts. A whole team of oxen are sometimes destroyed by them; and the traveller may be left helpless with his caravan. The tsetse live in defined localities, one bank of a river being infested with them, whilst the opposite bank may be free. They inject a subtle poison with their sting, from which a slight irritation soon follows, though not so much as that produced by the gad-fly. But in a few days, the bitten animal is affected as if it had an influenza; emaciation ensues, with a flaccidity of the muscles, and sometimes with blindness and staggering; and at last, purging or atrophy causes death, in spite of every remedy that can be applied. Dissection shows that the blood has been vitiated. A singular circumstance is that calves are not affected by the tsetse so long as they are sucking; although dogs fed on milk perish like the cattle.

In a former place we have mentioned the white ant, which also abounds in these southern latitudes, and raises the mound of its dwelling to a height of thirty feet, on the top of which trees sometimes grow. It has also its notable enemy, the black soldier ant, which is met with in these districts. They are about half an inch in length, and march three or four abreast. They follow their leaders which, like officers, guide their troops, but bear no burdens. If you throw a little earth or water on their path, they lose their way, as they seem to follow by a kind of scent. They will not cross over the obstacle however small, but will wheel round till they recover their track. The white ants are greatly afraid of them. The black leaders hold their victims one by one, inflicting a sting which makes them insensible, and then toss them to one side, where they are seized and carried off by the troopers. They do not enslave the white ants, as some have thought, but they eat them; as may be seen by a little heap of hard heads and legs near the barracks of the soldier ants. Were it not for this relentless foe, the white ants would over-run the country.

Southward, we pass by large salt-pans, and finally ·

INSIDE OF A BUSHMAN'S HUT.

arrive amongst the Bushmen. Families of these men are found in marshy districts, where they are tall of stature and dark in colour. But the Bushmen of the Kalahari are short and of a light yellow complexion.

c c 3

They roam about this desert region, living in rude
huts of hasty construction, and subsisting principally
upon the game which they take in hunting. They
never cultivate the soil, nor rear any animals except
dogs ; but their women gather roots and other fruits
of natural growth.

Without such vegetables, the Bushmen could
scarcely subsist; for being esculent, they furnish
them with drink as well as meat. The greater portion
of this desert is very arid; so that during part of the
year the grass will crumble into powder in your hand.
There is such a sameness in the clumps of bushes
·which grow here, that it requires a well practised eye to
distinguish them, so as to recognise the locality, and
be sure of travelling in the right direction. But
these children of the soil know everything that belongs to it, and can detect the slightest difference in
the appearance of a tree. Through long practice in
hunting, they are so well acquainted with the habits
of the wild beasts, that they can follow and track them
out in their migrations.

In passing through this dreary country, you are
often at a loss for water: but your Bushman guides
will tell you where to dig in the sand, and you will
soon obtain a small supply. They will also point
out plants from which you may obtain refreshing
moisture. Here is a small stalk with linear leaves!
If you dig down a foot or foot and a half, you will find
a tuber as large as a child's head, filled with fluid
like a young turnip. Another creeper has several
roots of still larger size ranged in the circumference

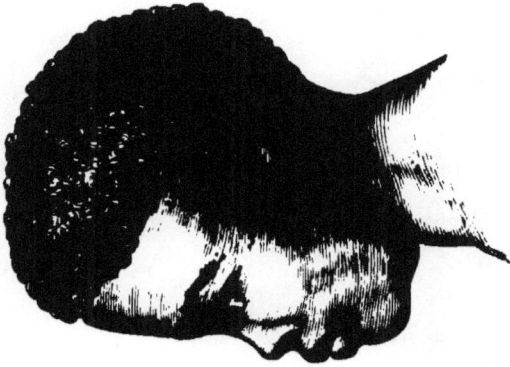

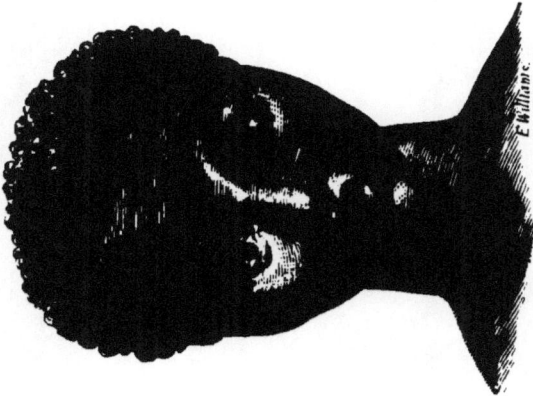

BUSHWOMAN.

E Williams.

of a circle about a yard from the stem. The natives strike the ground with stones, and know by the peculiar sound when tubers are to be found below. The water-melon, *Cucumis caffer*, abounds in some places, and is eagerly devoured, not only by man, but by all kinds of wild beasts.

The savage manner in which the Bushmen live, like mere animals preying upon their fellows, seems

BUSHWOMAN AND CHILD.

to have produced an unsightly degradation of their physical system. This is increased by the heat and thirst of the desert in which they rove. Their body is small, lean, shrivelled up,—ungainly specimens of human nature, of all the prerogatives of which they might seem to be destitute. Other creatures besides man possess cunning and sagacity in hunting and foraging, to which all the Bushman's faculties of body and mind are now limited. But his use of poisoned arrows, his quickness in deception, and the knowledge which he possesses of the habits of other animals, display a power of intelligence which might be exercised on the useful arts of life.

BAKALAHARI WOMEN DRAWING WATER.

The Bakalahari share the desert with Bushmen; but they live here as exiles rather than aborigines. They practise agriculture and rear domestic animals. They are a timid race, have thin limbs, and large protruding abdomens. For safety's sake they often choose their residence at a distance from water; and hide their supplies by filling up the pits, and even making a fire over them. The women draw the water with long reeds, by means of suction. An enemy coming to one of their villages, can find no water; but it will be speedily supplied to a friend. Whole bands of their enemies have been lost or led astray in this thirsty region, and have perished from drought.

The desert has thus proved a place of refuge to many tribes when over-run by powerful foes, who have vainly endeavoured to pursue them here, or have done so to their own destruction. We need scarcely say that the Bakalahari are as untutored as the Bushmen, that is, as wholly as human nature can be.

Our journey terminates here. The next people are the Bechuanas and other tribes known to the Cape colonists, and amongst whom Christian missions have been planted. We have run over the vast interior of Africa, through its utmost breadth in north latitude, and through its length from Barbary to the neighbourhood of Cape colony. We have seen the Moors and Arabs, both located and wandering, following customs which never change, and animated by dispositions inherent in their race. We have viewed the more pliable Negro, the proper inhabitant of these regions, under a great variety of forms, colours, conditions, and circumstances; semi-civilised, savage, Mahometan, pagan; wealthy and poor, master and slave, in power and under subjection; holding commerce with other nations, dwelling by themselves, and in the desert.

All these people are capable of civilisation, perhaps not of the highest type, but at least of a respectable form. It must be a Christian civilisation. Mahometanism has injured their tempers where it has improved their manners; and it has not benefited their morals. So, an increase of wealth in their pagan state has only increased their folly, cruelty, and other enormities. They need a civilisation which shall repress their vices, humanise their dispositions, and prove a bond of peace and amity. Then their facilities for improvement and happiness would be immense. Their teeming soil would support many times its present occupants, furnishing them with the richest fruits of nature, and producing the most valuable articles of commerce. Cotton, indigo, coffee, sugar, rice, vegetable oils, spices, farinaceous roots, and tropical fruits, could be grown to almost any extent that might be desired. The present exports of gold, ivory, beeswax, hides, dyes, and valuable timber, might be immensely increased. Then their imports would be on a similar scale of magnitude; for they generally desire foreign goods. The christianisation of Africa would enrich the mercantile countries of

Europe, and greatly add to or cheapen some of their luxuries.

Late discoveries have nearly completed our knowledge of the main features of African geography, by the authentic accounts which we have received of the course of the Niger, the Lake Chad, the Zambesi and its tributaries, and the lake regions. The vexed question about the source of the White Nile and the Mountains of the Moon remains to be decided; but this refers to a very small part of Africa. It is ascertained that the centre of the continent consists of immense plains, watered by large rivers and lakes, with an occasional hill or ridge of low mountains. The level country has a rich soil, interspersed with vast forests and portions of desert land. On either side of this immense region, between it and the coast, are ridges of mountains, which are highest on the eastern side of the continent. Abyssinia is bordered on the south by the higher "Mountains of the Moon." Subsequent ranges decrease in altitude, till they again rise near the coast in Mount Kenia and Kilmanjaro, the latter of which is capped with snow, though only two degrees distant from the equator. Next follow the hills of Usumbara, which extend from the coast inward. Below them are the Ngura hills, running in a long ridge from north to south; which are succeeded by the ranges crossed by Captains Burton and Speke, lying farther inward. The hills of Babisa, and those nearer to the Zambesi are less elevated, and some of them are known to abound in coal and valuable minerals. South of the

Zambesi, a double range of mountains extending southward occupies nearly the eastern half of the continent, having the district of the Lake Ngami and the Kalahari Desert on their western side. Afterwards, one great range runs near the coast towards the Cape. The western coast of Africa is also bordered by mountains, which seldom branch far into the interior; though we have found that they do so near the equator.

What will be the future of Africa, when its rivers and lakes shall be covered with steamboats, and its rich plains intersected by railways, — when the labours of the engineer and agriculturist shall have rid it of pestilential miasma, — when its fruitful soil shall support a teeming population, and abundantly furnish those commodities which Europe desires to import?

THE END.

LONDON

PRINTED BY SPOTTISWOODE AND CO.

NEW-STREET SQUARE

www.ingramcontent.com/pod-product-compliance
Lightning Source LLC
Chambersburg PA
CBHW031825270326
41932CB00008B/550